WILL'S GUIDE TO BUILDING THE $9,000 HOUSE

$9,000

WILL'S GUIDE TO BUILDING THE

HOUSE

By William Cruz

Illustrations by Eric Mathes

UNITY PRESS
SANTA CRUZ

Published by Unity Press
113 New Street, Santa Cruz, California 95060

Illustrations by Eric Mathes
Design by Richard Bigus
Cover photograph by Franklin L. Avery

Hangen, William S 1947–
Will's Guide to the $9,000 House
1. House construction–Handbooks, manuals, etc.
I. Title. II. Title: Guide to the $9,000 House
TH4813.H36 690'.8'1 78-5183
ISBN 0-913300-25-X

Typeset in Trump Medieval and Helvetica by
Chapman's Phototypesetting on the Merganthaler VIP

Printed and bound by Delta Lithograph
Printed in the United States of America

DEDICATION

This book is dedicated to my wife Terra for her diligent proof-reading and typing and to my two year old son, Colt, for not eating the manuscript while it was in vulnerable stages.

The journey of a thousand miles begins with a single step.
Lao Tzu

Failure is more frequently from want of energy than from want of capital.
Daniel Webster

TABLE OF CONTENTS

PSYCHING YOURSELF UP

INTRODUCTION

From the first time I helped a friend design and build a house right up to the time I built my own home, I noticed several things about traditional house-building books.

First, the imaginary builders for whom these books are written never make any mistakes and therefore never have any problems. I always thought this was because the readers were supposed to be professional tradesmen and therefore magically gifted with superhuman skills (likewise fees). So seldom do the books deal with all-too-human screw-ups that I found I learned more from trial and error.

Second, the technical language in these house-building books often seems strangely reminiscent of *Catch 22.* It winds itself into knots and refuses to be understandable to the average person. I now suspect it's all a very sophisticated conspiracy to keep the lay person working in the Dark Ages.

Anyway, my third and perhaps most important complaint about the house-building trade books is that the authors usually don't tell how to save money. You would think that the average house builder is the Shah of Iran if you listened to most authors on the subject. It's really a wet blanket when you're told you need at least $20,000 to build a 1500-square-foot house.

Who needs all that room anyway? Retired people, small families, and couples need approximately 1,000 square feet for starters. An additional room or two can be added later. I say move into your own house and save money you would have spent on rent for additions—why give it to the landlord? This book, then, is dedicated to those who haven't great funds to help them on the road to their own house but who want more than simply a rental in which to live.

Before we get too far out of the starting gate, there is one more important thing I'd like to bring up. That's the subject of difficulty, both physical and mental, experienced while building a house. At some point you'll be thumbing through *Better Homes and Gardens* looking at houses and you'll think, "Does Cruz really know what he's talking about? After all, look at all the funny roof lines and staircases. Look at that crazy floor plan. How could I ever hope to do that?" Well, my answer is "Don't." Leave the flying buttresses and sunken Japanese baths to the pros. Plan a simpler and more economical floor plan that can be expanded later with all the custom features you would like. You'll have a better understanding of your materials, your abilities, and your tools after you build the central building.

I feel anyone can easily build a 1,000-square-foot house for less than $9,000. (The figure $9,000 represents the house itself; excluding the cost of your land, sewer or septic system, carpets, furniture, etc.) The cost will vary, depending on how much is splurged and how radical the building site. Nevertheless, even in California or Hawaii it's possible to come close to $9,000. The several designs I present are for attractive, completely legal houses built to last and to be maintenance-free. All the construction details in this book are easy to understand, and if you have problems not covered here, common sense will guide you through.

Contrary to the myth, it simply isn't that hard to build a moderately sized and designed house. There are several solid reasons why I can say this. For one thing, in proposing low-cost house-building, I have used many modern ideas in conjunction with traditional techniques. Most of my houses are basically three-bedroom, one-bath designs based on the most practical use of space possible. Furthermore, modern building materials have also greatly improved the ease and quality of installations. Examples are aluminum windows, plywood flooring, and prefinished paneling. The list is limitless, and with reasonable care when buying you can keep the quality of your construction as high as if you had built it the old-fashioned way.

Another big money-saver is that plumbers, electricians, and other tradespeople will come to your site and help "rough in" your work. Given a few hours of their time, your work will be of professional quality and your savings 50 percent or more. More about that later.

I've tried to make this book as clear and complete as possible, telling you what to watch out for, where and when to get bargains, and virtually every other thing you need to know. You'll find sections on things such as well drilling and septic tanks, large chapters on plumbing and electricity, and even a whole chapter on buying your land.

If at first you seem to work slowly, don't worry. Your basic skills such as hammering, sawing, nailing, and leveling will develop in the first simple stages of foundation and floor laying. By the time you get to the walls, you'll be able to drive a nail in your sleep!

I hope I've convinced you to start building or at least to start planning. Whatever the case, I hope you'll read the whole book through completely because every chapter has things you should know.

Good luck house building—

William S. Cruz

AUTHOR'S NOTE

Prices and building codes quoted in this book were compiled with as much accuracy as humanly possible. However, any individual intending to build a house should check these details for timeliness before including them in their plans. The $9,000 figure will be affected by inflation. It would therefore be wise to add a suitable inflation figure to your calculations for each year past the publication date of this book.

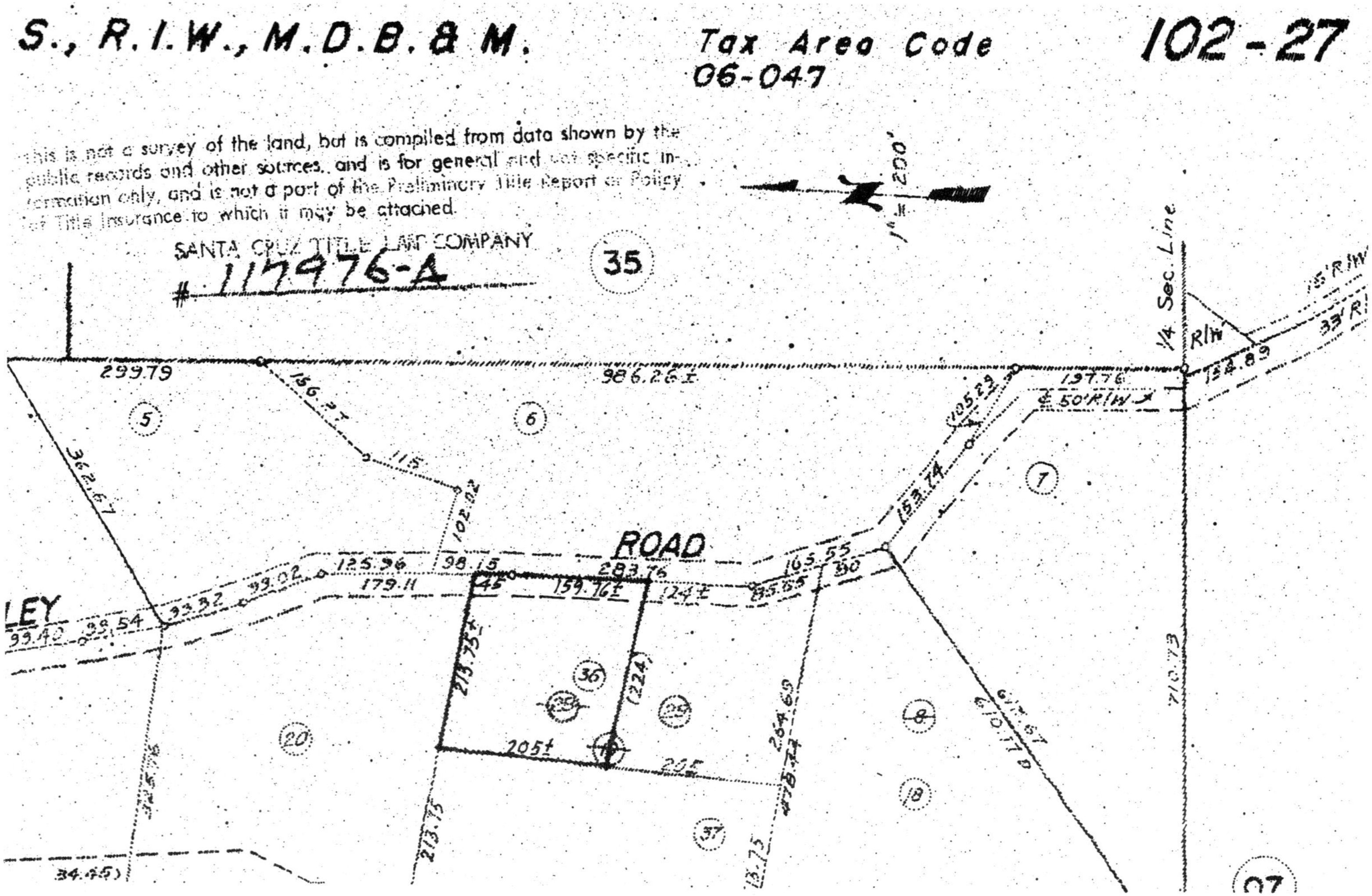
S., R.1.W., M.D.B.& M.
Tax Area Code 06-047
102-27
this is not a survey of the land, but is compiled from data shown by the public records and other sources, and is for general and not specific information only, and is not a part of the Preliminary Title Report or Policy of Title Insurance to which it may be attached.
SANTA CRUZ TITLE LAND COMPANY
117976-A
1" = 200'
35
1/4 Sec. Line
R/W
15' R/W
33' R/W
299.79
986.26±
197.76
50' R/W
ROAD
LEY

Parcel Map

LOOKING AROUND

CHAPTER 1

It wasn't like I'd always passionately wanted to build a house. It just sort of happened. Some people are driven to create with their own hands nearly everything that they work with, live in, or eat. I am not that way, at least not totally. When I first told some of my carpenter friends I was going to build a house for less than $9,000, I may as well have hit them over the head with a 2×4. Some said I wasn't skilled enough, some said impossible, and some just stared.

I was a little shaken. I mean here were *professional tradespeople* telling me, the lowly dreamer, that I could not build a house for $9,000. You can laugh but the road to building a house looks very long and steep when you decide to go it alone. Many a good man and woman have been talked down from building a house by doubting friends, but let's put that behind us while I share with you some things I experienced and learned.

It all began when my wife Terra and I were traveling in Europe for a year, enjoying the ecstatic flush that comes after finishing college, having spent too much time with books and not having enough time in the here and now. England, France, Austria, and Turkey all passed before us, and no place was too hard to get to or too remote. We traveled by plane, train, mule cart, boat, motorcycle, van, car, and bus, by foot and by hitch.

After a prolonged depression from homesickness, diarrhea, and bad water we turned our thoughts toward "settlin' down," as Terra's folks always so quaintly put it. California, Hawaii, and Washington State seemed to pop up repeatedly in our talks, so without delay we said "au revoir" to Paris and struck off for Hawaii. We soon decided to leave Hawaii to the developers and tourists. Washington was too cold, so it was back to California.

With certain fondness I remembered a little town I had passed through on a backpacking trip along the California coast. Even its name had that sweet Spanish taste: Santa Cruz. Definitely it had potential. Santa Cruz has an ocean that, like a beautiful lover, sleeps curled up against the rugged backbone of coastal mountains. Winter is mild there, but you know its presence. Summer is like honey on pancakes—warm, sweet, and golden with that sort of flowing feel.

I filled Terra's ears with wonderful tales of endless beaches, surfers, mountain streams, redwoods. As we drove down from Washington along the coast route, we talked about finding a house. Terra insisted it would be a shame to pay rent, that we'd only be giving money to the landlord and would never see it again. If we could put money into a house of our own, we'd get it back when we sold it.

"Money," I told her. It took money to get a house. Or to build a house.

"How much?"

I had been waiting for that. "$30,000." Actually, I wasn't sure how much it cost to build a house. The figure sounded good and padded.

"I'm not talking about Versailles. I'm talking about a cozy wooden house with a few large rooms."

I shrugged. I didn't want to back down from my original estimate. Besides, the thought of building a house nearly made me pee in my pants.

And yet, the seed of the idea sat in my frontal lobes for awhile, then blossomed into the mysterious phenomenon known as The Vision. I remember how it happened. I was walking along a quiet, overgrown street in Santa Cruz after a spring rain when I saw a rustic house set back amid the trees and bushes. "That's a nice house," I thought. "They must be okay people. Looks like they built it themselves." Click—The Vision. I saw myself standing proudly in front of my own house, Terra in the background hanging laundry in the bright sun, sheets flapping in the wind, a cat chasing a butterfly, and as always that sun shining down like honey.

The house I saw so clearly in my head was redwood paneled and had a rectangular look, like early pioneer cabins. Simple to build, yet easy to add on a wing at any side when the need arrived. Unfortunately, The Vision didn't tell me how to build this house or where to get the money, but it did tell me that I *had* to build it, and that's a very essential part of seeing it happen.

I became a familiar figure at the library, checking out every book they had on how to frame, plumb, and electrify. Terra brought home additional volumes, and I pored through them taking reams of notes. While reading these books, I realized that none were for people building on a budget and that most were cold and impersonal concerning methods used. I thought about chronicling my building experiences and trying to get some human levels established in the cold world of salespeople and tradespeople.

Perhaps in all honesty I should say that I had had some experience with carpentry in high school. One of my wood shop projects had been a knife rack for my mom's kitchen. It had consisted of a wooden box with a glass front and slots in the top. One day the glass fell out and five razor-sharp Sabatier knives had danced around the kitchen floor for awhile. I'm sure my mother had dire predictions about my future in carpentry.

Undaunted by past problems, I began leaving my detailed drawings all over the house and became obsessed with terms such as *butt end* (nothing what it sounds like), *header* (not a toilet), and *hot line* (not the one to Russia). I sent away for everything the *Whole Earth Catalog* recommended and brought the wrath of the post office down on our mail box. Reams of advertisements came, solicitations from lumber companies and contractors by the hundreds. It was difficult to turn away offers such as installation of a built-in sauna bath with cedar and brick for only $2,000, but a look at the ol' bank book closed the case every time.

SELECTING THE LAND

Of course this sounds like I had the house half built and the roof up, but in reality I didn't even have land yet, and I was still looking in the Santa Cruz Mountains every spare moment

I had. If you have a couple of thousand dollars and big plans you are going to have to look for a long time. There *is* such a creature as good land at a cheap price; it is not a unicorn. There are usually several compromises though in such a deal: the access road is dirt and under 2 feet of water most of the year, the property is a 90-degree hillside with a great view and straight drop, or the land is directly over an earthquake fault.

The last compromise may not sound like anything major, but in Santa Cruz it was extremely important. One parcel I looked at was right on the San Andreas Fault, and I mean precisely on it. You could see the fault line slash through the property and weave off into the surrounding hills. It was scary just standing there. I could easily imagine the sleepless nights if I built there.

Another place I saw was just like the Hollywood set for *Lost World.* It was back in the woods several miles and nothing was available—no electricity, access roads, or neighbors—just lots of trees. It was cheap, but we didn't want to be lost to mankind, so another pass-up.

One fantastic place we looked at was really cheap and included 2 whole acres, trees, a creek, and a good road. Unfortunately, there had been several unsolved murders in the neighborhood. Another pass-up.

Every morning I'd get a Santa Cruz paper and look through the classifieds for land. A lot of dimes went to the phone company before a small ad caught my eye. It didn't look like much, but the day was sunny and I figured a ride in the country would be nice. After calling the realtor and getting the parcel's location, I packed a lunch and drove out of town. As I thought back over the ad in the paper, I grew a bit dejected. It didn't seem we'd ever find the right land for us. My interest increased, however, as I drove up the little lane toward the property. On either side redwoods lofted toward the sky, and in the background an occasional house peeked out of the trees. The noonday sun became more and more remote as the trees grew larger, and I began to wonder where on earth that "sunny acre" was that the ad spoke of.

Suddenly my car emerged into sunlight and entered a small valley. Open to the southwest but enclosed on all other sides, the valley held a few scattered houses and a handful of barns. Ancient redwoods rose around the creek that sparkled across the valley floor, while all about the warm air rang with sounds of birds and insects. I slowed the car to a crawl and enjoyed the passing scenery.

Coming around a sharp corner, I looked up toward the hills on my left and saw a small grove of pines clustered together with what looked like a "For Sale" sign tacked to one. As I pulled my car over to the side of the road and got out, it occurred to me that everyone in America must have a dream, however deeply hidden it may be, of a homestead acre with a nice rustic house surrounded by an orchard and a garden. The Vision, I think, is in all of us. The craziness of the world would be too much, I fear, if that simple rural dream didn't function as a relief valve for so many people. What can beat the sound of the word *homestead*? The effect on a person's mind is tranquilizing and refreshing. *Home-baked bread* is another term like that—as are well water, crickets, and owls—all of them inspirations to the tense and rat-raced city dweller.

When I finally reached the approximate area that fitted the realtor's description I sat down and really studied the landscape. From this elevated view I looked to the horizon and saw a shimmer of blue ocean beyond the valley's low hills. The spring greenery was in full blossom and the hillocks rolled toward the sea as if someone had thrown a large rock into the earth and set off a series of waves. On a far peak I could see an all-glass house, and for a second I envied the magnificent panorama they must enjoy.

As my eyes wandered about, I realized that I preferred being in the valley with only its partial view of the ocean. A Chinese tale I had heard came to mind, about a man who bought a large piece of land on a hill overlooking the vastness of the coast and the China Sea. He built his house on the top of the hill but to the amazement of his friends proceeded to plant up the land with trees so that the ocean could no longer be seen. One day his friends came over to admire the house, and they remarked privately among themselves what a shame it was that he had destroyed the view. Just then one of them leaned over to drink from a low water basin, and under the foliage he caught a glimpse of the ocean. While in the humble act of stooping for a drink of water, he gasped at the greater beauty of the ocean's presence and realized the profoundness of the moment.

GETTING DOWN TO SPECIFICS

After I walked the land some more, I drove into town and stopped to ask a few questions at the county building. I knew I had to exercise some caution when buying land. The beauty of it could sweep hard facts under the carpet. I knew what I wanted to ask, so it didn't take long. I asked the clerk for the parcel map, and then I checked these points, which you should do too:

—Did the plotted location coincide with what I saw? It's important to measure out distances to geographic landmarks, such as curves in the road, poles, and fences.

—Were any liens or back taxes unpaid?

—Who owned the road, and were there fees for its use? (There were on my land, since it was on a private road—$50 per year.)

—And most importantly of all, was it legal to build a house on the land *plus* put in a septic tank or sewer hook-up legally? (See the building department and sanitation department for this information.)

It's a good idea to have two copies made of your parcel map, since they cost only a few dollars. Then you are ready to do some measuring. Take the realtor up to the land with you, but take all his or her glowing descriptions and grandiose measurements lightly. Verify for yourself all of the items mentioned above, because once it's your land it's extremely difficult to get your money back, if not impossible. **NOTE:** If you buy from a realtor, the fee is usually 10 percent and the seller pays it, but of course the commission is added to the asking price.

As I listened to my realtor talk, I envisioned milk and honey flowing from the land and wood nymphs cavorting in the pines. With great restraint I measured the land and the *road easement* (the amount of land the county or the road owners can legally use in the future for road expansion).

WATER

My next project was to determine how deep the water table was. To do this you must check two information sources: Go see your neighbors and find out how deep their wells are, then go talk to the county environmental department. It also might help to see a well drilling company, even if there is surface water. Often the powers that be (county or state) may not want to let you drink out of that emerald green pond you hope to use. Remember that surface water can often be unsafe to drink because of agricultural or livestock run-off. If you can't afford to drill down to the water table, you might want to look elsewhere for land because hauling water is a horrible project, as friends who do it have often told me.

I drilled 100 feet of well for my place and found water at 85 feet, so I was lucky. However, another person in my valley who lives on top of a hill had to go 400 feet deep at six times my cost.

Water is essential, and you'll need a spring or well that produces at least four gallons a minute. You might consider a hand-dug well. Of course, it will not be as deep, but it will save you hundreds of dollars on well drillers and all. (See the diagrams for spring box and pumps and tanks, page 29.) It can't be said strongly enough: Use all resources to find your water, and take all the old timers' opinions with a grain of salt.

One last possibility is to get someone to "water witch" (dowse) the land. Some people think of this method as pure superstition or magic, but if you think it's worth a try, by all means go ahead. I did and the results were good. Try to get someone with a lot of successful experience to do the witching. Besides knowing the thrill of ancient folklore in action, you just may hit water. Most witchers do well-drilling too, so be careful that they don't get too optimistic (for instance, a 20-foot-deep water table in the desert). You usually must pay even if the hole is dry, so bear that in mind when you're not sure about water's presence.

WHAT SIZE PARCEL?

How much land you want is directly related to your intended use. I am not a farmer so I didn't want much land, just enough for a vegetable garden, maybe a horse and a stable. I've had my land for some time now, and I haven't regretted having an acre (approximately 210 feet by 210 feet or, more exactly, 43,560 square feet). In fact, most people tend to overbuy and then have to pay higher and higher taxes when other people start building in the area. Try looking in back issues of *Organic Gardening* magazine, *Mother Earth News,* and government pamphlets to get an idea of homesteads and gardens. There are excellent homestead layouts for 1, 2, and 3 acres. You can grow enough food for six families on 1 acre, and that's with room to spare. So unless you like to know that your land extends from horizon to horizon or unless you plan to farm, don't overbuy. (See the diagram of a possible homestead, *Fig. 2–A*.)

If you are going to settle communally with a group of friends on some land, remember that one person leaving or not making payments—no matter how good his or her intentions—could mean the loss of the whole piece for everybody. I recommend getting a lawyer for $100 and subdividing the land into separate parcels, all legal and above board. Then if someone has to leave or wants to sell out, it's easy and painless.

You may consider buying a 10-acre piece, building a house, and then selling 5 acres for a nice profit. This is a good plan if you like the idea of tying up money in real estate. Sometimes it is easy to sell, sometimes it literally takes years, but there is a definite pitfall to consider. Many counties are trying to discourage overbuilding, and they usually do it in two ways: They refuse to issue septic tank or building permits, and they won't let you subdivide your land. You should know what your county is doing now, and even though you can't predict the future precisely, it pays to ponder it.

KNOW THE LAND

Land taxes are something you must know beforehand. Let's say you find a cute little oceanside plot at such a low price it's an obvious steal. Nine times out of ten, that little lot costs $1,000 a year in taxes, plus maybe a bond issue or two. A *bond issue* is a tax added to your regular taxes by a local public vote, and it is usually in the nature of $5,000 to $50,000 over a ten-or-twenty-year loan period. You must pay your share of this supplemental tax, and you will have it added to your base tax. So be forewarned and scout around at the tax assessor's office.

It pays to be cautious in relation to the nature of your land and also how nature relates to it! You like cliffs, huh? Well maybe you should see a local geologist before you put your house on the edge. Or that peaceful river flowing by in the summer—can it cause killer floods in the winter? These are not just idle questions. Open a newspaper and you'll see how bad planning and taking stupid risks can wipe out your life's biggest investment, or even you.

Now away from the bad stuff for a moment. Relax and get the feel of the land. I found the best way is to pack up a couple of sandwiches, some beer, or whatever, and take a picnic on it (with the owner's permission, of course). Find out if the land is too rocky or if you like the extreme shade it offers. How about good southern exposure for a garden? Is the grazing area relatively flat? Beforehand, make up a list of the things essential to you and then check them off. Remember that taking a few days and doing a little research can save you a lot of misery.

A word of warning about realtors. While most of them have basically good ethics, all of them tend to tell white lies, such as "you'd better tell me today if you want this beautiful lot because another couple is going to submit an offer tomorrow." Now this may be true, but usually it is not, so don't rush. Take enough time to consider carefully. If you miss it, even better land will turn up. I know . . . it happened to me.

MAKING THE PURCHASE

Now let's assume you've found some land and you like it enough to build on it. But then you remember all those tales about how it takes years to get the papers and all the red tape out of the way. Most of these stories are myths, except in rare cases where the problem of a civil action suit or lost deed pops up. If the title company is efficient, they will find the deed and title papers in a week and send them to the county offices. Usually it's a two-to-three-week period until you get the title. If you finance, add on the time it takes to get your loan.

Now you face the question of whether it is better to pay outright or to obtain a loan. There are advantages and disadvantages in each course of action, and your decision will be based largely on your amount of available money, your credit rating, and your desire to sink yourself in debt. Most banks are reluctant to loan on unimproved land, but you may want to try agriculturally oriented banks. Sometimes they are more liberal in policy.

I wanted to pay cash for my land and get a clear deed, then build the house gradually with cash I saved along the line. Some friends did it the other way; they bought the land on credit and then financed a house too. They have pretty good jobs, so the risk for them is minimal on a twenty-year loan. You have probably heard that good money managers finance everything because the value of money borrowed is increased by inflation and real estate appreciation. This is true, but to figure the growth of money value you have to know the market values and be able to plot a speculative increase. This is not impossible to do, but the details are beyond the scope of this book. Talk to your banker if you are curious.

Sometimes an individual selling the land will "carry the papers." That is, he will accept payments directly from you. If he will do it and it's legally drawn up by a lawyer, be sure you understand the terms. Missing only a few months' payment can mean you lose your down-payment *and* land!

The advantages of cash are more obvious: the simplicity of the transaction, a clear deed, the secure feeling of really owning the land, and finally, the saving of the interest you would normally give the bank. But if you don't have cash, get a loan. Why wait?

PROTECT YOURSELF

Most states require you to have insurance on the title to your land, in case your ownership is challenged. It isn't a bad idea to have it anyway, since the fee is $40–50 and you only pay once. The title insurance company then takes your deed and records it, making all the past papers on the land available to you in chronological order. This is handy because you may, for instance, want to know if an old well is any good, and you can find the past owner who dug it and ask him about it. In some states the state government will insure you and do the paperwork. In others you will need a lawyer, due to red tape involved.

If you neglected to find out if anyone has easements across your land (e.g., the power company, neighbors who need access, and lumber companies) you might get an unpleasant jolt now. Get the title company or proper agency to explain the terms and stipulations of the title papers. You can always challenge an easement in court, but court action can be very expensive, and you probably won't win anyway. Remember, a realtor often won't tell you about these hidden clauses. You must find them out *before* you buy, to be on the safe side.

This is also a good time to talk about insurance. I know, you say all work and no play. Well here's what happened to me. I put off getting liability and damage insurance, which protects you in case someone breaks their neck or something on your land and wants to sue. I just couldn't seem to find the time to make it down to the insurance man. A few months after I had bought the land, a fifty-year-old man delivering wood to me slipped while carrying a load. Luckily, he broke only one leg. All the way to the hospital he kept saying to me, "I sure hope you got insurance, buddy." I didn't have the heart to tell him I didn't, because I had visions of that man soon owning my land. Anyway, we settled out of court and to this day I regret not having had insurance when I needed it. Imagine the cost of getting out of the jam if a small child falls in your septic tank hole! Check on fire insurance also, if there is any risk of a fire destroying your construction in progress. Insure right away, don't rely on luck!

Assuming you have found some land, checked it out, and bought it, you can roll up your sleeves and proceed to the next chapter.

Fig. 2–A The One-Acre Homestead

GETTING THE LAND READY

CHAPTER 2

This is the appropriate time to draw a scale-size aerial view of your land on a large sheet of paper. On another piece of paper draw an *elevation plan* (side view cutting through your proposed area). *See Fig. 2-B* .

If the area on which you want to build is very steep and has no flat space for the house, you will have to consider cutting out a ledge with a caterpillar tractor. If you build on posts that elevate part of the house, you will need to secure the rear of the house with a concrete footing. Include the posts and concrete footing in your drawings. *See Fig. 2–B.*

Now draw the compass directions on your aerial drawing. To easily visualize the sun's path, write *setting sun* on the west edge of the paper and *rising sun* on the east. Only in the dead of summer does the sun pass directly overhead, so to get its correct path, draw a rough sketch resembling the one below. Be sure your plan shows the correct topography of your land. *See Fig. 2–C.*

As you can see in the drawing, the winter sun in North America still rises from the east to west but it leans far south, making the days shorter and shadows longer. This altered winter path is most important in relation to your land. Let's say you put a garden behind the north wall of your house in June, where it receives good sun in the summer. When the fall comes and the sun leans south, your house's shadow will be cast across the garden, depriving the garden of light.

Your house is similar to the garden, in that a well-planned house receives a good amount of direct sunlight in the winter months, cutting your heating costs and lighting bills. If you plant tall trees to the south of your house, you will receive very little cooling shade in summer but a lot of harmful shade in winter.

There are other reasons for carefully planning your sunlight orientation. Consider the important psychological advantages of direct winter sunlight. Imagine getting up in a cold room and looking out at the tall trees or cliffs shading your house. Next imagine that same house filled with warm bright sunlight when you wake up.

As a rule, open southern slopes are best for gardens, since they receive sun all day. Regarding your house, the sun all day in summer means trouble with cooling. You can cool your house naturally by planting shade trees to the west of it and slightly favoring the north quarter. If you have the opportunity to observe your land in summer and winter, by all means visit your proposed house site from time to time and jot down a few notes as to where the sun sets and rises in the various months. Record this on your aerial land drawing, and it will be invaluable when you plant your trees and gardens.

Other land features in combination with weather conditions will influence your land drawing. If, for instance, you live in a valley as I do, you do not receive sun until later in the morning. Also, cool night air sometimes is trapped in the pockets of the valley until noon. Land near the ocean is swept with wind blowing onshore in the morning and offshore in the evening, creating heating and cooling problems for the home builder. Land in the mountains has its own peculiar features too. Some of these are updrafts, winds, little direct sun, and clouds backing up on slopes. In this regard one of the most important things you can do first in planning is to take your drawings to a local weather service and geological station and try to get some advice on local conditions. It will pay big dividends to

Fig. 2–B Elevation Plan and Appropriate Foundations

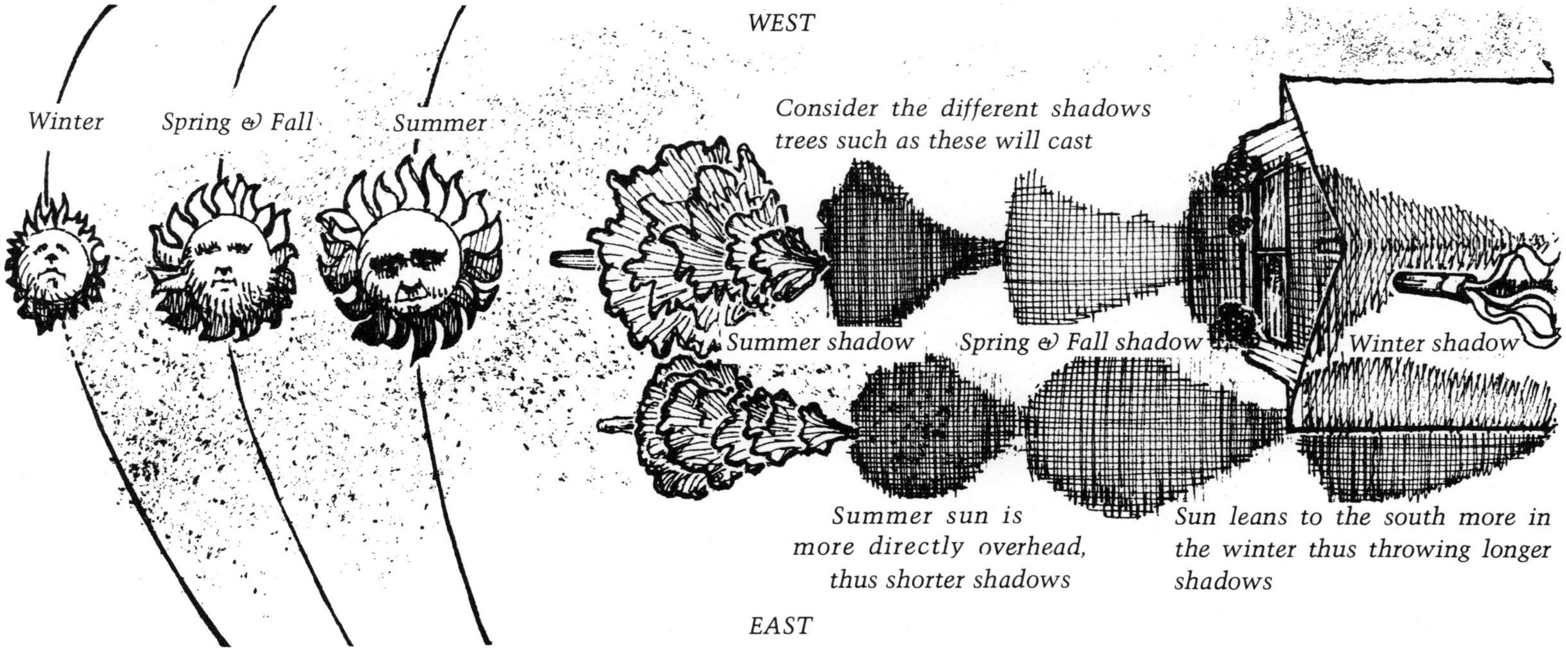

Fig. 2–C The Sun's Path

you later if you plan correctly at this stage.

Let's take up the subject of sunlight in the house once more, now that we better understand the importance of house placement. Keeping in mind the previous discussions, you might decide to plan east-facing bedrooms for the people who get up early. Since the kitchen is also used early, you may also want to put it on the east side. If you get beautiful sunsets, place a picture window facing in that direction. During all this preliminary planning note down ideas in the corners of your land maps. When the time arrives to do the formal blueprints, you'll have a page full of good ideas. One excellent book to use at this stage is Ken Kern's *The Owner-Built Home.* It provides a wealth of environmental ideas plus construction details.

GRADING

The steepness of the slope in its relation to the house and its proposed foundation is something the builder must take into consideration. For instance a forty-five degree slope can be cut with a deep notch if the soil and house design permit, or a shallow notch can be cut and long poles can be used to support the front of the house. Since a forty-five degree slope would be considered by most builders to be a very challenging slope, the layman should consider something less steep. If you have insurmountable problems see an architect versed in slope houses.

If you now know what the land needs to make it buildable, call the earthmovers and set up a date. Be there for the work, because you'll personally have to direct the cutting at every stage. The work will probably be over before you realize it, but *remember this:* Have them dig everything possible in one trip, and you won't have to pay the delivery time fee again. Here is a check list of things they might be able to do for you:

1. Grade or cut out road and driveway.
2. Cut and grade house pad and garden spot.
3. Rip out medium-size trees to help clear land (see it to believe it!)
4. Dig large leaching trench and hole for septic tank.
5. Dig sewer line trenches.
6. Dig culvert trenches for roads, paths, and retaining walls.
7. Dig pond.
8. Shave a steep bank back so it won't collapse.
9. Move large objects or tear down sheds, bushes, and other obstacles.
10. Pack down loose fill dirt.

If you are lucky and have fairly flat land and not a lot of rainfall, you probably won't need to put in a road and parking space. But more often than not, it's necessary or preferable to put in some sort of access. In the summer months it's easy to get a big cat tractor on your land to cut a road for temporary use; later you can pave or oil it if you want. In the winter it's a whole different story, depending on how soupy the soil is, or how steep the slope. Sometimes you just can't effectively use land until the dry season comes. My advice is to wait until springtime or later to put a road in, because cutting it in the fall could mean it would be washed out totally by March.

How much does it cost to have this big machinery crash around on your land? First, there are several different sizes of caterpillar tractors available, and the size of the job should determine which you use. I prefer the big one if any amount of land cutting is to be done, and this runs from $25 to $40 per hour, depending on who's available. The smaller cat with a back-hoe is fine for light cutting, tree pushing, trench digging, and grading, and it usually runs from $20 to $30 per hour. These monsters are so powerful that almost any job never takes more than two hours on an acre or two of land. Tractors are well worth the money if you know what you want done before they arrive.

WATER DEVELOPMENT

Water is your most important concern now, and there are many choices of development available. The first that occurred to me and usually does to everybody else is to share a neighbor's tanks, creek, well, or whatever and then split the costs. I know people who have done this, and I've been told that it works if a legal form is drawn up by a lawyer *exactly* designating the sharing procedure and costs. Near my house in Santa Cruz, several water wars have been viciously fought, and they are colorfully reminiscent of the range wars waged in the old Southwest.

If you have a river or creek, you will have to check its drinkability at your county water department or fish and game bureau, or get a chemist to analyze it ($20). You might have to invest in a treatment system.

Livestock wastes or septic tanks must not be allowed to contaminate springs. If necessary, the area should be fenced off from cattle, pets, and wild animals. Periodic cleaning and maintenance of retainers and *well points* (screened intakes) will be necessary, along with yearly chemical checks on the water's drinkability. Sand has a nasty habit of clogging the flow, so gravel in the bottom of the spring might help. *See Fig's. 2–D, 2–E & F.*

Water holding tanks are made of either steel, concrete, or wood. Any of these materials is satisfactory, but concrete insulates best and is most durable. A redwood tank made of heartwood will last 50–100 years depending on wood quality. Steel is equally durable if it is well galvanized. A 300–500-gallon capacity is what a normal household needs. Expect to spend a couple of hundred dollars on your tank.

WELLS

When no surface water exists, the next major alternative is to dig some sort of well. Before you decide where to locate your well, remember it will have to be 100 feet from any part of the septic tank in order to be safe. This means you should have enough room later to put in a septic leach field. Be safe and put the well over to the side of your parcel of land, away from the septic tank.

The cheapest well, but not the best, is hand dug. These old-fashioned wells are easy to contaminate and hard to treat chemically. They also can present a danger to small children and animals who stray near them.

If your water table is near the surface, I recommend renting a home well-drilling outfit, which is available from rental companies in most large cities. The outfit drills to a depth of 50 feet and consists of a small gas motor, bit extenders, and

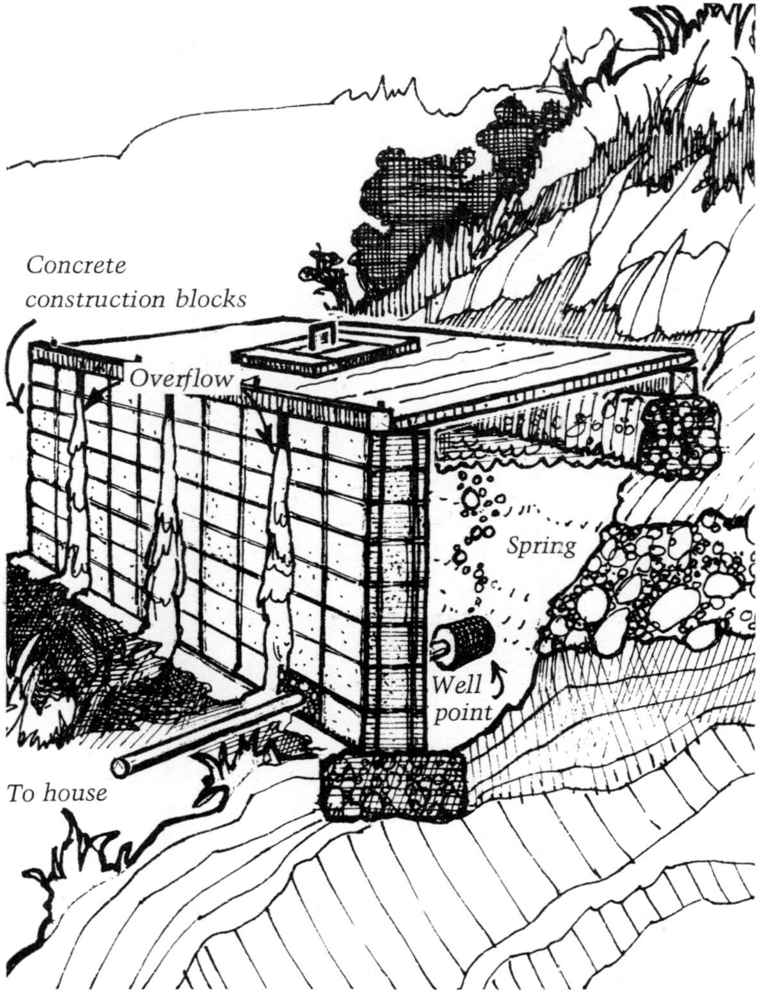

Fig. 2–D The Excavated Spring

Fig. 2–E The Excavated Spring

cutting bits. When you're finished drilling, you put in your own perforated pipe, gravel, and submersible pump. The equipment rents for approximately $30 a day, and one day should do it. This type of well is safe, clean, and just as cheap to install as the hand-dug type, when you consider the time and effort put into digging a well by hand.

Pumps

One type of pump is a *surface pump* that suctions the water up out of the well. Surface pumps cost $80–$300, depending on size and capacity. These are okay for shallow wells (60–75 feet deep), but the deeper the level from which they have to pump, the less their capacity will be. Surface pumps are used with perforated plastic or metal pipe sunk in the ground, and usually you pack the hole with pea gravel and seal the top with a load of concrete.

The most commonly used pump and also the most expensive is the ½–1 horsepower *submersible pump. See Fig. 2–G.* You can expect to pay anywhere from $150 for the smallest (120-volt) to $500 for the large-job 220-volt pump. You can install these yourself if you can drill a well hole at least 6 inches in diameter—preferably larger. The pump is 3–4 inches wide, and it must fit inside the plastic perforated pipe slipped into the hole. This pipe is glued together with plastic couplings and special adhesive and is lowered almost the whole length of the hole. The submersible pump is efficient because it does not rely on a vacuum suction to pull the water up, but instead pushes the water up to the surface from the bottom of the well. *See Fig. 2–G.*

Submersible pumps seem to work reliably and are excellent for maintaining a constant pressure high enough to fill a pressure tank to 60 psi (pounds per square inch). Usually 60 psi is sufficient to supply a very large house with excellent pressure

Fig. 2–F Spring Box with Pressure System and Gravity-Feed System with Submersible Pump

at the faucets. A submersible has one drawback that a surface pump doesn't have. When the submersible pump is worn out, you must pull the power cable supply pipe and pump out of the hole to replace it, which can cost considerable money if a well repairman does it for you.

When putting the submersible in, say, a 100-foot hole, you normally must keep the pump 10 feet or more from the bottom of the hole. Your well hole will collect sand and gravel in the bottom for a while, and if the pump is sitting on the bottom it could be buried. Sometimes after a few years, you will find that even a pump placed at 10 feet from the bottom starts to suck up sand. It must be pulled out, and the well must be sucked free of sand with special pumping equipment.

Don't be too discouraged if your well is slow refilling at first. Drilling can temporarily clog water flow channels in the ground, and the channels must have time to reopen.

Hiring A Well Driller

Now that you have decided what type of well best suits your needs, maybe you've decided you will need the help of a well driller. Go get some price quotes. Start in the *yellow pages* and go right down the line. Prices can range from $6 to $20 (rare) per foot, depending on the diameter of the hole, the method of drilling, the type of ground, and the depth you must go. Some drillers will sell you a pump at cost to get your business, so balance that price with the others offered. When you've got a good quote, find out the cost of a well if it misses water. This probably won't happen, but you'll have to pay something if it does.

Set up a day for the well driller to arrive and be sure to have a good passable road with a fairly smooth, level spot for him to park the drill rig (which is usually on a truck bed). You'll want to stick around for awhile, naturally, to see if you get

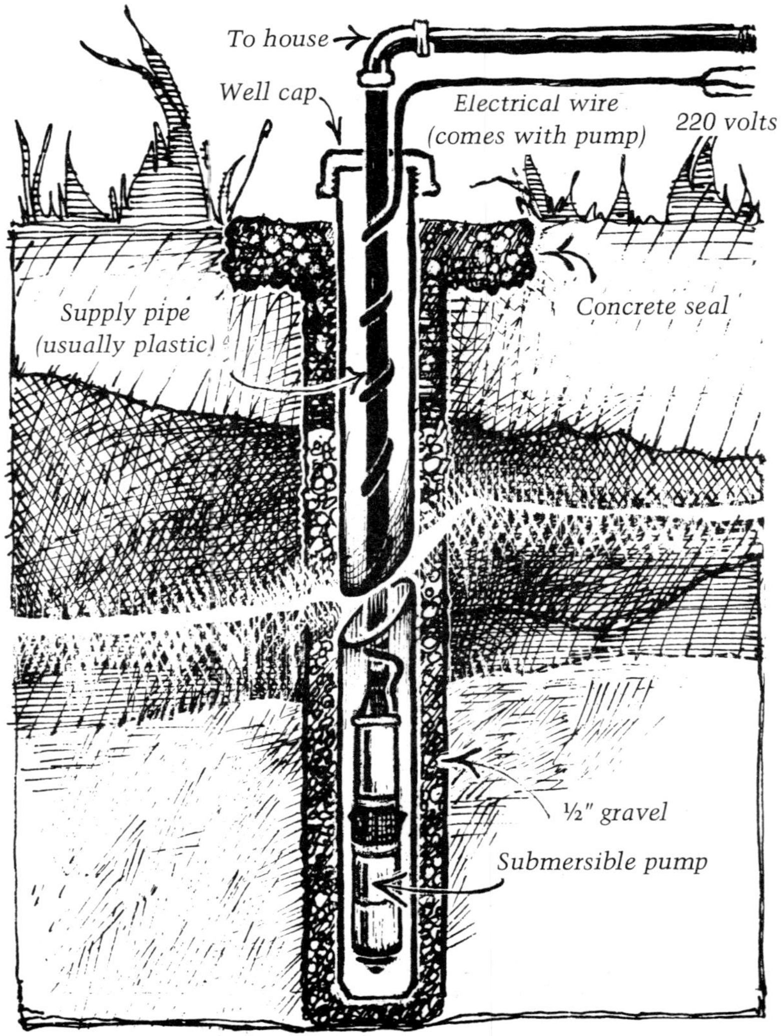

Fig. 2–G An Example of a Submersible Pump

water. Often, setting up the rig takes more time than the actual drilling process.

After the driller finds water, he'll probably drill a little further, then draw out the bit to measure the depth. You'll want to know this measurement because the depth is directly related to the cost of the hole. Next he'll probably put the 6-inch perforated pipe in and fill the hole surrounding the pipe with pea gravel. Leaving a foot or two of pipe above the ground, he'll lower your pump into the hole by its power supply cord and a 1–1½-inch plastic supply pipe or hose. If it's a surface pump arrangement, he'll lower a pipe or hose and hook it up to the surface pump.

If the driller feels it's necessary, he may mix up some concrete grout and fill the space between the pipe and hole for a depth of several feet from the surface. This is a seal against surface contamination. See previous Figure.

Power For The Pump

After the driller has completed testing your pump with a generator or power supply line, he'll pump it out for a while and then leave. You'll have a few problems on your hands now. First, if you don't have temporary electric power, you can't run your pump. Second, 1 or 2 feet of unsightly pipe will be sticking out of your land. There are two solutions to the power problem: Buy the appropriate-size generator or have the electric company give you temporary power for building.

A generator is a good solution if you have the money for it. If your electric company is slow moving, or if they have to put poles in to your area first, you may not have any alternative. Generators/alternators are extremely expensive, so you might want a stiff belt of something before you decide to buy one. There is *good news* though: since used generators are much in demand, you will be able to get back almost all of your money in a year or two, if you aren't in a hurry to sell to the first bidder. I paid $400 for a 220-volt alternator in 1972 and got $350 for it used in late 1974, so it actually saved me money on electric bills! Get one with enough power (watts) and the correct voltage (120 or 220) for your application.

A temporary power pole on your property is easy to put in, but good luck in getting quick service, unless there already is a company pole right across the street. See your power company for a typical setup for temporary power.

Covering The Well

What about that big piece of well pipe sticking up? There are two ways to house the well-head. The first and easiest, but least protective and permanent, is a wooden box built over the pipe head. Use this for a temporary cover only. *See Fig. 2–H.*

The best way to protect your well is to sink a cement well box into the ground around the hole. You will need to build some forms out of particle board or scrap plywood for the concrete pouring, but this will get you used to working with hammer and saw! *See Fig. 2–I.*

If you decide to run some pipe for your water supply, consider that any permanent pipe must be buried at least 1 foot, usually more. If you are unsure where you want your water pipes to go underground, the best bet is to use garden hose to get water where you need it temporarily. At the hardware supply store buy a few new garbage cans (you can use them later for that purpose) and fill them with water. Then every time you need water for washing and various things you won't have to run the pump. This is particularly useful when mixing concrete—you can keep the water near the site you are working on.

Often people have asked me if they can live on their land in a semicompleted house while they build. The answer depends entirely on attitudes in your local area, what the laws are, and how well they are enforced. In some counties and states, you can get a one-year nonextendable permit to park a trailer on the land while construction continues. In other areas nobody seems to care if you ever intend to build a house or not. Of course, if you have land way back in "them thar hills," it's less likely you'll be discovered living in a tent or partially finished house. I would like to say, however, that the building inspectors and health department people are uncanny in turning up illegal acts, and for some reason they often find sadistic pleasure in tracking you down in even the remotest areas. Remember that these people have exceedingly dull jobs and probably look at this side-line detective work as a hobby.

Some friends I knew in Big Sur, California built a 10-foot by 10-foot sun deck in a rather well-hidden and private glade of trees. Since it was summer they slept on their land and did a little cooking every weekend until they could afford to get their house up. One weekend they pulled up to the site and discovered several red tags fluttering from the edges of the sun deck: *This construction is condemned! All building on this site must cease and desist!*

California inspectors "red tag" illegal and unlicensed construction, even if you just want to put up a fence! However, my friends were lucky and no fine was levied against them.

Oddly enough, I was able to stay in my house for weeks on end, even though the exterior wall sheathing was not finished. The building inspector knew I was living there and also that I was surreptitiously setting up my kitchen and bathroom behind the house. So it really just depends on your inspector's attitude toward you.

Remember, if the inspector sees your car, he will assume you are around, and if he sees your car there at night, he'll assume you are living there. You'd be surprised how often

Fig. 2–H Wood Box to Cover Well Head

the building inspectors casually pass by your land and construction. Mine "just dropped by" so often that whenever I made a mistake during construction, I would unconsciously look over my shoulder to see if he was watching!

At this point a certain "manifest destiny" graces your land. The house pad is cut, you have a water supply, and the human hand shows upon the earth.

If the time to build is upon you, this is when you begin to lose some sleep or worry a little (or a lot) about the actual work

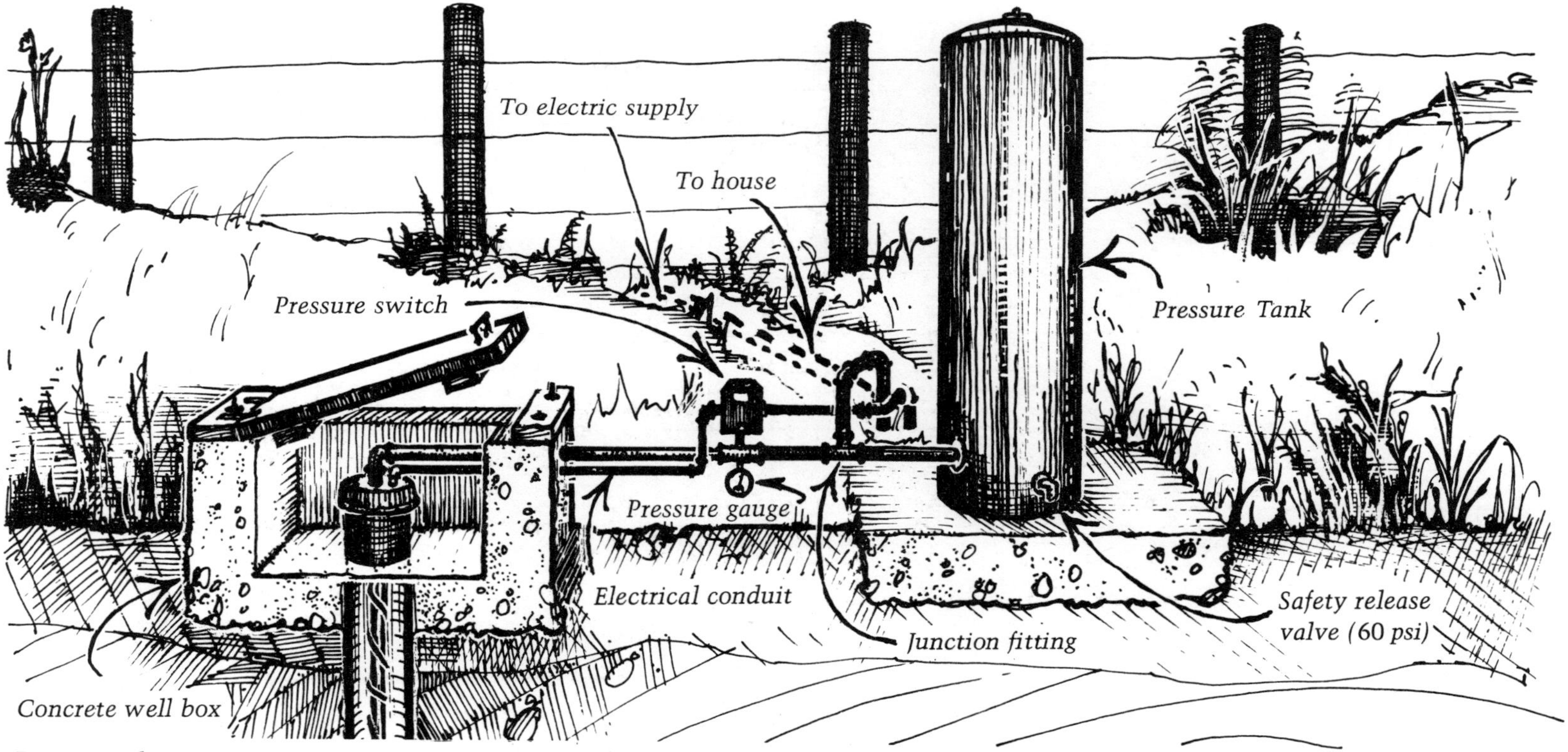

Fig. 2–I This Is One Common Pressure System Used Everywhere

involved. All I can say is keep the proverbial chin up. I went through this phase too, and looking back on it I realize that I needlessly worried. I had planned well, I knew my abilities, and was willing to learn the new ones. This is the point on which I hope my book succeeds most: Keep at it and don't lose heart. Dig into your work and all the doubts will vanish.

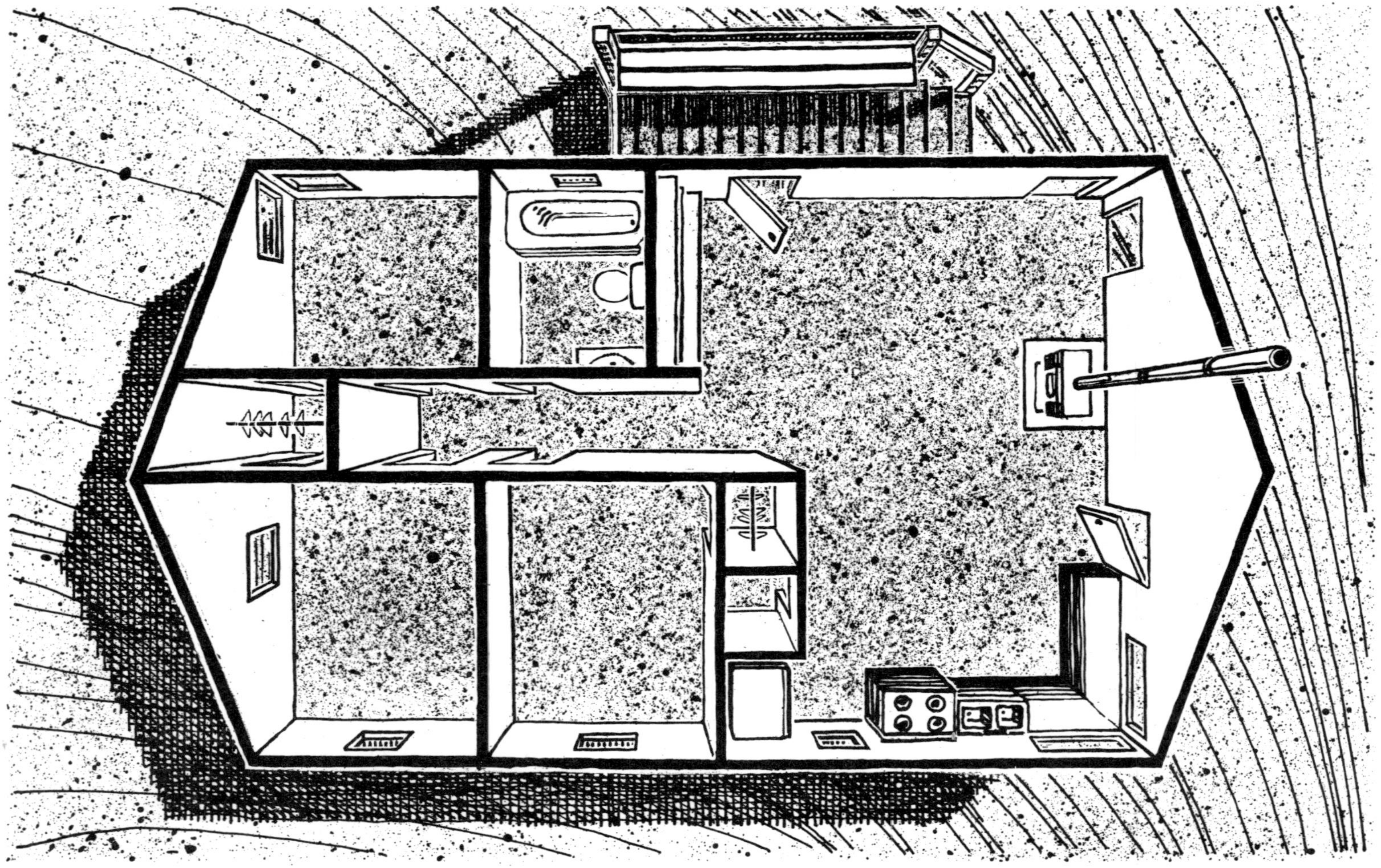

Fig. 3–A The Basic $9,000 House

DESIGNING AND DRAFTING A PLAN

CHAPTER 3

With some of the groundwork out of the way, you'll have time to go over your land and see in a more objective light what you've purchased. You'll probably notice a lot of things you missed when the other person owned the land. Get the feel of the place and visualize the kind of house you'd like to build.

A tape measure stretched across your building site will help you get a more specific idea of how much room a house will take up and will also help you to fix it in your imagination.

You don't have to be an artist to sketch out an idealized drawing of what you'd like your house to look like in ten years' time. If you keep it, you may be surprised at the sketch after only a few years. I certainly was.

As I said at the outset, this book aims to give those people who have no great funds some inspiration to build their own homes. Another major goal is to detail feasible designs that will adapt themselves to amateur construction.

With house designs in magazines or architectural sketch books, the first thing to strike the eye is the size. Usually people associate 1,700 interior square feet with the word house. While the three-bedroom, two-bath ranch house is most often presented as the perfect house, this concept is valid to a minority of people with larger families. Today the trend is toward smaller families and more economical use of space. With our growing ecological concern, we have begun to demand less wasted space and more concentration on the problems of efficiently housing people in smaller homes. Just as the large American luxury car with V-8 engine is rapidly becoming a dinosaur, the rambling mansionesque American ranch house will follow. People are also becoming more involved with their life support systems and wish to take the reins from unseen hands, such as architects, contractors, and tradespeople.

Your concept of the house you will build should be based on one simple tenet: *Build what you need as you need it, while always allowing easily accessible expansion routes.* The general format I have chosen is predominantly rectangular based with a great deal of sloping roof. The round or geodesic house is beyond the scope of this publication and there are several fine books already dealing with it in detail.

Here is my final reason for building on a modest scale, particularly if you are a beginner: A 1,000-square-foot finished house is a heck of a lot more useful than a 2,000-square-foot foundation that you can't finish.

For the most part, the construction details you'll find presented here are acceptable in all the states. However, *always check carefully your local building codes before planning.* Many building codes get updated or changed and you should know these changes in your area.

To get an idea of what type and size of house you want to build, you have to know a little about yourself, your personality, and your future. A single male may want a small bachelor pad initially, but even the best-laid plans go awry. So leave those avenues of expansion ready, even if you now abhor family life.

HOUSE DESIGNS

THE BASIC $9,000 HOUSE

For the family of four that wants a compact house with almost 1,000 square feet of living space for less than $9,000, I recommend the basic house I designed and built. *See Fig's. 3–A & 3–B.* It consists of three bedrooms, a bath, a large kitchen, and a living room. The latter two rooms are the biggest since they hold the most people most often. The bathroom is larger than average, and the kitchen is full of counter and storage space. There are plenty of large windows, which make it seem larger than it really is. This nuclear design is the lowest-cost design possible to build that is still aesthetically pleasing inside and out. The use of high, open-beam ceilings will lend airiness and will eliminate that boxy feeling. I used this design for the first house I built, and I live in a similar version now.

Remember that a more varied look will occur when it's time to expand with additional rooms, dormers, porches, or whatever you want. *But first get in that house!*

The materials used in the basic house are extremely variable and can range from a wood shake roof (expensive) to an industrial hot tar and gravel roof (good and cheap). The interior rooms can easily be juggled with no serious design problems once the essential technique of wall framing is understood. Exterior wall sheathing materials, windows, and doors are also varied and will be discussed in appropriate chapters.

The interior walls may be covered with a number of different materials such as sheet rock, plywood, or old barn wood. Before you choose materials, keep in mind that dark woods will tend to make the rooms look much smaller. I believe the key to keeping your house roomy and airy is to hold the decor to whites and pastels, with some dark trim for contrast.

In making preliminary sketches try not to be too ambitious. Remember, if you draw an elaborate fireplace system in your plans, the building department may hold up your final approval even if you actually don't have enough money now to build the fireplace system. Be modest on the drawing because you can always put that special feature in later.

If you become confused in planning your house, you may want to consult an architect. For a small fee he can straighten you out and put you on the right path.

Assuming you have fairly normal land to build on and it's not too steep or too cramped, many alternate designs are possible. Bear in mind that any departure from basic simplicity will probably increase construction time and costs. However, if you use your imagination and scout around for materials carefully you can produce an extravagantly unique house for less than $9,000.

THE L-SHAPED HOUSE

A second design to consider is the basic L-shaped house. *See Fig. 3–C.* It has the advantage of bedrooms isolated from the

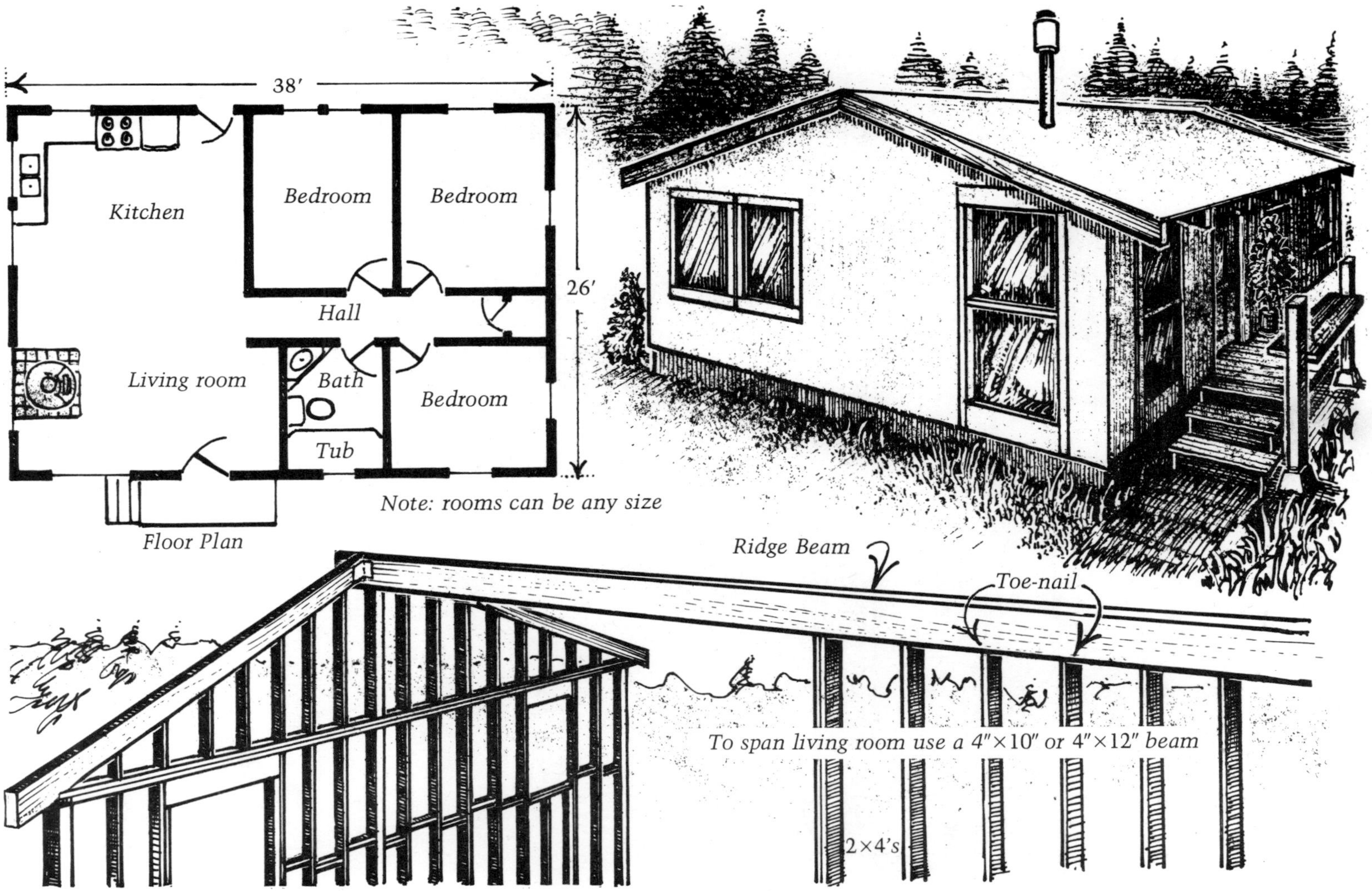

Fig. 3–B Basic House Design #1

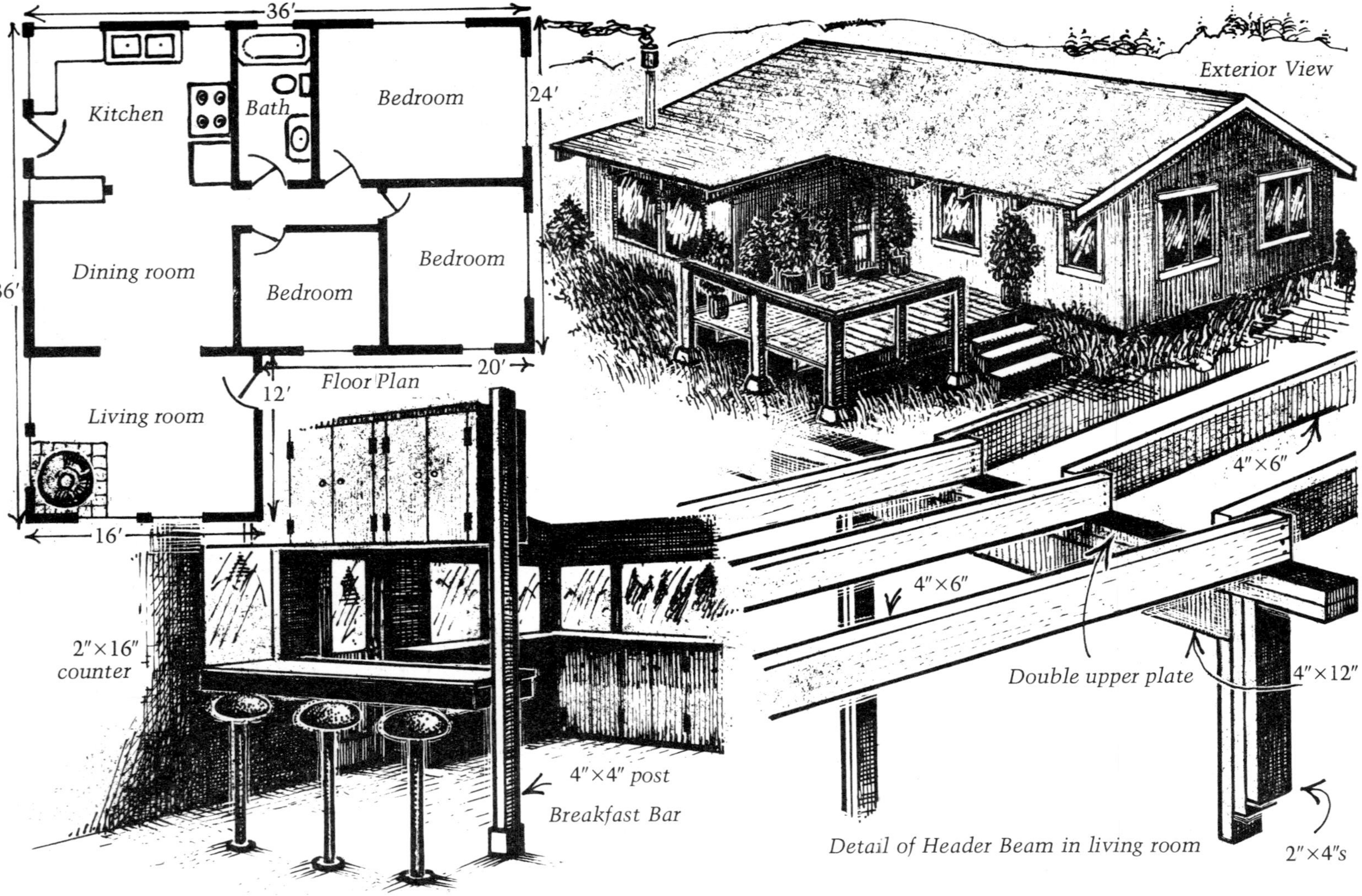

Fig. 3–C L-Shaped House Design #2

rest of the house, making both areas more private and quiet. This design also creates a pleasant mixture of lines and forms, particularly when viewed from the outside. The L-shaped design can also be juggled about to produce the desired area and can be contracted or expanded easily. The roofing on this house is slightly more complex, so care must be taken in design to hold the costs down. (Ideas on how to make it look unique on a beer budget later.)

Large windows will increase the overall feeling of openness in the bedrooms, particularly if the view is nice. The same applies to every other room, and if you are the sort of person who likes a cozy closed-in feeling occasionally, shutters or heavy drapes will work nicely to close off the large windows. The interior of the house suits itself to expansion quite well, and a livable porch usually can be built for a fraction of the cost of an additional room.

THE MODIFIED BASIC HOUSE

Here's a design very similar to the first one I presented, except that the major rooms are dominated by unusual angles. *See Fig. 3–D.* This is an excellent technique to use because the walls are perfect for large glass panes overlooking a grand view. Building with glass is not really much more expensive than using all wood and in some instances is even cheaper. If heating presents a problem, consider using double pane windows (double glazed) to reduce heat loss.

A deck or porch increases the usable area effectively and adds a nice contrast to the glass of the walls. An interior load-bearing wall again provides major savings in money and construction time and throughout this book will be the major roof-support system I advocate using.

THE ONE-SLOPE ROOF

This is one of my favorites, even though it's really a large cabin with a one-way sloping roof. *See Fig. 3–E.* It's the ultimate in useful space and economic construction. A one-slope roof house can easily be built for a few thousand dollars and in addition forms an excellent nucleus for expansion. Simplicity in construction is a feature that I particularly like, and I've seen this design built in approximately five weeks' time, complete with plumbing and electricity.

This house is excellent for a beginner's first project or a second home. You could build it on your land in addition to your house and be assured of a month rental income to help pay the bills. At a later date a room could be added to efficiently expand the livable space, in effect creating a two-bedroom house.

The features of these various houses can be interchanged freely from one design to another, with a little planning on paper first.

Consulting the library for books on house design and architectural drawing will help you grasp the techniques should you want to depart into new territory. Several good magazines are published that feature contemporary ideas and styles, and often you can find inspiration in these pictures. I happened to see a picture of a house with wood shakes around the raised foundation. Since I was building on a hill, I had to cover a rather large foundation area too. So I relieved the tallness on the front of the house with a random pattern of wood shakes. It looks fine now, and I owe that idea to the magazine I saw it in. (The problems of hillsides and their solutions will be discussed later in the book.)

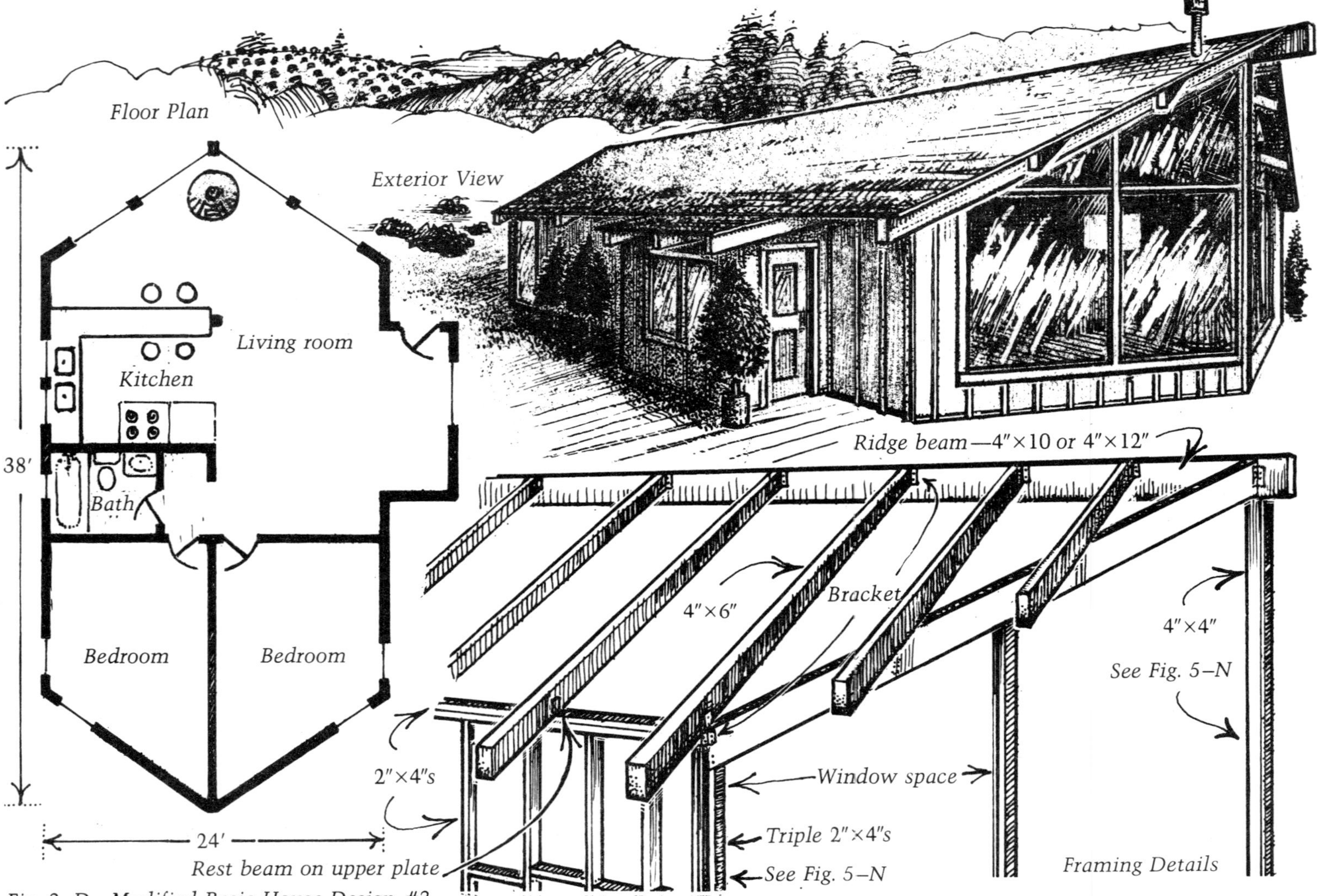

Fig. 3–D Modified Basic House Design #3

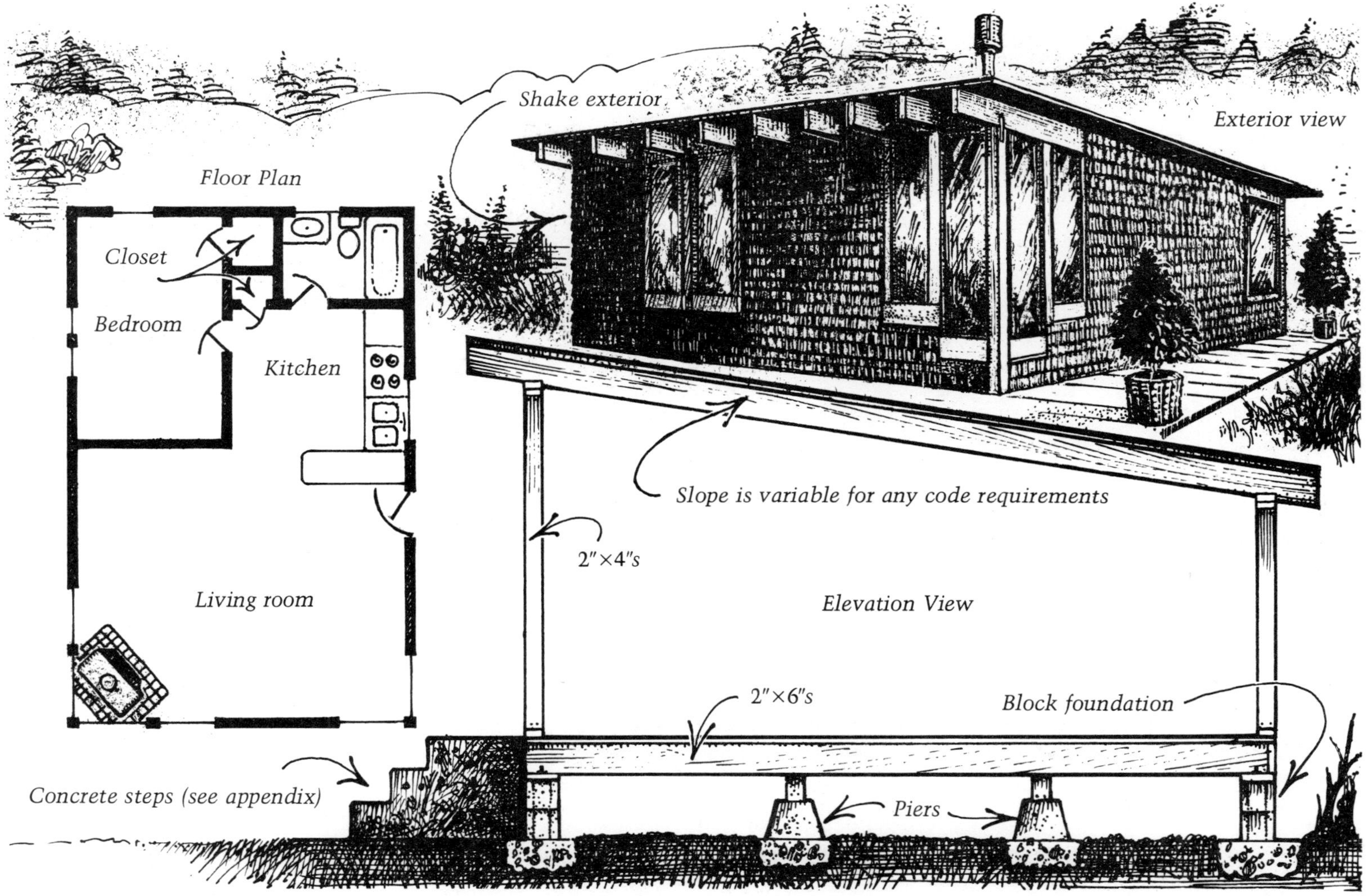

Fig. 3–E One-Slope Roof Design #4

DRAWING YOUR PLAN

The time must inevitably come when those house sketches you've been leaving on matchbook covers and dinner napkins will have to become more substantial. Drawing, or *drafting* as it should be called, isn't hard to learn. The drawings are really just common-sense diagrams of what you are going to build in somewhat chronological order. I was quite surprised to find that architects don't regularly use those boxy letters but instead print like everyone else, only perhaps a little more legibly.

NOTE: House walls are often planned in units of four feet. This is so you won't waste plywood, which comes in 4-foot by 8-foot sheets. Planning this way also speeds up construction time considerably.

Perhaps the greatest problem is knowing what to draw, rather than how. The solution is easy: Go down to the county building department and ask them to give you the fact sheet, if they have one, and also a copy of the building codes (usually $2).

If they have some spare time, get the building department people to show you approximately what they want. Please do this when it's slow for them. It pays to stay on their good side by not inconveniencing them. The inspectors and the building department office people are like no other people I know, and you will soon find out what they're like in your own local area. Throughout this book I will have numerous occasions to comment on them.

The next thing to do is trot on down to the nearest drafting supply store and buy several sheets of prebordered and ready-to-draw translucent paper (a real time-saver), but stay away from those fancy German steel rulers and Rapidograph pens. You don't need them. I bought it all and switched to dime store supplies, which I found more efficient, cheaper, and less messy.

You will need:

—A couple of #2 pencils and a few #3 (lighter shade) pencils.
—One plastic or wooden 1-foot ruler.
—A yardstick (make sure it's straight).
—A 39¢ T-square, if you want to get fancy.
—A lettering template, if you're really a sloppy printer.

Now this is hard to do, but when you get home put all that nice stuff you're itching to draw with in the closet and close the door. Practice first on large sheets of plain paper with your ruler and pencils until you think you can use them neatly and you're sure you know what you want to draw. Tape some pennies to the bottom of the ruler to raise it off the paper—that way you won't smear the line.

At the building office, you'll probably be told you need five 2-foot by 3-foot sheets of drawings. Usually they are as follows:

Sheet 1—*General plot layout,* designating lot size and shape, location of the house, septic tank, well, and anything else major. Give compass directions and indicate nearby lots by number.

Sheet 2—*Floor and foundation plan,* including front and side view of foundation and small detail drawings.

Sheet 3—*Elevation plans.* These are side-by-side drawings of the sides and front of your house after it is sheathed or covered. Windows, doors, and outdoor fixtures are shown.

Sheet 4—*Floor plan with all rooms,* including walls, doors, and windows. This is a top view down into the house. It usually shows wiring and plumbing.

Sheet 5—*Construction plan and details.* Often this is not required, but it's a good idea to include it. The plan is a collection of detailed drawings of complex joints and cross-sections of the construction. Some of them may be represented in an isometric projection style of drawing (three-dimensional).

When you get ready to draw, remember it must be neat and orderly. Start drawing at the top of the page and work down, so that you won't drag your arm across your lines.

Scale rulers are not necessary for this job. Just use a regular ruler and allow ¼ inch to represent 1 foot.

Line up your drawing in the center of the sheet and feel free to box off a little section in the corner to show details or write a little explanation (no sonnets or witticisms, though).

If you feel unconfident, use a #3 pencil when first lettering the words. Then go back and fill it in with a #2 pencil later. Of course, you must underline your lettering lightly with a #3 pencil to get it straight on the page. You can erase the line later.

As you walk into the building and inspection office with your fresh plans under your arm, you will undoubtedly feel like the first person ever to design and draw a house in human history. Remember that the building inspector sees *hundreds* of drawings every day and he isn't that easily impressed. He'll probably tell you that you have not made something clear enough or that the figures don't jibe with the lines, so take a deep breath and DON'T ARGUE. Go home and wipe the tears from your cheeks. Make the corrections or redraw whatever is necessary. Unfortunately, it's seldom, if ever, you win an argument with these people, and God help you if you ever do.

When your plans are accepted, you will be required to pay for the building permit, so take along your checkbook. The fee could range from $50 to $200, so find out beforehand. Now you're ready to think about buying lumber and other materials.

Fig. 4–B Tool Box with Trays

BREAKING GROUND

CHAPTER 4

In a previous chapter I spoke about the nervous qualms you'll suffer before you actually begin construction. Well, here's the second big scare: prices. I'm sure a lot of houses never get beyond this stage, and as much as I tried when I built my house, I could not find a word about how to save money when buying supplies. It must be the old Midas touch syndrome, but most authors of do-it-yourself books and magazine articles seem to think their readers have easy access to Fort Knox. There is some good news, and it took me some thinking and searching to come up with it.

First, it's no secret that lumber companies stand to make a lot of money on the lumber and supplies necessary to build a house. Often they'll even come out to the site and offer you all sorts of inducements to buy the whole shot at once from them. They may promise free delivery, 10 percent off, or possibly free construction guidance (usually a dozen-page throwaway pamphlet). If your checking account is fat and you're dying of impatience, take them up on it—but you're not going to save as much money.

The bottom line is the thing to remember in lumber prices. So before you buy anything, scout around to different lumber companies and get a feel for what the prices are on the supplies and materials you'll need. Write them down so you'll be able to recognize a real sales bargain when you see one. Familiarize yourself with the different grades of lumber and their price differences, but keep your checkbook in your pocket or purse. At this point patience is your best friend.

LUMBER AND MEASUREMENTS

Before we get into saving money, let's discuss the materials you'll be using. A very large percentage of your home-building budget will go for lumber and plywood. It is essential that you know the types of material available and the variations in their quality because building codes specify certain grades of wood for different aspects of construction. You will want to be sure that you get the grade of wood specified for the job.

One thing that will surprise you if you are a beginner is the *actual dimensions* of the lumber you purchase. For instance, did you know that a 2×4 is actually measured closer to 1⅝ inch by 3⅝ inch? That 2×6's are actually 1⅝ inch by 5½ inch, and 4×12's are 3½ inch by 11½ inch when tape-measured? This apparent rip-off is just the standard size designation for

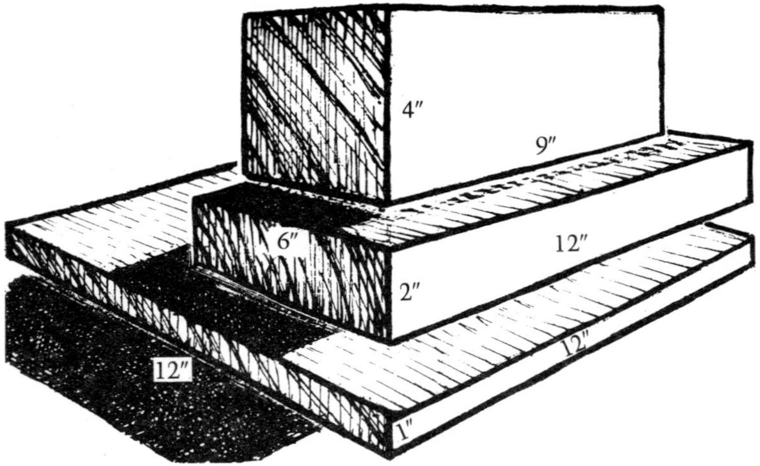

Fig. 4–A Examples of One Board Foot

rough lumber before it is planed to a finish.

Lumber is sold by the *board foot* most commonly. This isn't the same as a square foot and should not be confused. A standard board foot is 1 inch thick, 12 inches wide, and 12 inches long. Likewise, if you have a 1-foot long 2×6 you'll have 1 board foot. *See Fig. 4–A.*

Prices will often be quoted by the 1,000-board-foot quantity, so divide by 1,000 to get the board foot price.

Lumber is graded in categories of 1, 2, and 3. Number 1 is best quality, smooth and suitable for finishing and framing work. Number 2 is more knotty and is for utility nonstress work. Lumber yards will often mix grades 1 and 2 together in what is called a *mixed grade.* If your state allows it, use it. Number 3 is very rough and knotty and is usually suitable for fences and small projects. Find out each specific use in your locale.

Plywood is sold by the square foot, and there are different grades with hundreds of wood finishes readily available. *Finish quality* is best. It is also stamped Grade 1 occasionally. *Utility grade* is the next, and this is often more knotty and unfinished in appearance. *Exterior use plywood* is treated against weather damage and is also called *sheathing. Interior plywood* is also called paneling and is generally thinner. All trim wood is sold by the running foot and is almost always finish grade.

SAVING MONEY

Salvage or second-hand lumber can be a real money-saver, provided first of all that you can find it, and second whether your local building code allows you to use it. Find out by all means—if you think you can get your hands on some. But keep these precautions in mind. Even where its use is allowed, the grade stamp must still be visible. If it isn't, you may be able to get by the building inspector by having it checked out and approved by an architect or building engineer—in writing. Always look closely for signs of termite damage (press a screwdriver or other metal tool firmly against random spots along some of the boards—if the tool sinks into a channel or network of holes, bid the seller a polite goodbye). Nail holes are okay if the wood is otherwise structurally sound. Here again, it pays to know your prices of new lumber. Don't take for granted that the seller is offering you a good deal automatically or you may get taken to the cleaners. Don't be afraid to bargain and don't be at all hasty about prices over 50 percent of retail as compared to new stuff.

My favorite technique for saving money on lumber takes a little time and planning, plus the help of a big-city Sunday paper. While your deed for the land is being readied, or you are waiting for the winter storms to finish, look around for good lumber deals. Lumber companies are deluged in spring and summer with new shipments of wood, and any old and discolored or beat-up stock must go. Ads will read something like, "25% to 50% off on 8-foot framing studs" (very common to see) or "plywood paneling $5 a sheet—construction grade." Check these prices against a master price list you have created from all other sources.

When you finally see one or two stores offering good prices on studs and plywood, borrow a friend's truck or rent one and get all the sale items you need for building your house. You will need a flat bed or a big van to haul it all. Sometimes you can get the truck and driver cheap by asking around farms for a flat bed, then making an offer for the trip into town. (Call the store first to see if they have what you want.)

When you get to the sale, check to see if the grade is stamped and is clearly readable on the lumber. When transporting and storing your wood in harsh weather, be sure to cover it with plastic. All that pretty plywood will quickly discolor and stain if the rain douses it or the sun beats down on it.

There is another method for saving big money on wood. Go directly to the mill, if there is one reasonably near. Often the people there will sell you lumber if you say you are an owner-builder contractor. Ask them if you can see any weathered studs or beams out in back that they might sell cheap. There's a good chance you'll find a pile of straight lumber that has nothing wrong with it but some sticky sap and a little grayness from age. You can get this stuff supercheap and cut your cost at least 50 percent. Most likely you'll have to pick it up and haul it yourself, but it should be worth it. **WARNING:** Beware if this wood has too many knots, warps, or no grade stamps!

To find odd-size pieces of lumber for doors and cabinets, go around to construction sites and ask the boss if you can clean up the site a few times a week and keep the scrap lumber. You will need a pickup truck, and within a few weeks' time will have a handsome pile of scrap lumber that is very useful on any job. It is not uncommon to find at construction sites handfuls of nails dropped on the ground from broken bags, large discarded pieces of plywood, and discarded electrical and plumbing supplies.

One trick for saving money is slightly illegal, but the nice part is that absolutely none of the risk falls on you. When you have a plumber, carpenter, or electrician come over to do a small job, ask him if he'd like to buy electrical, plumbing, or wood supplies for you. He'll probably agree if you offer him $10–$15 to do it. He will be able to use his contractor's number and save you 50 percent, and he'll make some easy money for just cruising downtown. Have your list ready and you'll be on easy street, because even in the unlikely event that something goes wrong, no blame will be associated with you. All of the tradespeople I personally know do this, and at first I was shocked by the casualness with which they do it. One disadvantage of buying this way is that you can't return an item if it's the wrong size or whatever, but remember your savings will be *hundreds of dollars* if you buy your materials at once.

Back on the legal side of the tracks again: Remember that *it is possible* to save money, and that every penny you save will get you further along if you're tight for funds.

TOOLS AND TOOL BOXES

After spending all that money, you'll be ready to roll up your sleeves and dig in. There is a really satisfying feeling about watching a big pile of lumber turn into a house.

It's crossed your mind, I'm sure, that you are going to need a panel truck just to carry all the tools you'll need. This is another myth. I keep all my tools in a tool box 1 foot wide and high by 2 feet long, except, of course, for my electric drill and saw and a few other items. How can I do that, you say? For the plumbing I rented the equipment for two days at $10 a day. For the cement driveway I rented all the tools I needed, thereby saving money by not buying equipment I would only use once.

Sometimes tool chests can be bought at flea markets or pawn shops. I picked up mine for $15, and it was packed full of tools. When I sat down and figured out the savings, I came up with $120 on that one tool box. If you buy tools that are rusty—maybe a saw or a screwdriver—you can restore their original beauty with a piece of emery paper and some light oil. Take dull old saws to a good saw sharpener, and they'll come back as sharp as new.

It's great to have one big tool box for everything. That way you don't have to run back to the car every few minutes to get something you left in the other box. Just be sure the box has a lift-out tray. That way small tools are easy to find. Here's a simple plan for a tool box I built of plywood (particle board would also be good) in three hours. *See Fig. 4–B.*

FOUNDATIONS

The most expensive space to construct in a house, considering today's prices, is the basement. I'll assume here that you will forgo this luxury. Many homes built today do not incorporate basements, due to difficulties of excavation, bad natural lighting, leakage, and heating problems. Providing you have at least a couple thousand square feet of land, you will have room to expand without going underground.

SOLID CONCRETE PAD

Four types of basic foundations are presently in use. The first is the solid concrete pad. While an excellent foundation, it is the most expensive. You can expect to pay thousands for a 1,000-square-foot house pad. Once it is in, the beginning plumber has put all his eggs in a concrete basket, so to speak, since the plumbing is covered up permanently. See a professional for this type of concrete foundation and floor.

POLE FOUNDATION

This second method of foundation construction is rapidly becoming illegal in many states due to abuses of its simplicity. Check to see if you can build a pole foundation in your area. Perhaps by saying your house is a vacation house you will be able to convince them you can safely use this method. The ease and low cost of pole construction is the major advantage. However, it is not as strong structurally as a concrete foundation, and it tends to lower your overall house value.

If you are using long foundation poles on a hillside, or if you want to raise the house on stilts, you will have to embed the poles in the earth. Check to see what the local specifications are for this operation. Then proceed as you would with the normal pier construction technique explained next. *See Fig. 4–C.*

PIER AND POST FOUNDATION

Pier and post foundations are cheap to build and strong enough for all situations involving fairly level ground. Your site must be reasonably level, but it does not have to be graded perfectly.

Your first step in building a typical pier foundation for the 1,000-square-foot house is to stake off the foundation measurements. Begin by driving two stakes at one corner of your site (a). *See Fig. 4–D.*

Tie strong string to one of the stakes and run the string to one of two stakes (b) at a distance exactly equal to the *exterior* length of your house. Next estimate as best you can the 90 degree angle and measure off to the next two stakes (c). Do it

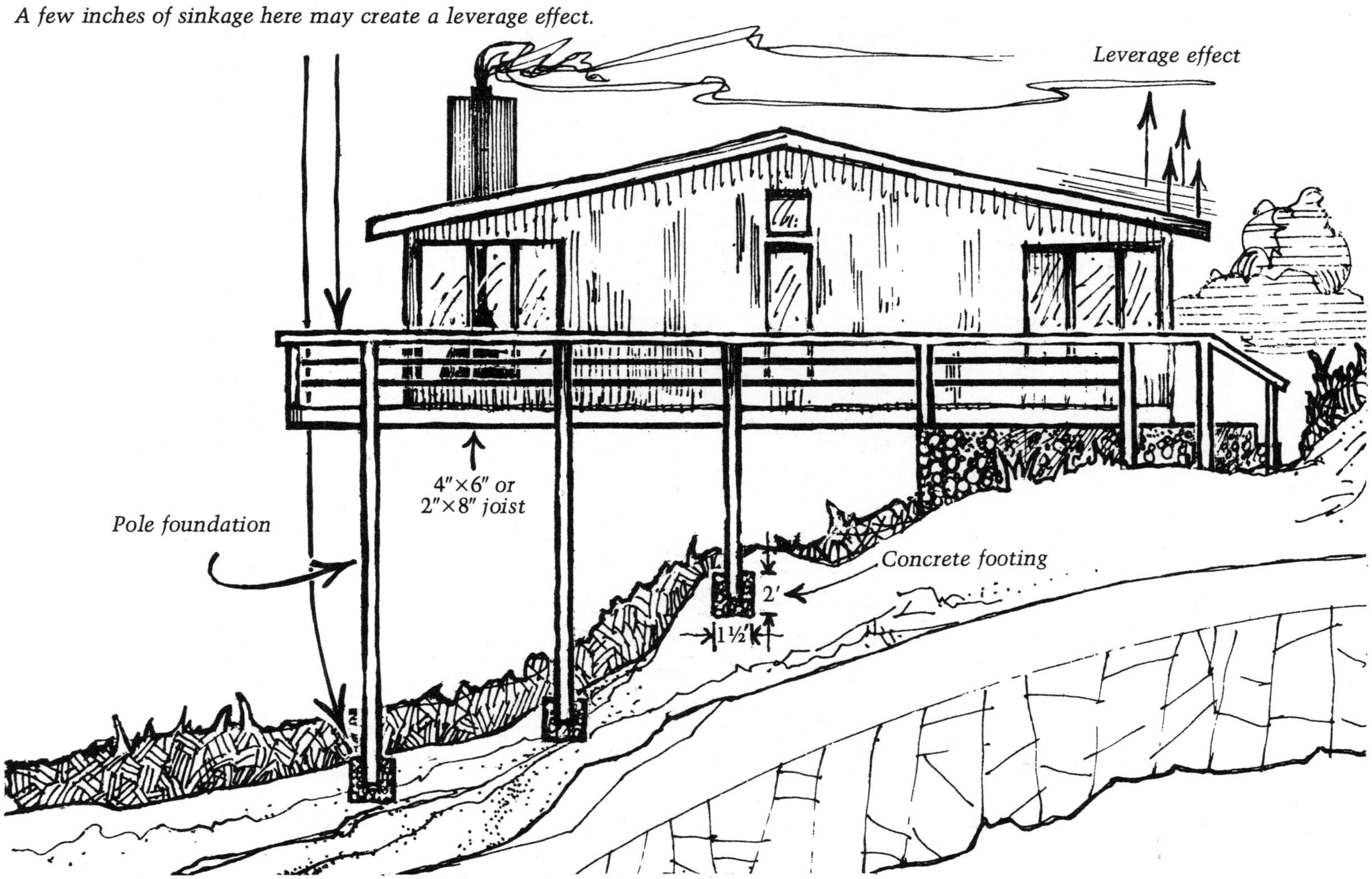

Fig. 4–C Embedding Foundation Poles

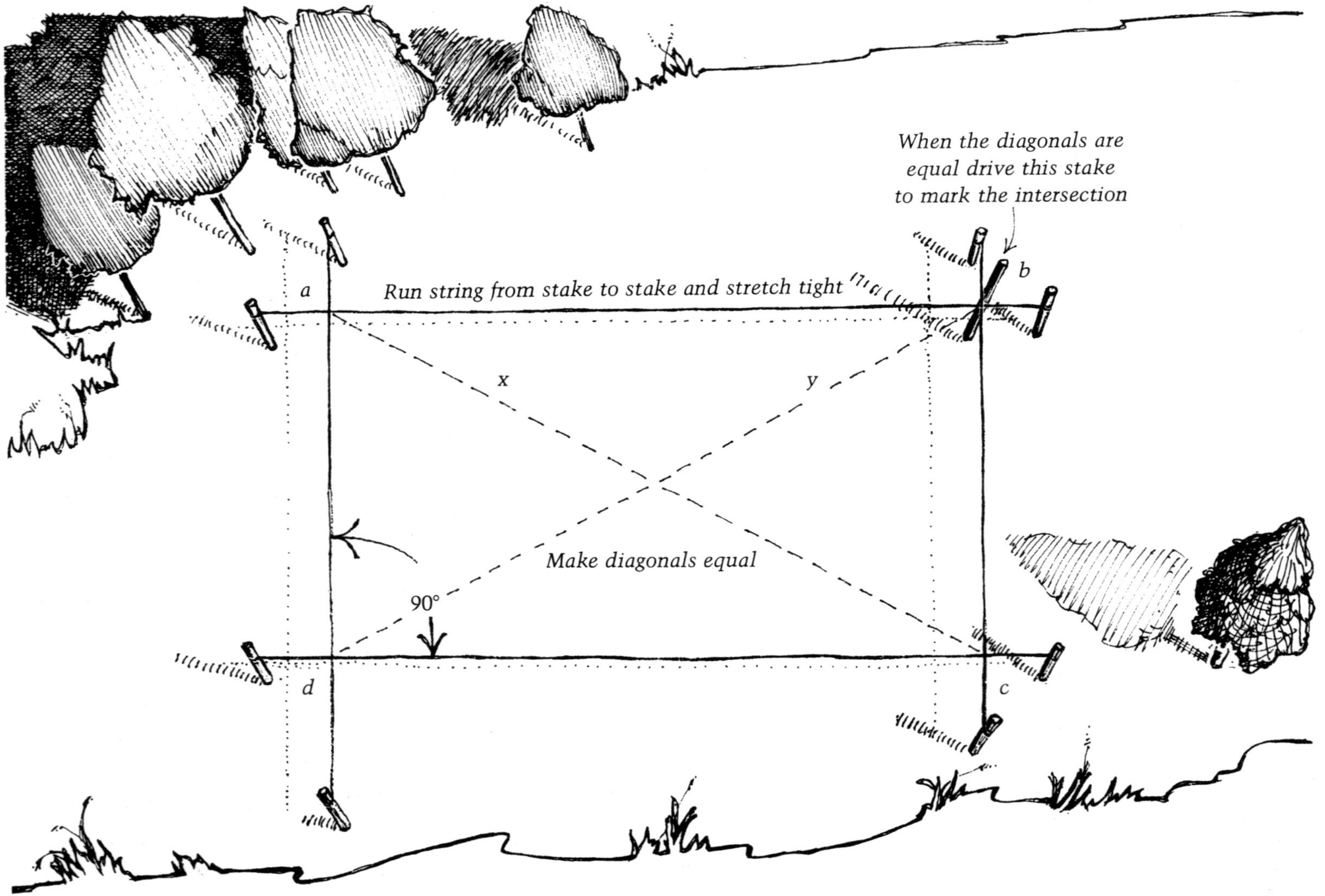

Fig. 4–D Laying Out a Foundation

twice again (d and a), and you will have four strings intersecting each other in *approximate* right angles. To get the angles exactly 90 degrees, you must measure diagonally (x and y) across the rectangle. (See illustration.) These diagonals will be of equal length when the house is square (x = y = 90 degree corners).

Drive a stake to hook the tape measure on at the string intersection of (a and b). You can then run a tape over to the intersection of (c and d). Do the same for the other diagonal and move the string stakes until the diagonal lengths are exactly equal (x = y). When this occurs you will have 90 degree angles exactly. *Don't skip measuring the diagonals.* It is important to have a square-cornered foundation later, when the floor goes up!

I like to slide the strings down the stakes until they touch the ground. If you want, you can use the traditional chalk line mark, which means you need chalk powder and other stuff. I prefer to buy a can of cheap white spray paint and spray 3 inches from the ground a narrow line all around the perimeter of the proposed foundation. You can walk over this line and it will remain discernible, plus it gives you the advantage of visualizing your foundation's size very easily.

Next you'll want to find out the local pier spacing requirements for foundations of this nature. Mark off the center to center spacing for the piers, using measuring tape and spray paint. *See Fig. 4–E* which shows the usual spacing for a single family dwelling.

Two methods of flooring are commonly in use: the *beam and plywood system* and the more traditional *joist and plywood system.* Advantages of the beam and plywood system are ease and speed of construction. The disadvantage is the springiness supposedly inherent in this type of floor (largely canceled out if you use foam-backed carpets).

The advantage of the joist method is the solidity of the floor. The disadvantages are mainly the extra time and money involved in construction. Both systems are equally strong overall.

If you use the beam and plywood system, you will need the number and size beams your plan specifies. You will also need 4-inch by 4-inch redwood or other suitable wood posts, preformed foundation piers, and a quantity of concrete. *See Fig. 4–F.* Line up one row of holes along one exterior wall. Keep the holes on the line so that the pier will sit on the concrete-filled hole and the post will be even with the paint line. After the piers are firmly embedded in the hardened concrete, nail one measured and cut post to the pier. *See Fig. 4–G.* Set the floor beam on top of the post, and going over to post C, set a level on top of the beam. Move the end of the beam up or down until it is level. With a pencil in your free hand, mark a line on the side of the post where the beam lines up level. Set the beam on the ground and saw off post C at the pencil line (use a carpenter's square to get an even cut). The beam should be set upon posts A and C and its height from the ground should be very close to that specified on your blueprints, usually 1½ feet from the ground. Do this again with another beam from C to E. *See Fig. 4–G.* Toe-nail them (see glossary) with 3-inch nails. Afterwards, cut and measure posts B and D.

When you do the second beam (F, H, and J posts) be sure to place a 2×4 edgewise across A and F to get the floor level across all the beams. *See Fig. 4–G.*

CONTINUOUS CONCRETE FOUNDATION

A fourth type of foundation is the continuous concrete foundation. It's the most popular and the one I recommend as a happy medium of strength, simplicity, and economy. It can be made two ways. The first is:

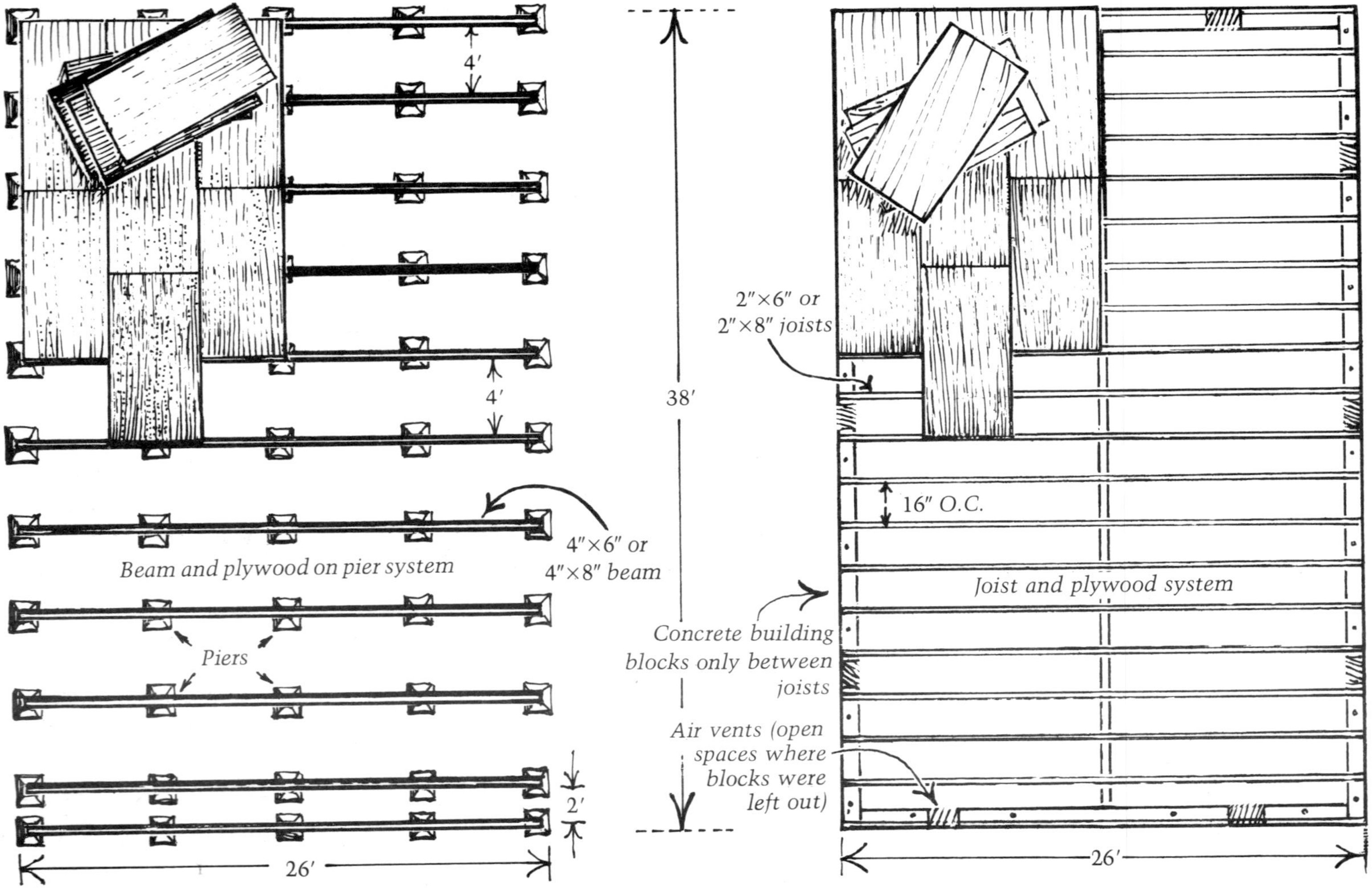

Fig. 4–E Two Types of Foundations Commonly Used

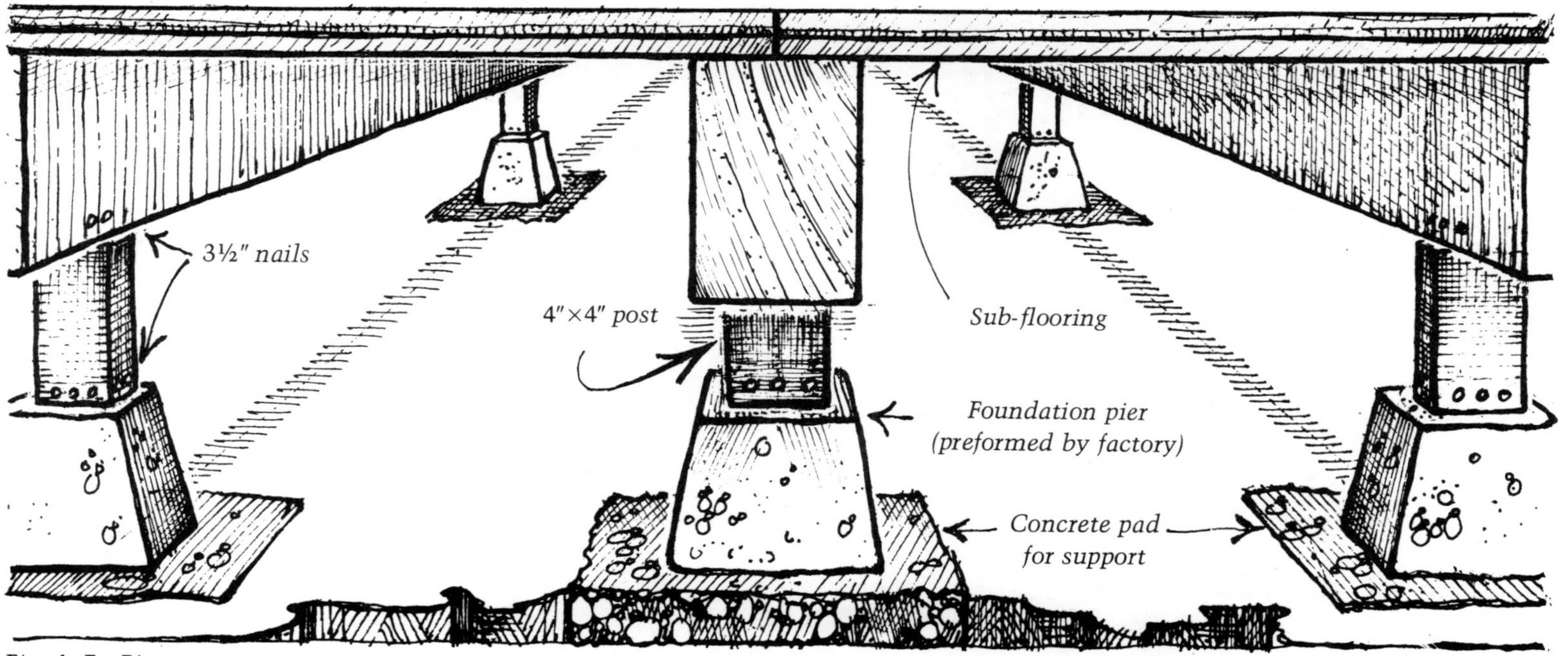

Fig. 4–F Piers

Formed Concrete Foundation

A common method of building up this type of foundation is to dig a trench and then to line it with forms to a few feet above the surface of the ground. Later, concrete is poured in the forms to make a solid one-piece foundation. The main thing that this technique has going for it is structural strength and clean lines. It also has a few drawbacks, as it is a tricky technique for the amateur or nonprofessional builder to tackle. The beginner lacks the experience of knowing how concrete flows and how the forms should be. If this scares you, use the next method of form construction. If this didn't scare you or you happen to know what you're doing, here are the directions.

A trench must be dug to the required depth and width of the county regulations, and in the trench you must suspend ½-inch reinforcement bars with wire or small wooden blocks. *See Fig. 4–H.* This *form and trench construction* must extend all around your house, except that every 10 feet you must

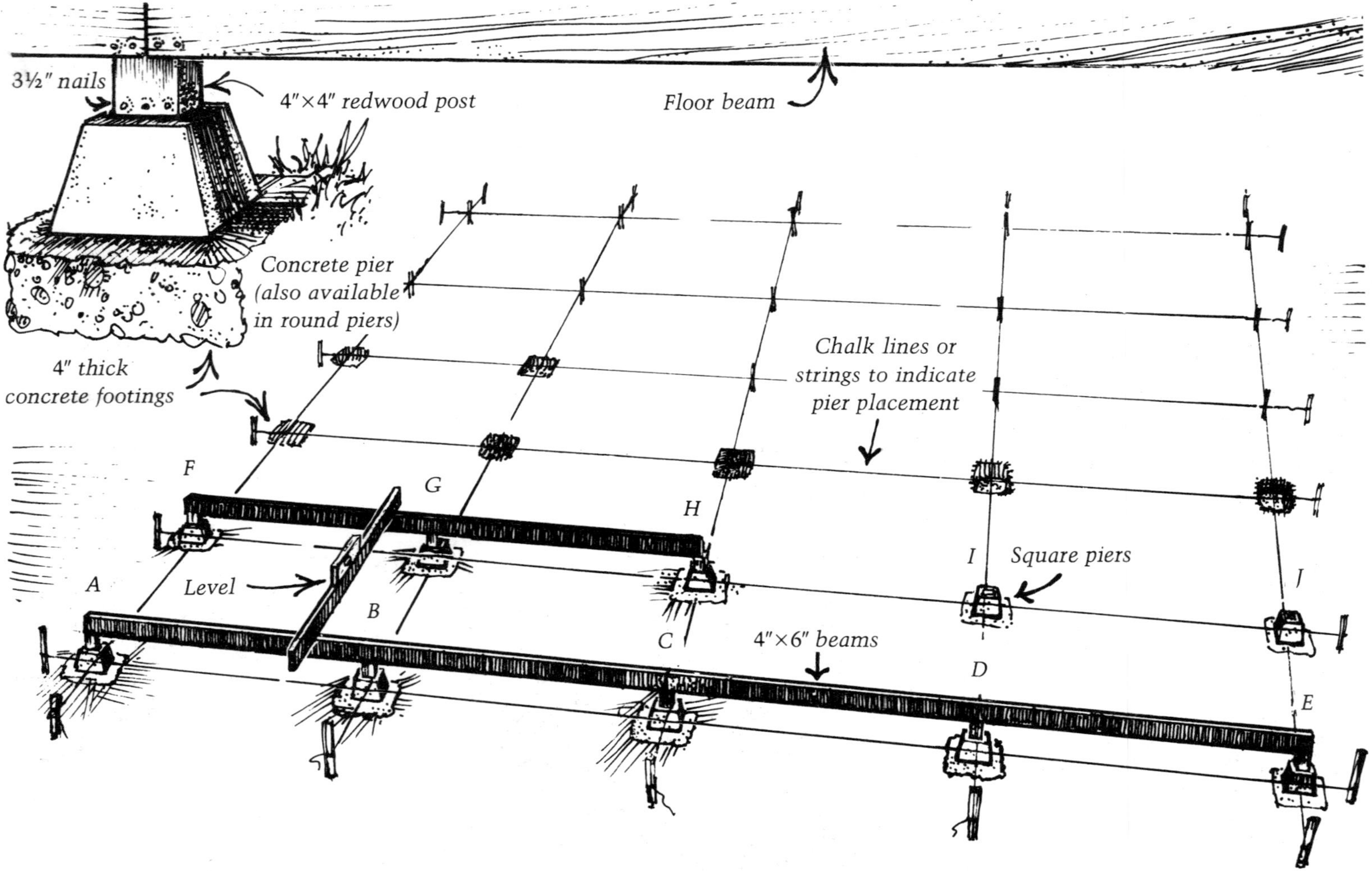

Fig. 4–G Laying Out and Bedding the Piers

leave a small 1-foot by 1½-foot opening for ventilation. Using *Snap-ty* form bolts, you can easily get the required width for your foundation—the bolts come in 6-, 10-, and 12-inch sizes. These handy items break off inside the cement and eliminate the need to saw off hundreds of bolts. Your plywood for the forms should be ½ inch or ⅝ inch thick. *See Fig. 4–I.*

When making these forms, you can usually rip the 8-foot plywood into two halves lengthwise, giving you 8 feet of form.

Premade forms are occasionally available in large cities with rental agencies, and for $50 you can get everything you need at considerable savings. It is also common practice to use the plywood forms as a part of your subflooring—just knock off the excess concrete when you remove them.

Concrete Block Foundation

Forms are not usually necessary when you can pour the wet cement footing right in the foundation trench, and then use construction blocks. *See Fig. 4–J.*

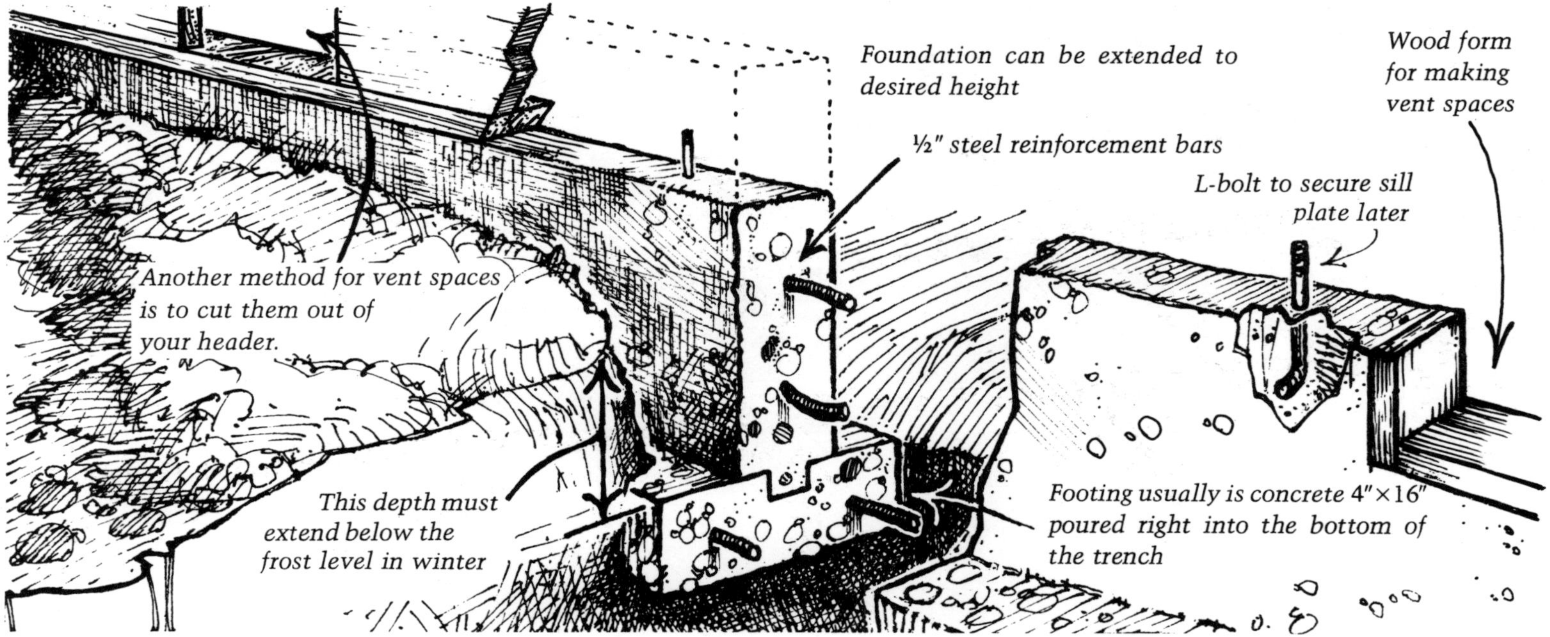

Fig. 4–H The Concrete Foundation

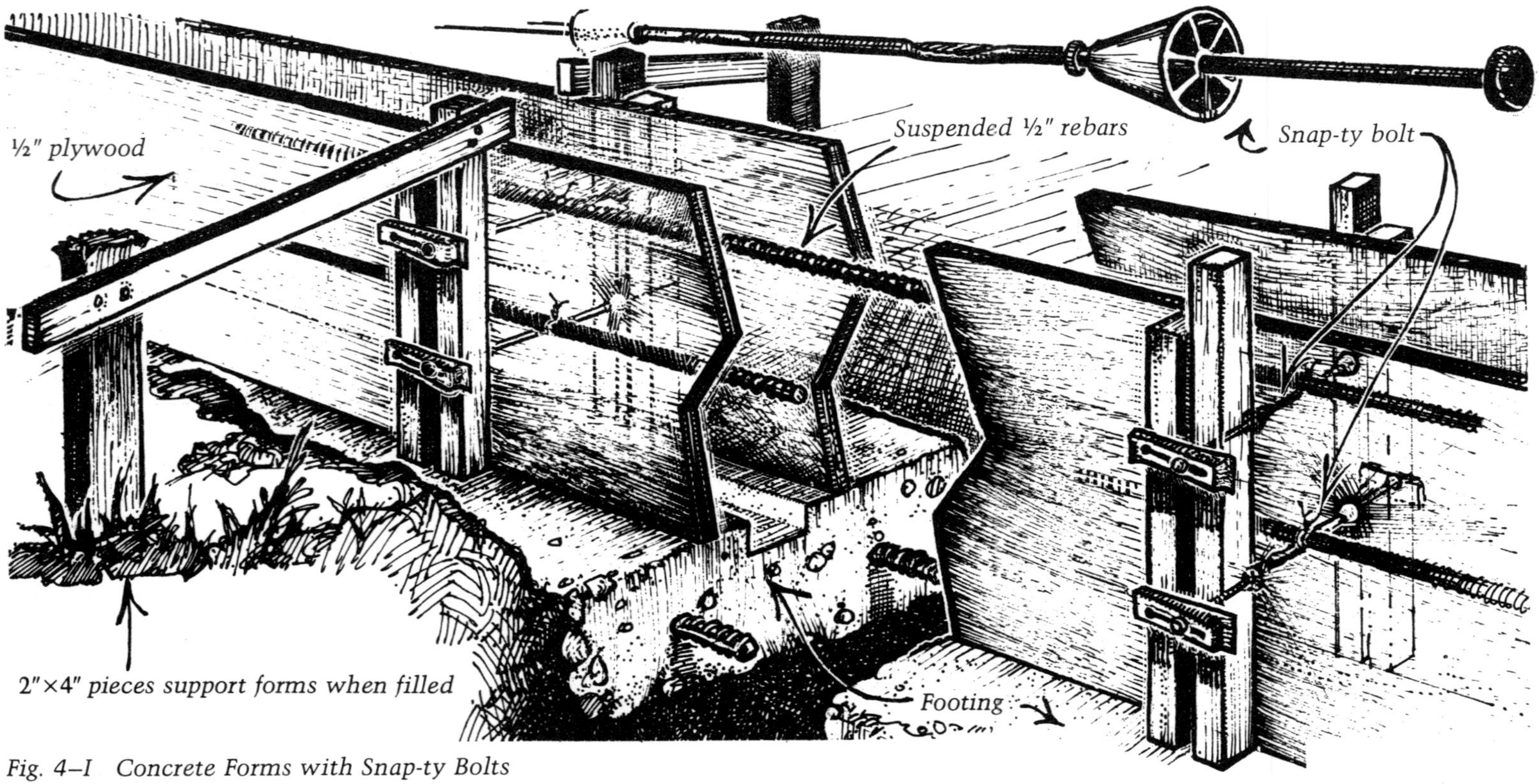

Fig. 4–I Concrete Forms with Snap-ty Bolts

Using the same technique as shown before, mark the perimeter of the foundation and then by hand or with a back-hoe dig out the trench to the required depth and width. Next have a cement mixer or truck ready to fill the trench to the depth your plans specify. With a level and a long 2×4, level the concrete all around the trench while it is wet.

After the cement has set in a day or two, return and build up a continuous block foundation, using mortar to bed the blocks level. One ½-inch steel reinforcement bar must run the length of the top row of blocks. Usually there are knockout sections in the center of the block that will accommodate one bar. A bar must stand vertically every few feet if the foundation is very tall.

Two rows of blocks are sufficient to raise the foundation

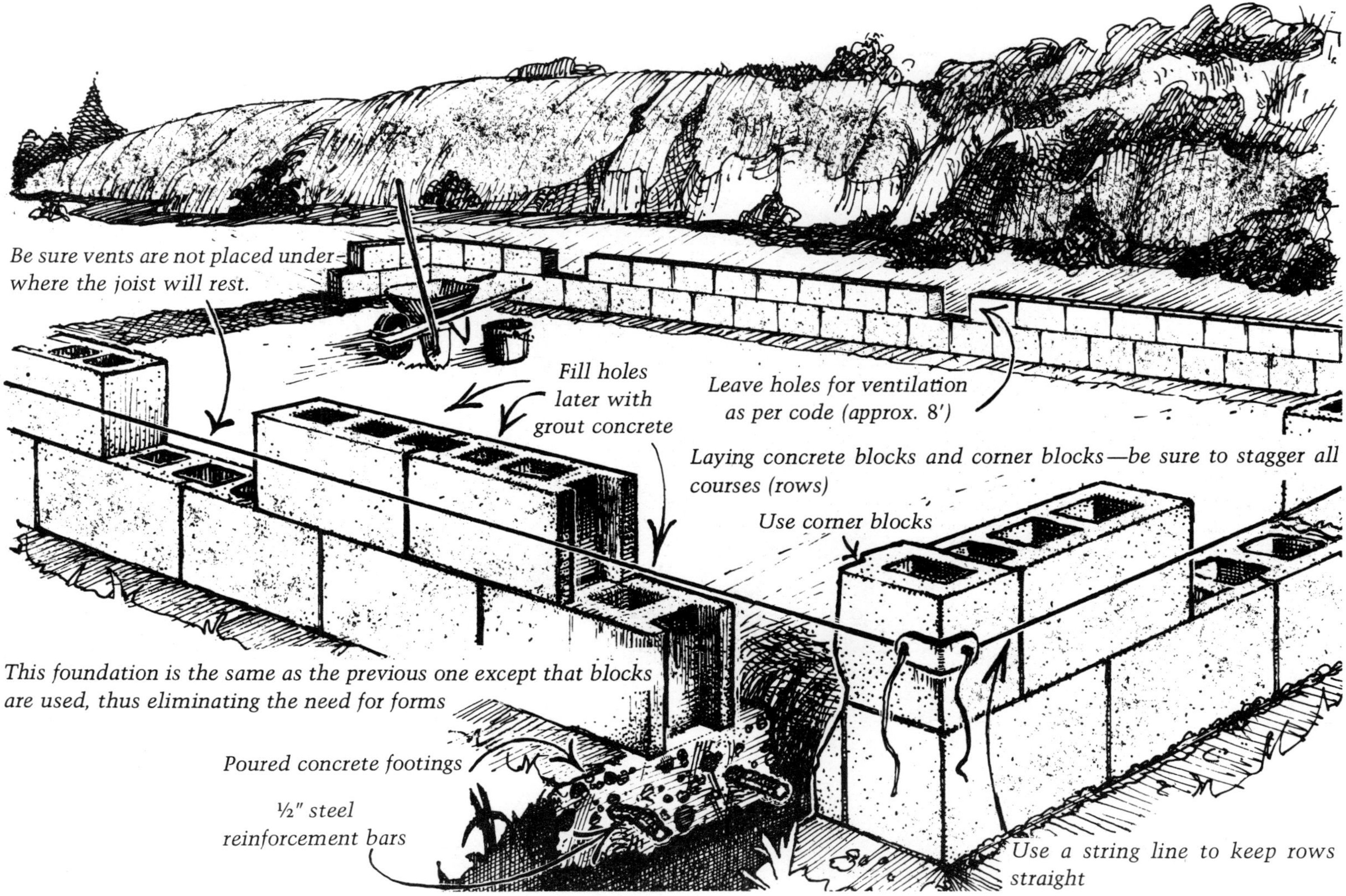

Fig. 4–J The Concrete Block Foundation

beams far enough off the ground. Leave out a block every 10 feet for ventilation. Later you will hook up a screen over the space. You can also cut openings for the vents in the space between the studs.

To get the blocks level, which is extremely necessary, you must use a system adaptable to your project. Some people build up a frame of 2×4's for reference. For no more than five *courses* (rows), I prefer to use a string line attached to the end of each course. Proceed with the block laying as described below, but first check the appendix for additional information on block masonry and mortar mixing.

1. First lay out a course of blocks to see how many you need. Remember that you will stagger each course.
2. Lay each opposing corner block using a liberal amount of mortar.
3. Run a string line between the blocks and check for levelness.
4. Lay the first course by bedding it in mortar and tamping it level.
5. Pour *grout* (slightly runny cement) into the blocks' holes.
6. Be sure to use corner blocks on the corners.
7. Lay the second course following the method used on the first. *See Fig. 4–J.*

When the top course of blocks is level, fill the holes in the blocks with a grout mixture of concrete. Into the wet cement grout shove 8-inch-long sill bolts every 4 feet. (See glossary for *sill.*) Be sure to leave 3 inches or so length of the bolt sticking up. Let the concrete harden for twenty-four hours. Next

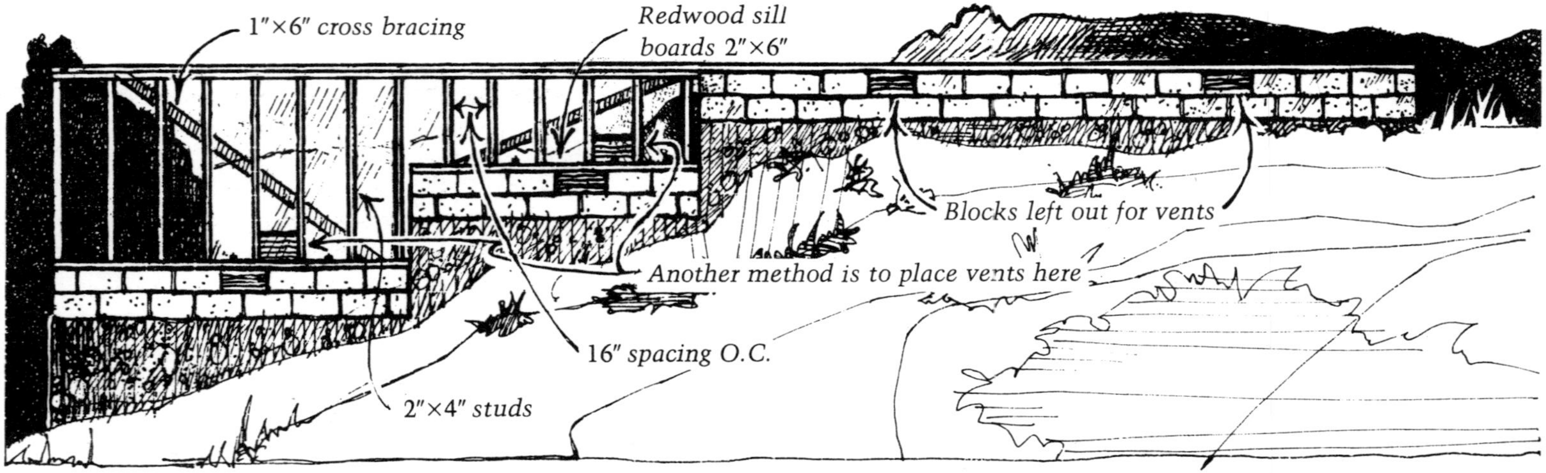

Fig. 4–K An Example of a Stepped Foundation

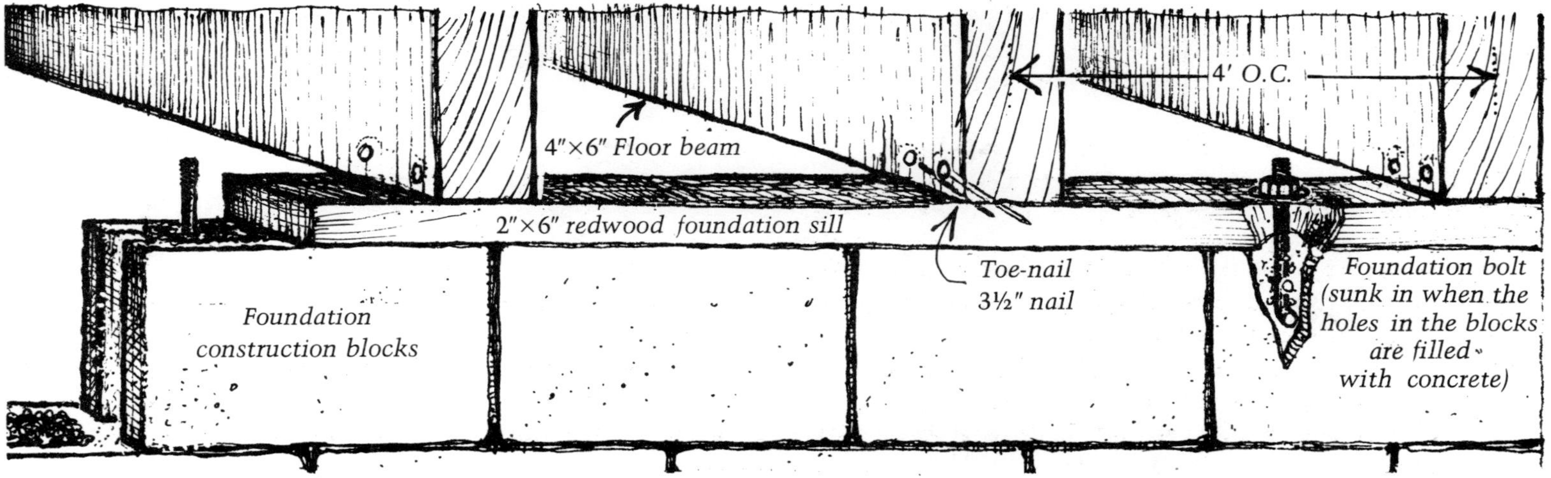

Fig. 4–L Toe-nailing the Floor Beams

buy enough 2×6 redwood to lay all along the top of the continuous foundation as sill boards. The easiest method I have found for determining where to drill the holes in the redwood is to place the board on top of the bolts and, when it's aligned properly, whack the board with a hammer. This will leave an indentation at the proper spot to drill. After drilling the holes slightly oversize, bolt down the 2×6 sill boards.

HILLSIDE FOUNDATIONS

If you're one of those fortunate people who owns a hillside lot with a view, there are a few drawbacks with which you will have to cope in laying a foundation. You probably cut a house pad if your grade is too steep, but possibly you will have to perch the front or back of the house out over the hillside. This is done quite frequently, and many solutions are possible. Check around your neighborhood to see how other people solved their hillside problems.

My favorite method, and the one I feel is easiest, is the *continuous stepped footing and frame method.* Basically, as you can see, this is just a stepped foundation with studs rising to the level of the floor. *See Fig. 4–K.*

You should find out from the building department how high you can build the frame foundation. You'd probably be surprised at how high some people will go—often high enough to get two separate floors under the house!

Be sure to use good quality 2×4's and cross brace your corners with 1×6's. (See framing section in Chapter 5.)

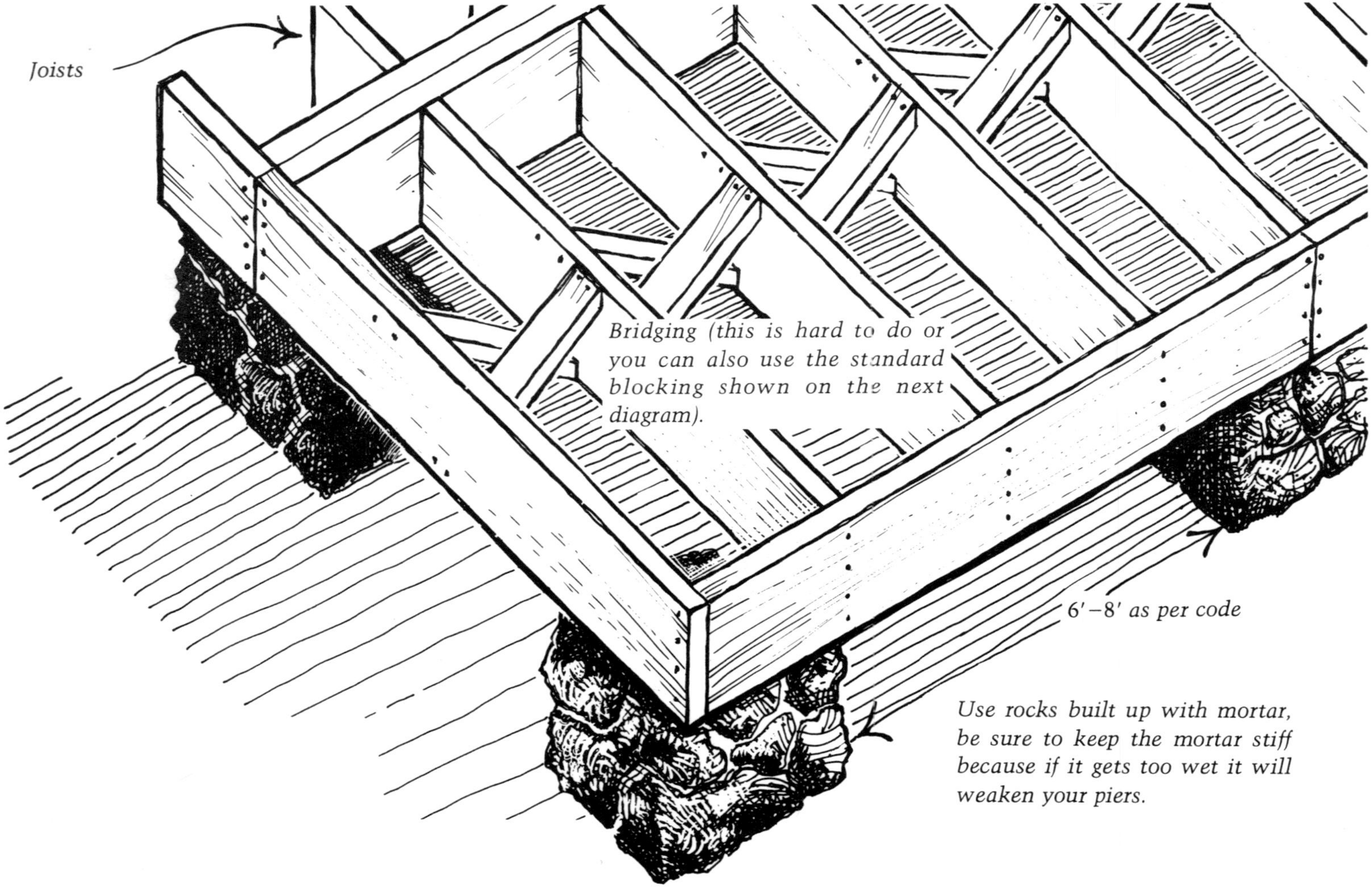

Fig. 4–M Using Natural Rock Piers

PIER PLACEMENT

With the sill boards secure, you can now dig the pier footings in the proper places. Proceed as you would with the pier foundation system, but put the ends of the beams on the top of the sill and toe-nail each beam with six 3-inch nails to the sill. *See Fig. 4–L.*

Butt the beam flush with the outside of the sill. Later you'll come back and nail a 2×6 *sash board* over the spaces between the beams, or cover it with plywood.

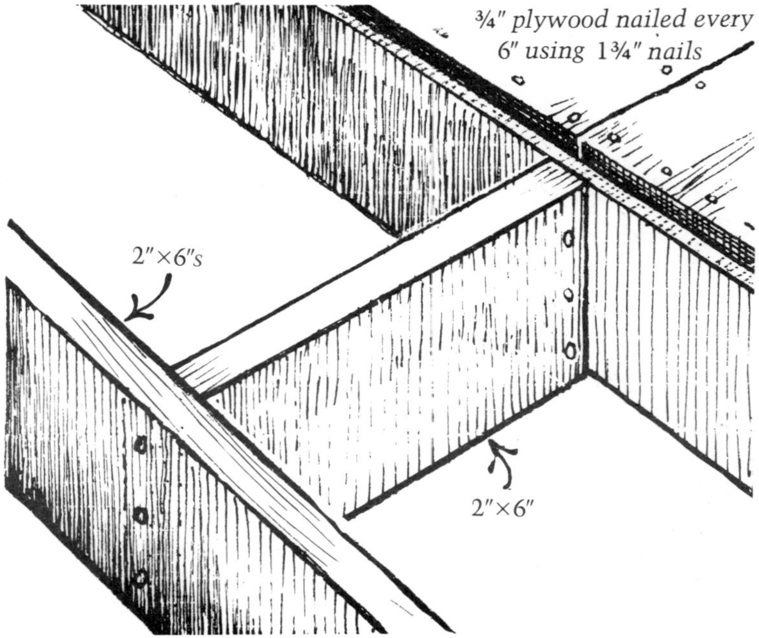

Fig. 4–N Blocking

Be sure you get all the beams level on the sill and the piers. If you took care to get the foundation level, this part should be easy.

SUBFLOORING

The house as it stands now has a foundation and floor beams. The time has come to put down the subflooring. Your budget is the major factor in determining which type of subflooring you use.

JOIST FLOORS

One traditional and still-popular method of subflooring is to use the *joist and planking system.* Instead of beams you use 2×6's or 2×8's laid on their edges. *See Fig. 4–M.* You can usually run these 12 feet without a beam for support, but check local codes for specifics. Be sure to use either bridging or blocking on every joist. (See glossary for bridging.) It should occur approximately every 8 feet. Use 2-inch nails to fasten ¾-inch plywood and use 3-inch nails for planks or anything thicker. *See Fig. 4–N.*

PLYWOOD FLOORING

Plywood sheets ⅝-inch thick, laid two deep, are good if you want to do the job twice, but now a new plywood has made it easier. The new plywood is 1⅛-inch thick, and one-sheet thickness is all that's needed, even if your beams are 4 feet apart. Usually a couple dozen 4×8 sheets will lay a floor, and although the cost is high, it's still cheaper than the alternatives ($18 a sheet in California).

Instead of using plywood at all, you can use 2×6 tongue-and-groove wood nailed at right angles to the joists.

Now is when you get a few blisters nailing down the floor. Employ a 20-ounce hammer with a *waffle-type head* (a framer's

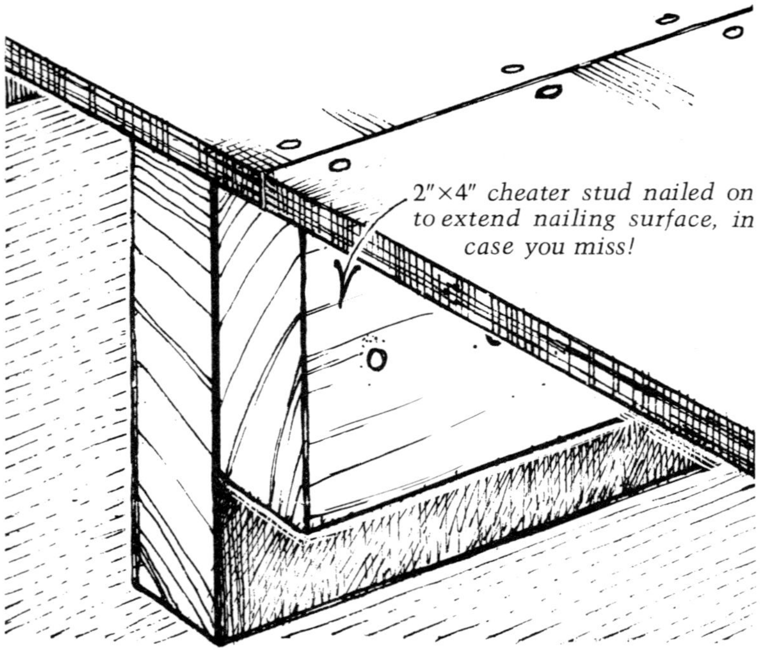

Fig. 4–O Cheaters

hammer). This will take some getting used to, but will soon become your favorite tool. Those little 16-ounce finishing hammers are fine for bookcases and trim, but a heavy hammer will drive a 3-inch nail in two strokes, as opposed to eight.

If your 1⅛-inch plywood is difficult to mesh together, don't hammer on the edges directly. Put a piece of wood against it, then bang it into place.

Use plenty of nails, and hammer them every 6 inches, being sure to drive the plywood down against the beam. Then crawl under the floor and check to see if you can find any gaps in the flooring, where it's not seated properly on a beam.

Here is a hint you will seldom find in a regular carpentry book. If you miscalculate by a few inches when you put the beams in and don't discover it until half of your floor is down, you're going to feel pretty sick. Here's a solution that doesn't require you to rip out your work. If the plywood misses the beam by ½ inch or 1 inch, nail a 2×4 flush with the top of the beam along the problem area, thus extending your nailing surface. *See Fig. 4–O.*

If you find you have a piece of warped plywood or a warped beam, and you need a little extra pressure to hold your flooring down, buy a hundred 2½-inch screw-type nails and whack those in to hold it down. These screw nails are difficult to pull out, but they'll hold until long after you're gone.

After you finish the flooring, you'll experience a moment of pride when you see the real floor plan of your house stand out. You have made a little order out of that wood pile out back.

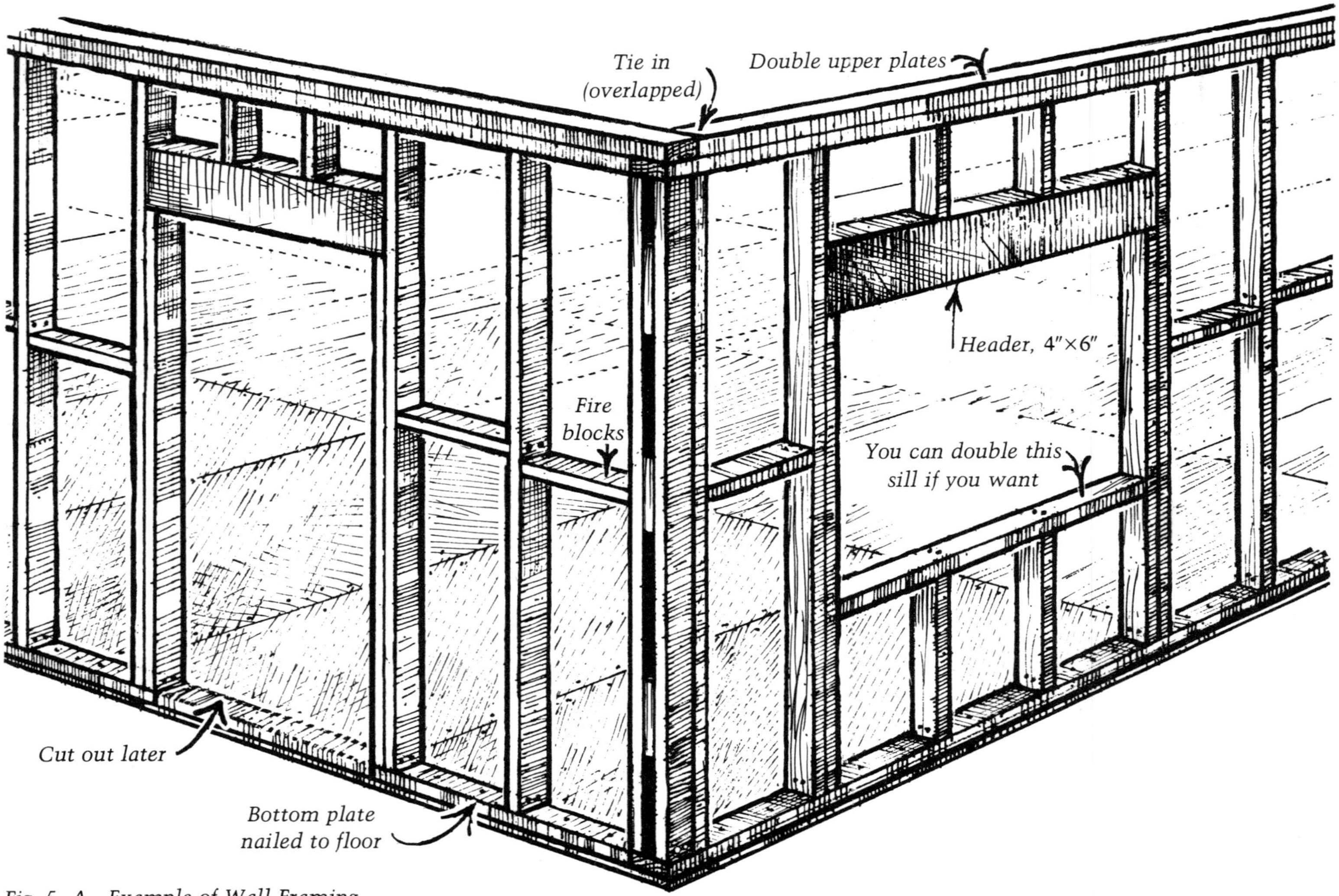

Fig. 5–A Example of Wall Framing

RAISING THE WALLS AND ROOF

CHAPTER 5

FRAMING

Framing a house is the most climactic and satisfying step in the building process. In one day you see the wall studs go up, the next day, the ceiling beams, and a few days after that, the roof.

The walls will shoot up magically from the floor . . . that is, if you do it properly and plan a little first. All your wood should be on the site—including *lintels* (crosspieces over doors and windows), beams, and studs. Have a good bag full of 3½-inch nails plus a couple of handfuls of larger spikes.

You'll want to refer constantly to your working blueprint during this phase, so keep it handy for reference.

For the first example of framing, let's assume you are going to build the basic design I recommended in Chapter 3. This design makes all the details of framing exceptionally easy. There are no obtuse or oblique angles, except at the roof gables, and a little common sense is all that is needed there. For figuring your roof angles, see rafter section. Keep in mind that the interior wall dividing the bedrooms from the kitchen and living room is designed in your plans to carry part of the weight of the ceiling. This wall must be built to the same specifications as an exterior wall: All the studs must be 16 inches on center apart, and the studs should be construction or mixed grade quality.

On the house floor line up all the studs so that they are 16 inches center to center. Where the windows go, put in either a 4×6 beam or a 2×6 beam for a lintel and use two studs to support it. *See Fig. 5–A.*

Do the same with the doors, being sure that the space you leave is equal to the size of the door jamb you are using. All the doors and windows should be right on the site for easy measurements . . . if they're not, it could mean you have to tear out work later!

NOTE: Eight-foot studs are the normal precut size, but if you want to use regular 8-foot siding, you must make the studs 4⅞ inches shorter to compensate for the *bottom plate* (see glossary) and double *top plates* (1⅝ inch each). This way you will have an 8-foot-high finished wall. *See Fig. 5–A.*

When cutting the studs and beams, you must be extremely careful to get them square. Use a carpenter's square and draw the lines directly on the wood, to assure a good cut. When the

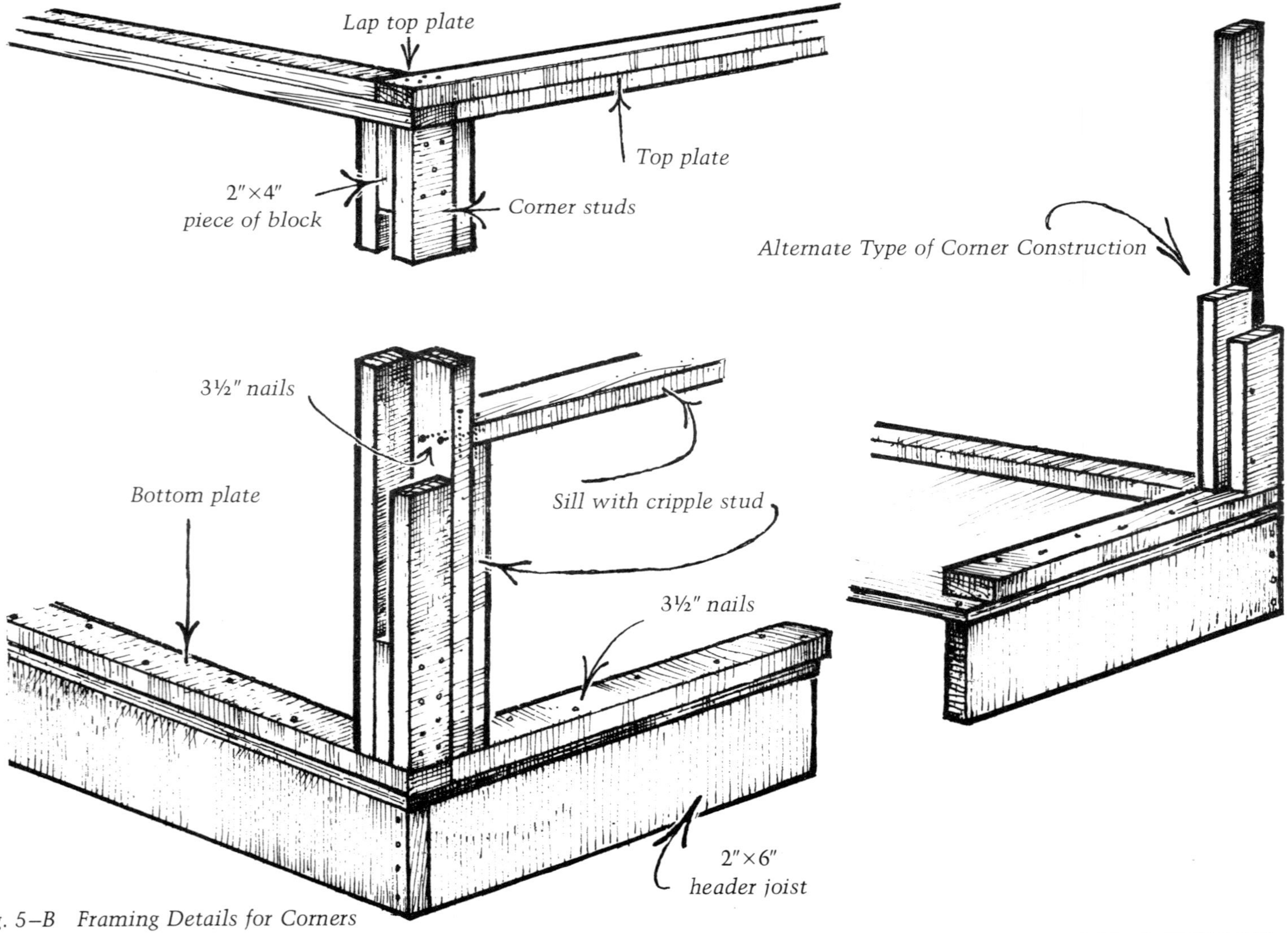

Fig. 5–B Framing Details for Corners

studs are laid out and cut, you can begin nailing with 3½–inch nails. Use four per joint. *See Fig's. 5–B, C, & D.*

Keep the bottom plate back from the edge of the floor by approximately 4 inches, so that it will be easy to tilt up the walls. Double-check the studs using a tape measure to see that they are still on center when you finish nailing. Check both top and bottom.

Now you can go over to the opposing wall and nail that up the same way.

RAISING WALLS

With two walls framed but still lying on the floor, you need the help of a few people at this point to tilt up the walls. Hopefully earlier you moved the bottom plate back from the edge of the floor by approximately 4 inches, making it easy to tilt the walls up.

Before you tilt, nail three or four short lengths of 2×4's to the edge of the floor. The reason, and a very important one, is that when you tilt up the wall, it won't slide over the edge and fall while everyone watches helplessly.

Also, have some ten- to twelve-foot 2×4's handy to use for braces to hold the wall up after you find the point at which it's true and perpendicular. *See Fig. 5–E.*

Up you go then, with everyone pushing. Three people are a necessity, as you will see. The person pushing in the center lets go while the other two hold. The center person then grabs the hammer and nails and secures the bottom plate. Next the braces can be put in while the wall is adjusted for a plumb vertical.

It's time to do the other walls now, and remember to space the double studs at the end of the wall so that you can nail the walls together once they're up. A nice trick for slightly adjusting the walls is to have a few people pull while you move the braces to the correct positions.

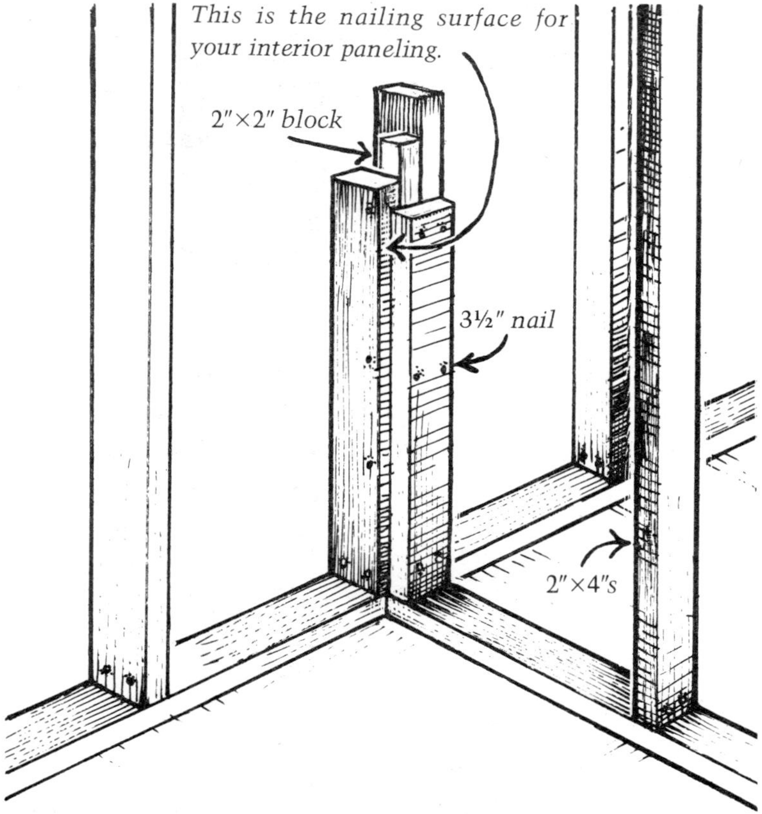

Fig. 5–C Butt Joint for a Partition Wall

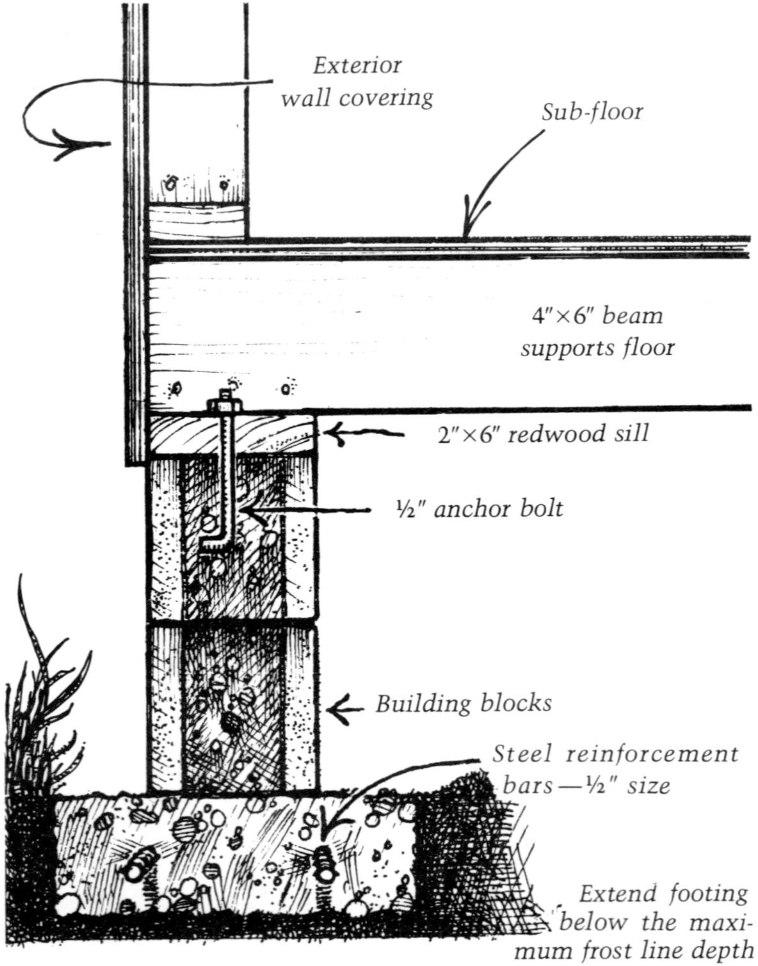

Fig. 5–D Cross-cut Detail of a Wall and Foundation

WALL BRACING

Usually all walls are required to be cross-braced at every corner. Codes also usually require that every long stretch of wall have a 1×6 cross brace. These braces must be *let into* the studs, that is, you must saw notches for them. *See Fig. 5–F.*

To saw out the notches easily, first lightly tack the brace across the studs you wish to brace up. Next mark with a pencil the angles the brace intersects on the studs. Then pull off the brace and saw out the notches. Use a wood chisel to knock out the middle part. Be sure to nail the brace securely with 3½-inch nails, and don't cut the studs too deep or they'll be ruined!

Last but not least, saw up some of the leftover 2×4's and nail in your *fireblocks* (see glossary). These will be secured to the studs with 3-inch nails. Fireblocks are supposed to help support wall loads and reduce fire hazard by cutting the air space in half. Code requirements generally require that fireblocks occur once in every space between studs.

THE GABLE ENDS & RIDGE BEAMS

When both the end and side walls are up and braced, your efforts should be directed towards building the gable ends and providing a solid place for your ridge beam to rest. In *Fig. 5–G* you can see that the ridge beam must rest on the 4×4 post in the gable end and that should in turn rest on the upper plates. It is also supported from underneath by another 4×4. Secure the ridge beam in the wall with heavy metal brackets, one on each side, as shown in the previous figure. The other end of the ridge beam will rest on the 2×4's you are using for your interior load-bearing wall. Be sure to double or even triple the first studs that receive the beam. After the beam runs for a few feet where it is supported by the wall, you can then use a 4×6 for the remaining length of your ridge beam.

Fig. 5–E Bracing a Wall

ROOF BEAM RAISING

You are going to be tired after that day of framing, so get a good night's rest, because if you choose to use ceiling beams instead of rafters the job involves great exertion. Again, three people make it easy.

Place the beam (4×6 or 4×8) onto the exterior wall first and then position a tall ladder at the other end of the beam. Usually one person can set the beam end into sheet metal joist hangers, which are nailed to the face of the ridge beam ahead of time using 1½-inch long nails. Beams are commonly spaced 4 feet on center (O.C.) for open-beam ceilings. *See Fig. 5–H.*

Care should be taken that the beams are set fairly even with each other. Place a 2×4 edgewise across them, then put a level on the 2×4. If the beams are out of line, you can place a wood *shim* (thin, wedge-shaped piece of wood) under either edge to adjust them.

I recommend that you let the beams hang over the edge to give you a few feet of eaves. This will cost you a little more money in roofing (approximately 5 percent), but it's worth it because the large eaves will keep the rain and sun off the sides of the house. Besides lowering future maintenance costs, it also adds a nice overhanging visual effect to the roof lines. An especially pleasing effect can be had by extending the roof beam past the roof decking by 1 to 2 feet, giving the house a Mexican adobe feel.

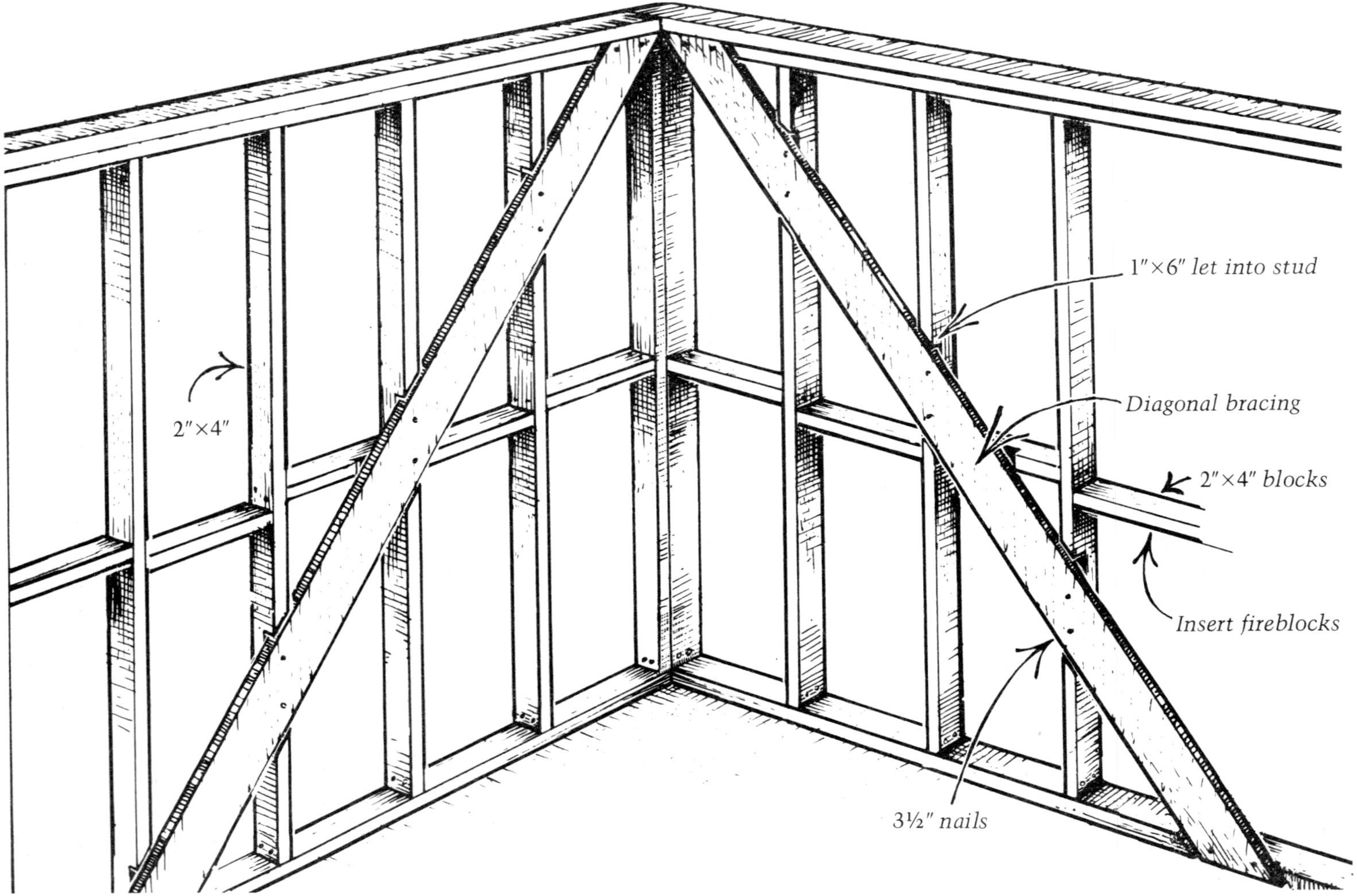

Fig. 5–F Corner Bracing

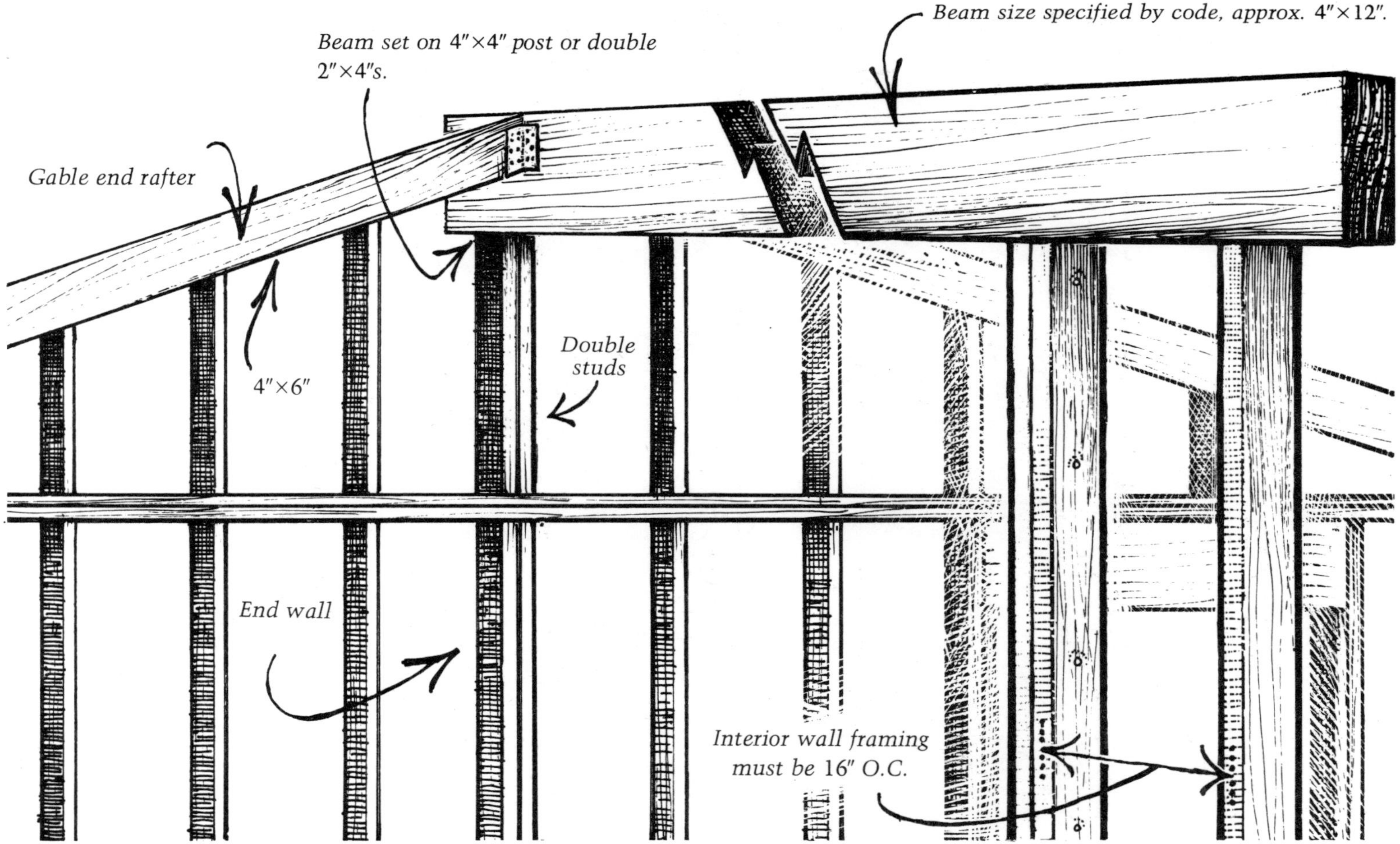

Fig. 5–G Spanning the Living Room with a Ridge Beam

Fig. 5–H Attaching Beams to Supporting Members

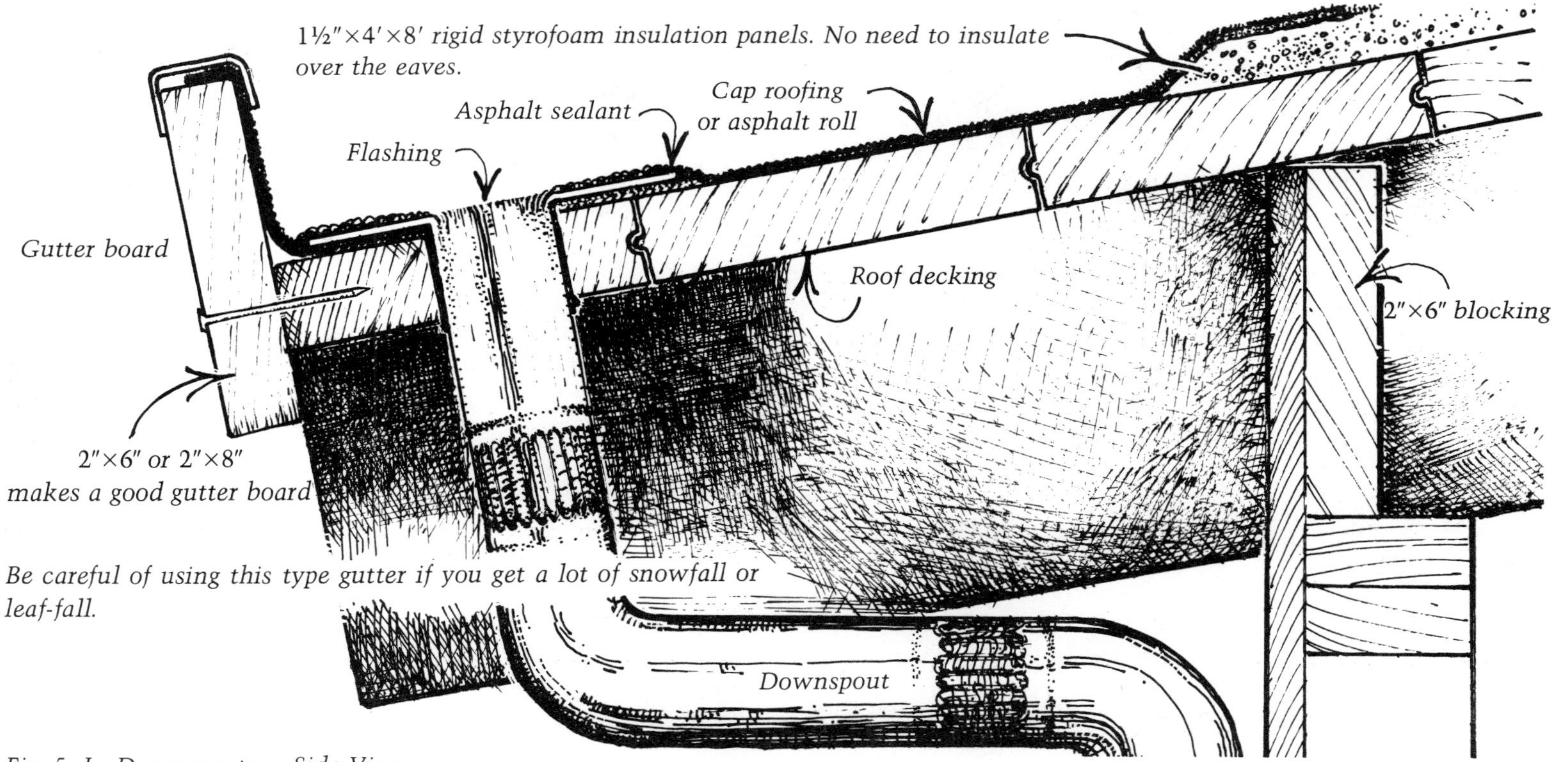

Fig. 5–I Downspouts — Side View

ROOFING

When you stand in your living room now, you'll get the feel of the rooms, even though the house does look like a giant grape arbor.

Your next job is to get the roof on, and this work resembles flooring quite a bit. If you have spaced your beams 4 feet apart, regular ¾-inch thick roof-grade plywood will be okay for the roof if you are on a tight budget. But let's see if we can't make that plain plywood a little fancier for you. There's a gimmick that works like a charm, but you will need a power saw. Stack up your plywood, and on the good side draw parallel pencil lines 6 inches apart down the length of each board. Now set your power saw so that it will cut 1/32-inch deep into the wood—that is, so that it just scores the surface with a clean line. Buzz down the lines you have drawn, and then with a soft pencil darken them to get a deeper visual effect. Before you saw the plywood though, get the building department's permission.

Now you have a very good imitation of planked roofing, and you have saved $200–$300.

If you are one of the lucky ones who can splurge and get a knotty pine ceiling, by all means do so. This is one of the most beautiful facets of a house, since the exposed surface shows a wonderful pattern of grained wood and knots.

Whichever material you use, run it out past the gable ends at least 2 feet to create side eaves. When nailing use 3½-inch nails, and if you have trouble seating the planks on the beams, use a 20-ounce hammer with screw nails for extra hold. Roofing plywood and panels usually have edges that interlock so that the builder can mesh them together for greater strength. These edges are called *tongue and groove.* Be careful to get the tongues and grooves tight, even if you have to bang them a little to do it—later when the wood shrinks slightly any gaps will get worse.

Saw all the way around the roof to get a nice straight line, and keep the scrap wood. If you don't want gutters, you can roof it like it is. Since most people want to keep the water from spilling down, I will illustrate a gutter design that I have used.

The easiest gutters, of course, are the kind you buy and tack up according to the manufacturer's instructions. These, however, are expensive. I prefer to run a 2×6 all the way around the roof. This 2×6 is nailed to the edge of the roof and later is covered by asphalt roofing. Next I drill 3-inch holes for the downspouts. *See Fig. 5–I.*

I recommend that you put down heavy building paper (tar paper), then lay down over the whole roof a 2-inch thickness of Fiberboard roofing insulation sheets. The sheets come in 2-foot by 4-foot lengths with water-proofing on one side. Using them will cut your heat loss on the roof by 40 percent, saving you $1,000 in several years' time.

In some areas more efficient insulation on the roof is legally required; in any case, it is desirable because much heat is otherwise lost through the roof of a house. More than 2 inches of Fiberboard can be difficult to work with, so I recommend using a new product called *Technifoam.* It can be used in various thicknesses and has a much higher insulating ability. Usually 1-inch or 1½-inch thickness is suitable for most applications. Technifoam also comes in easy-to-handle sheets, but they are extremely expensive right now. Perhaps when the newness of the product wears off, the price will settle down to a more reasonable level.

To put down Technifoam sheets, you must use galvanized nails. Using the appropriate length nail for the thickness you select, tack the sheets to the roof being careful to leave no gaps. Next nail plywood over the roof, using 4×8 sheets of exterior-grade ⅜-inch plywood. Now you'll have a greater and more secure nailing surface for your shingles or roll roofing.

FINISH ROOFING YOUR HOUSE

Perhaps I should warn you that if you plan to use roofers, they seem to be hard people to track down and get to work on schedule, since they're so busy all the time. Call them a week or more before you need them, and make an appointment. When you call they'll want to know if you desire a *wood shake* roof, a *hot mop* roof, a *shingle* or a *tin* roof. Let's dismiss tin for aesthetic reasons. Wood shakes are beautiful but expensive. If you can find them cheap (good luck) do the work yourself and save money. A shingle roof is also a good roof but the pitch

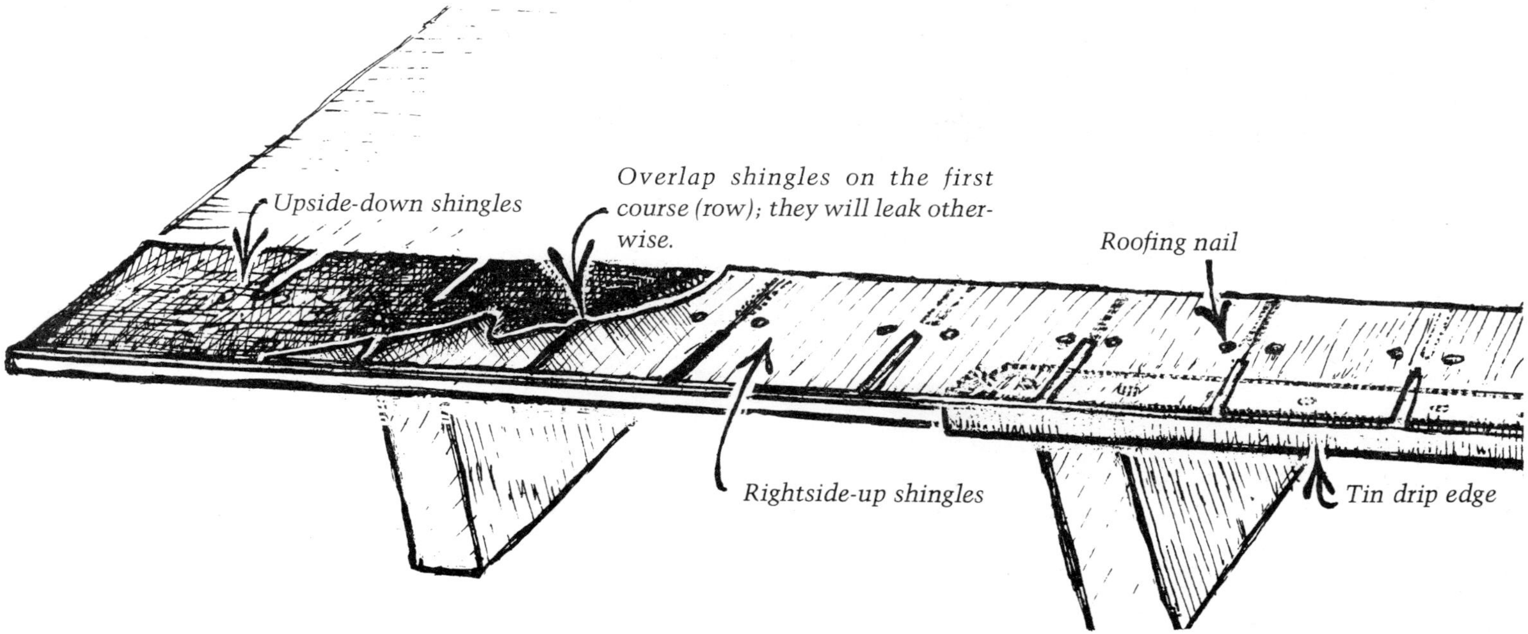

Fig. 5–J The First Course of Shingles and Metal Drip Edge

of your roof cannot be too flat or water will not run off properly.

SHINGLE ROOF

First prepare the surface by seeing that it is smooth and relatively free of protruding nails and large gaps in the wood joints. Lay down over the entire roof one layer of 15-pound building paper, which is tar impregnated felt and comes in rolls. Then staple the paper or tack it down with galvanized ½-inch roofing nails every 12 inches along the edges. Insert nails through roofing tins if you think the building paper might blow off. (Roofing tins are about the size of large washers, but are made out of tin.) Stretch the paper flat as you go, and use the white lines on the paper to align it horizontally. Seams should overlap.

If you like, you can install a metal drip edge to keep the water from running down the sides of the eaves. You can purchase it in 10- or 12-foot lengths, and it should be nailed on as shown in *Fig. 5–J.* Galvanized drip edges require the use of galvanized nails to prevent corrosion by electrolysis.

Notice how the edges are staggered; this prevents water penetration.

Fig. 5–K Laying Shingles

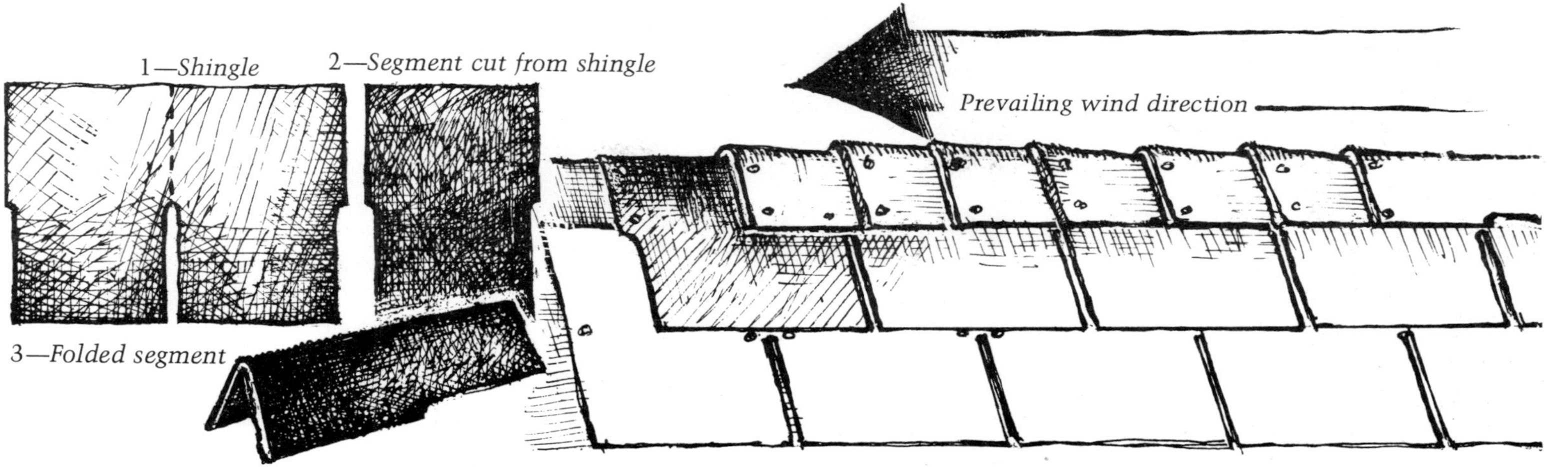

Fig. 5–L Doing the Ridge with Shingles

The actual installation of the shingles must follow the manufacturer's instructions. There are a dozen different types of shingles, but the most common is the *three-tab square butt.* These shingles are sold "by the square." You can cover 100 square feet of roof with *one* square, so it is quite easy to figure it all out. Many different colors are available, but the darker ones tend to make a roof warm and subsequently the space below too.

When tacking on shingles, use ½-inch galvanized roofing nails. Start the first course (row) at the bottom roof edge, then work upwards. In the first course the notches in each shingle should point upwards, so that there will be a solid layer of shingle under the first notches. *See Fig. 5–J.*

Be sure when laying the shingles to stagger the joints and overlap all shingles by 50 percent. This is called an exposure of 5 inches. Check the package wrapping and see the manufacturer's recommendations. *See Fig. 5–K.*

The fourth course begins in the same position as the first. To cut them, use a framing square and razor knife. Score each shingle and crack it back, but don't be too rough, as they can be damaged easily. After approximately six courses use a tape measure to see if you are keeping the shingles lined up. Do this quite often, because they get out of line easily and foul you up later.

After the sides of your roof are shingled and you are at the peak, the "ridge course" must be shingled. Take a shingle and cut it into three segments. Then nail each one to the ridge, remembering to overlap them 50 percent. *See Fig. 5–L.*

HOT MOP ROOFS

One of my all-time-favorite roofs is the hot mop roof. The major benefit of this roof is that it's extremely maintenance-free and preferred by most factories and industries, and they can't afford to fool around. It's also the most leak-proof roof you can get, and it takes just one day for "hot mop" professionals to put it on.

If you do get a hot tar roof, don't put down building paper. They'll just have to pull it off to do the job. If you like, they will sprinkle gravel on the finished roof for you, or they will roll gravel-impregnated roofing over the applied tar to finish it off.

Now your house is ready to stand off any minor rainstorms, and at this point you might consider tacking heavy construction tar paper to the exterior walls and moving in. Without the utilities, of course, you'd be camping out, but it won't be long now before you are finished.

ODDS AND ENDS

Now that the roof is up, you can place the bathtub or shower stall in its proper position and nail it to the studs and floor. Cover the bottom of the tub with building paper or cardboard so that you won't scratch it up when you stand in it. *See Fig. 5–M.*

If you chose to build the modified basic house design, you will find most of the construction details are the same, except that you will need to custom-cut the plates and studs where the walls intersect. *See Fig. 5–N.* For the roof beams, you can use one solid 4×10 or 4×12 beam. As you probably found out at the building department, the interior partitioning walls in most cases can be made smaller or can be eliminated by the addition of a thicker and heavier beam. *See Fig. 5–G.*

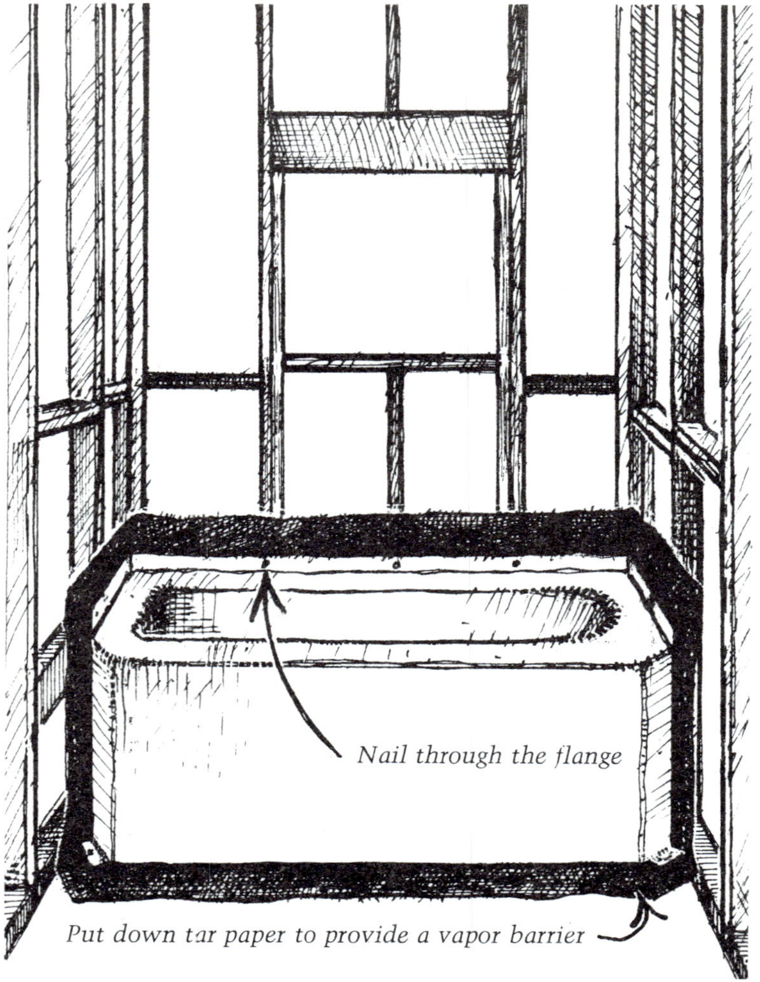

Fig. 5–M Nailing the Tub to the Studs

If you wish to bridge a very large room (such as a huge living room) with a strong beam, you might check into something like a steel I-beam. Of course, this is less pleasing aesthetically, but it can be painted or covered with wood later to improve its appearance.

The house with a one-slope roof is the simplest framing job possible. Just place the roof beams on top of the upper plate and then nail. This way you save the cost of joist hangers. The one-slope design is also very suitable for an add-on room connected by a breezeway to the existing structure. Using this idea, you can make the porch or breezeway into an additional room later if you wish.

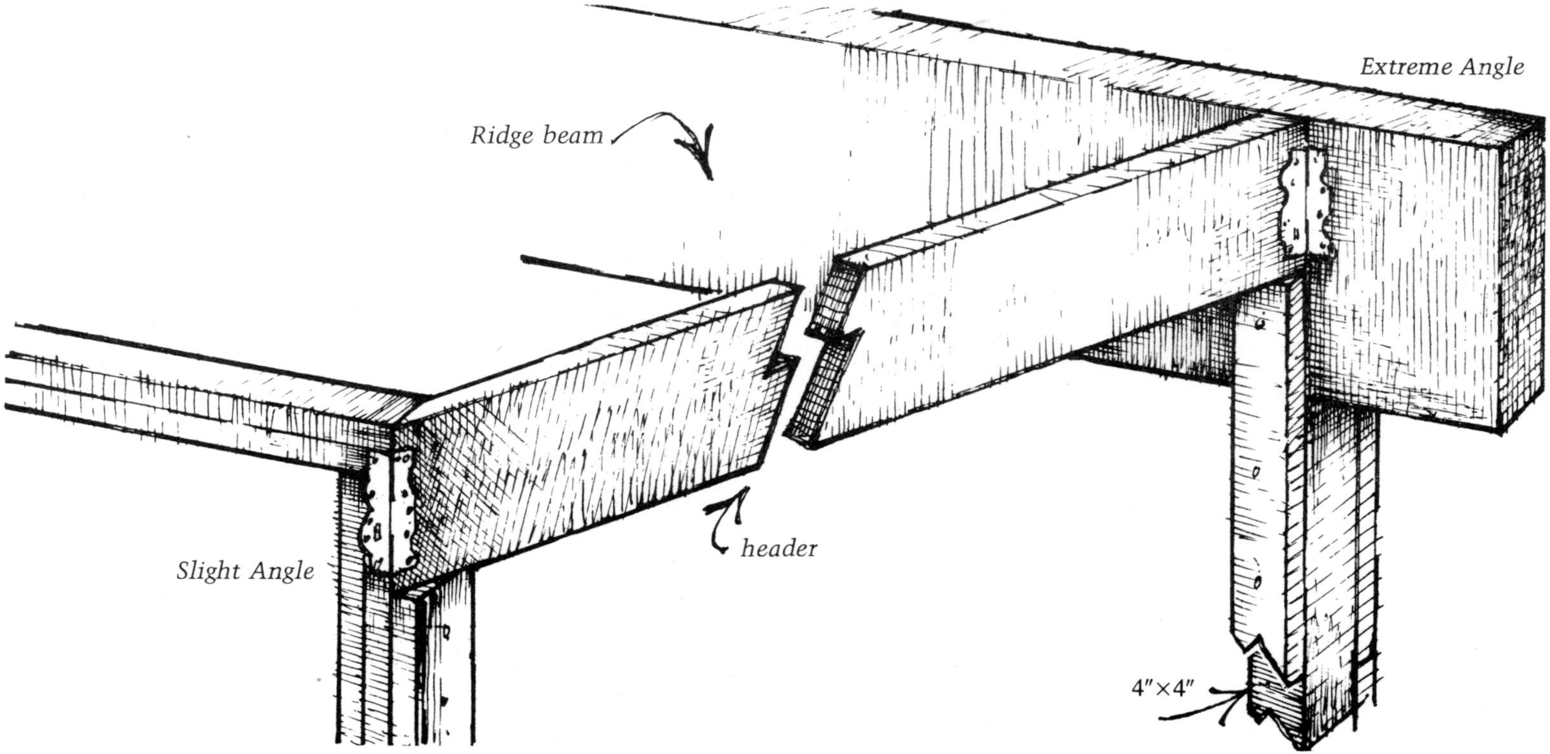

Fig. 5–N Corner Details for Design #3, the Modified Basic House

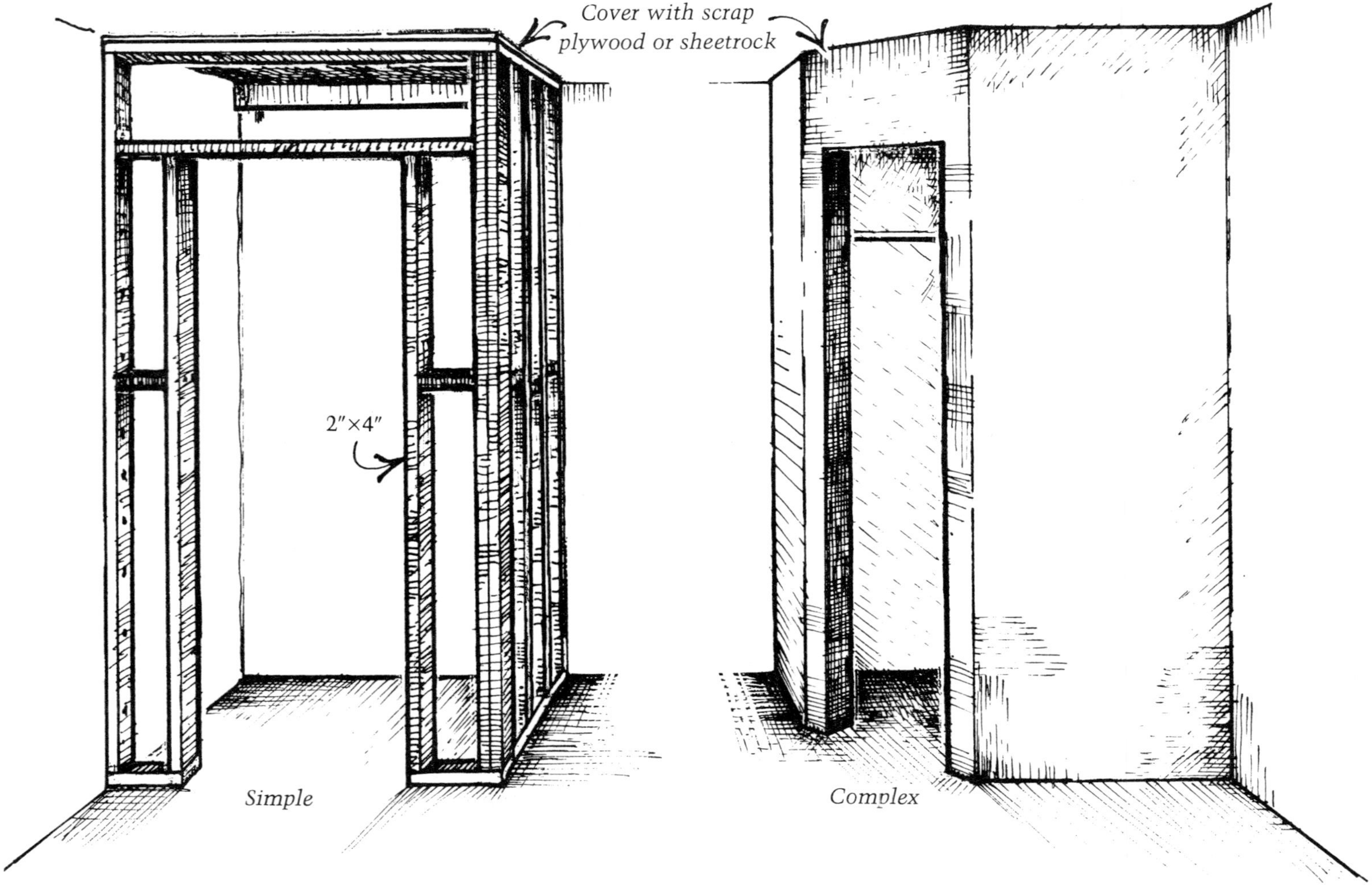

Fig. 5–O Two Types of Corner Closets

With the second structure built 15 or 25 feet from the main house, privacy will be greatly increased and noise transfer through walls will be eliminated. The one-slope design can be enlarged several ways, and this subject will be discussed in a later chapter on expansion.

CLOSETS

Closets are often built in with the framing, but I feel they can be added easily later. If kept movable, they can be taken out if you later choose to make a bedroom into a dining room or a sitting room. I personally like flexibility in features like closets and large cabinets.

If you'd like to make your closets and shelving permanent, you can cover them with wood or sheet rock. Also, you can save a little on closet doors by not using them. Make up some cloth drapes to cover the opening. You can make them more permanent later if you wish. *See Fig. 5–O.*

Save all of your odd piece wood scraps for use later, particularly the wood studs you cut. They often come in handy for closets and cabinets.

WINDOWS, DOORS, AND SKYLIGHTS

A cheap form of window is the fixed sheet of glass with no openings. This is well suited for windows that you wouldn't be likely to open very often. If you use it, consider that it's easier to make one big window than three small ones. If one side of your house faces a bank or high wall, small windows are preferable because they ease that packed-in feeling. Almost all good views deserve big windows, and I always utilize them in designs I draw, but the people living in the house have to decide how they feel on the subject. One lady I know is afraid of open spaces and even goes so far as to paint rooms dark maroon and brown. She has to pull the drapes on any wide

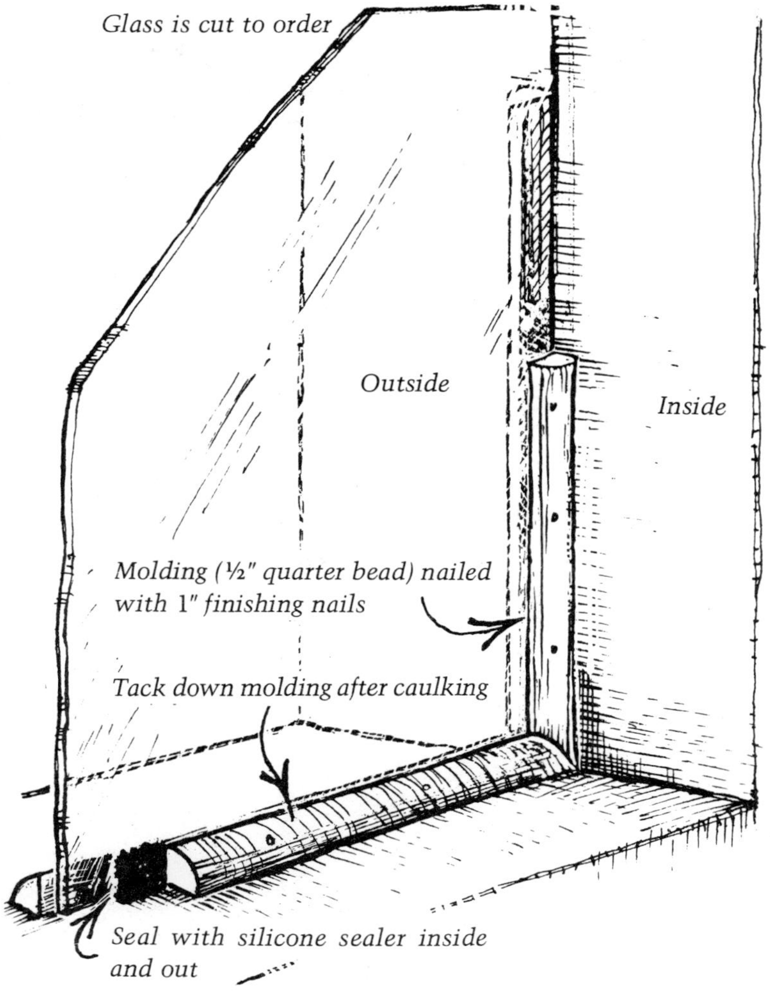

Fig. 5–P The Most Simple of Windows (Non-Opening)

views, so if I designed a house for her, I would utilize smaller and more numerous windows. If you're not sure how you'll feel, put in large windows—you can always get some heavy drapes if the view bugs you too much.

Setting a plain sheet of glass in the window opening between the studs is easy if you checked and double-checked the measurements before framing. Use plenty of putty or caulking to seal them tight, but don't tack the sealer in too hard. You might want to remove one some time. *See Fig. 5–P.*

Another inexpensive window is an old *sash window* (window that slides up and down) that you find in the junkyard or in the rubble of an old torn-down house. Unfortunately, many building departments frown on using any secondhand materals, except for decorative purposes. There is a way out of this, if you can convince them your used windows are very rare and are integral to the overall design of the house. I did this once, but after discovering the used windows I had bought were half rotted, I switched to new ones.

This brings me to the more expensive subject of new wooden sash or casement windows. Any house that has these installed definitely displays a touch of class, in this day of modern materials replacing old traditions. The owner of these pretty windows also has one other thing: yearly maintenance and eventually warped jambs. You should realize that if you put in wood casement windows you have to pay some dues to keep them looking nice.

Mostly I use dull-surfaced aluminum sliding windows, often contrasted to exterior wood paneling. This has a very harmonious effect and works nicely in all situations. I have had some installed for several years now and have only washed them to keep them clean. I heartily recommend aluminum sliding windows.

Typically these windows have large flanges, and you nail the flanges right to the studs. No caulking is necessary if you have a roof overhang because the sheathing and trim you add will form a water seal.

Used doors are another matter altogether, and most regulations allow them in all doorways. Doors are easy to find in junkyards and old houses if you ask around. Your savings will be big, and with a free afternoon and some liquid paint stripper, you will have good-as-new doors for a few dollars each.

WARNING: *Buy and measure the doors and windows before you frame.* I've seen so many people disappointed because they can't find the right size doors and windows after they've framed.

Used doors require jambs made for them individually. To make the jambs, use ¾-inch by 4-inch wood. You'll probably need shims to get the jamb the size of the door without getting it too tight. *See Fig. 5–Q.*

Whatever kind of door you install, be sure to leave ¼-inch to ½-inch on each side of the jamb clear of the stud, so the paneling will be flush with the jamb. *See Fig. 5–R.*

Lightly tack the jamb with a finishing nail or two. Then slowly drive the shims in or out until the door fits right in the space. Leave approximately a ⅛-inch clearance all around the jamb and door. Then nail the jamb in permanently with 2-inch finishing nails. Complete the job by sawing the shims flush with the door. Hanging the door is easy, but leave ½-inch at the bottom for finish flooring or carpets. Rout or chisel the place in the jamb where the hinge goes, and use ½-inch screws to secure the door.

You can buy new prehung doors if you want to make it easy on yourself, but they will cost $10–$15 more than plain doors. Just slide the door and jamb into place, shim it, and nail.

A heavy outside door takes two people to shim accurately. For that matter, it's a lot easier for all the door hanging if you

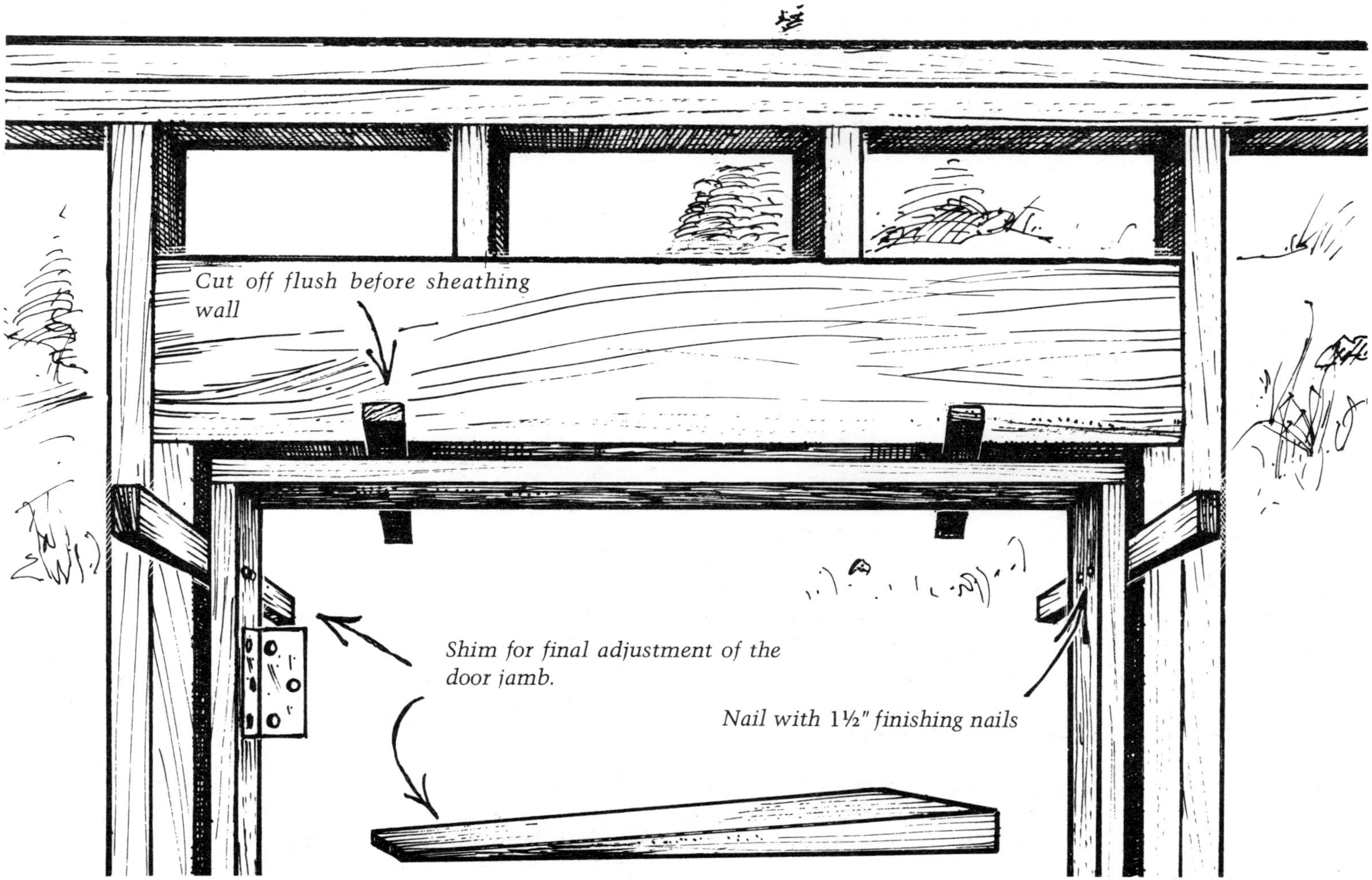

Fig. 5–Q Shimming the Prehung Door

have two people.

Skylights are good for lighting and make a small or medium-sized house seem incredibly larger. With modern designs and plastic, the age-old problem of leakage has been virtually eliminated. Designs range from simple to complex, and most of the new designs have a valid use.

The universal defect in plain skylights is that they tend to make a room too harshly shadowed. Oddly enough, by using a floodlight in the skylight, you can soften this effect. *See Fig. 5–S.*

The cost of skylights is often unreasonably high, so shop around until you get a good deal. If you get a simply designed one, you can easily modify it so that there's no lighting problem.

If you use plain sheet opaque glass set in the roof, you will save money, but be sure to smear on plenty of asphalt sealer anywhere it might leak. If you have expensive Chippendale furniture, don't put it under the skylight, as moisture sometimes condenses on the glass and drips down on the floor.

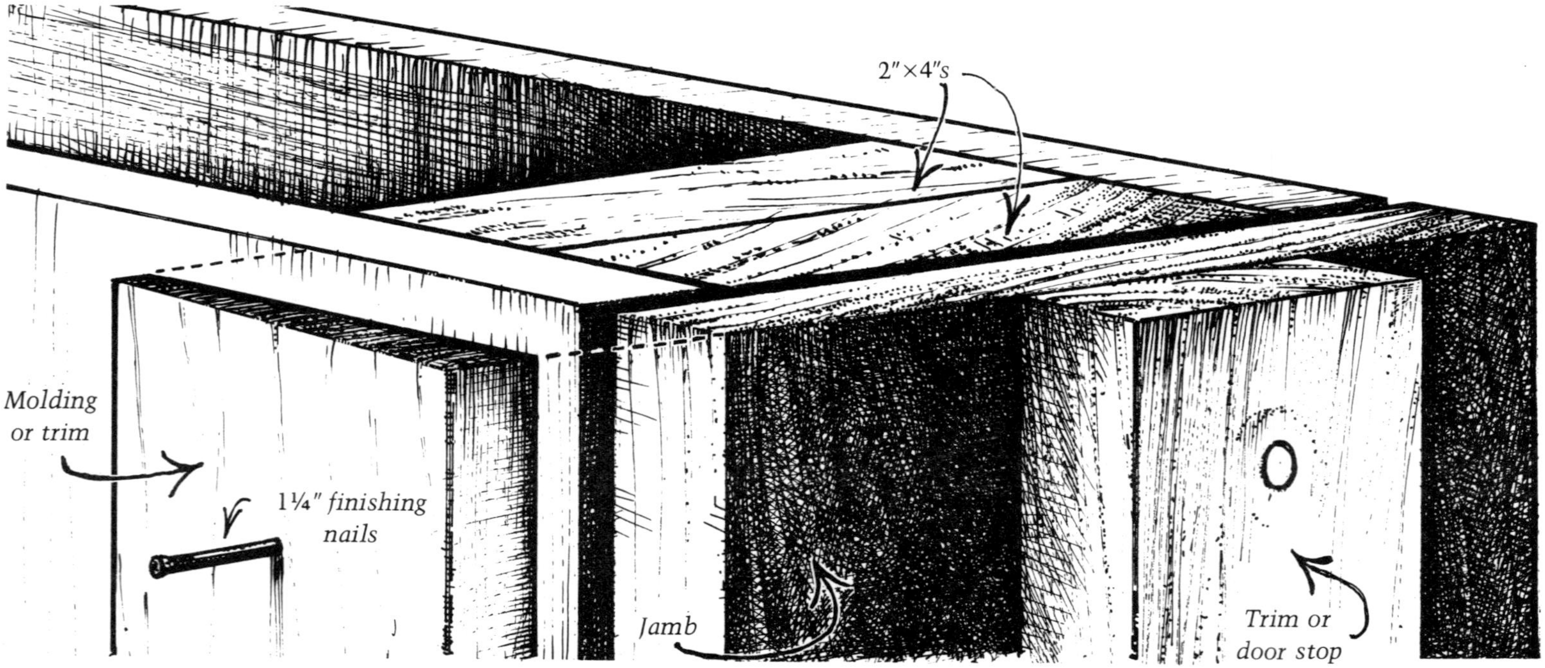

Fig. 5–R Close-up of the Door Jamb and Wall

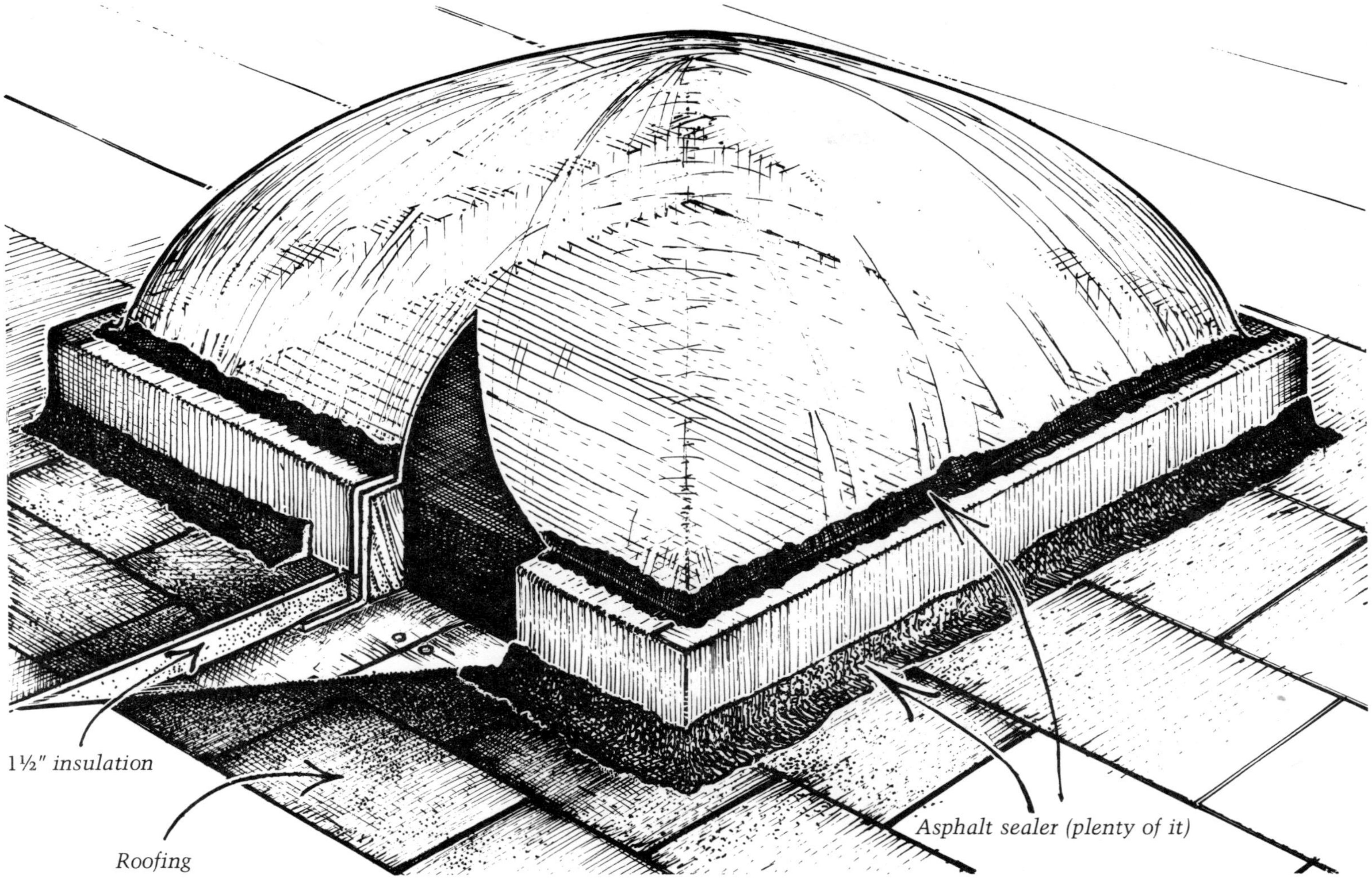

Fig. 5–S Pre-Manufactured Plastic Skylight (Clear or Translucent)

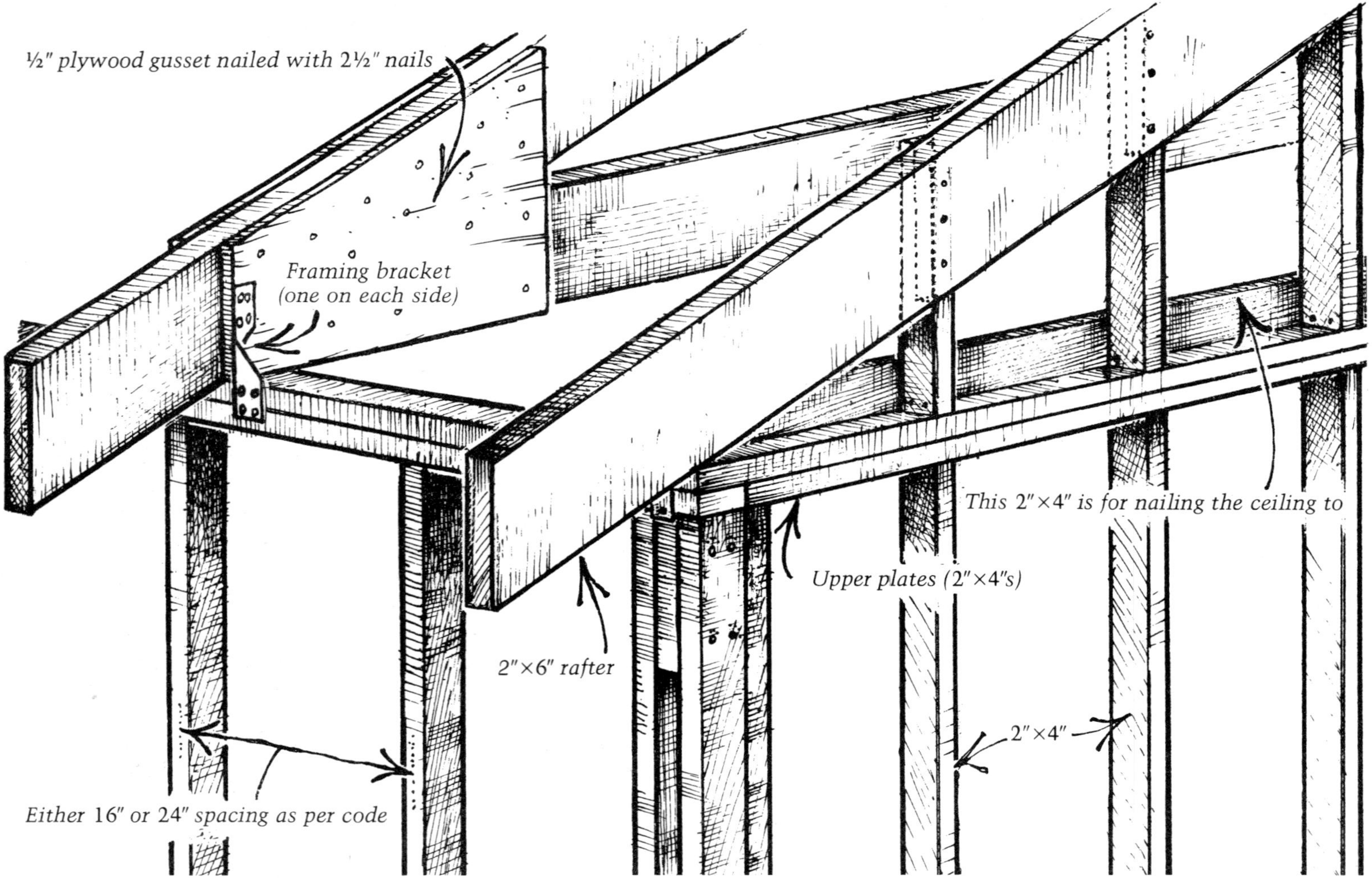

Fig. 6–A Endwall and Gable Framing

SYSTEMS OF RAFTER ROOFING

CHAPTER 6

My father and I added a porch to our modest surburban house in Ohio several long years ago. Of all the things he and I did that summer, I remember the rafters most.

My father, I should mention, wasn't religious in an orthodox sense, but he did have a lot of Quaker influence in his upbringing. Father never drank heavily, lost his temper completely, or swore profusely. That is, until we put up those rafters.

Now that I'm older and better experienced in carpentry I see the whole episode in a more mature light. Now *I* swear, drink hard liquor, and throw my tools around whenever I do rafters. A full circle you could say.

In the following pages I will describe the simplest methods I have found for roofing with rafters, and hopefully you will be saved some of the drastic personality changes my father and I have undergone.

Why should you want a rafter roof, especially since I heartily endorsed open beam ceilings in the previous chapters? Snow is a good reason. Snow tends to stay on and sometimes damage rooftops, and it's your job to see that it doesn't. Steep *roof pitches* (slopes) allow gravity to pull the snow off your roof to fall harmlessly around the house. Yes, you can make fairly steep sloped roofs with open beam ceilings—but think how high your ceilings will be inside, maybe 14–15 feet. If that idea sounds okay, stick with open beams. If not, consider rafters.

Two more reasons in favor of rafters are heat and cold insulation and attic space. The air space in the attic provides superior insulation against extreme hot or cold temperatures, especially when combined with between-the-ceiling joist insulation ("roll" or "blown-in" fiberglass). In addition, the space in the attic is useful for future storage or expansion.

The cost of rafters as opposed to beams can be favorable, but it will depend on how long you can afford to spend doing the job and how much timber and plywood you'll butcher in the process.

Before you say rafters or high-pitch roofs are for you, consider the last factor—height. How do you feel about hanging over a 15-foot abyss with a hammer in one hand and a 2×4 in the other? Enough said.

Usually for 20–28-foot spans, the wooden members for rafters are 2×6 top grade Douglas fir. The trusses (W-shaped parts) can usually be grade #1 2×4's, but check with the build-

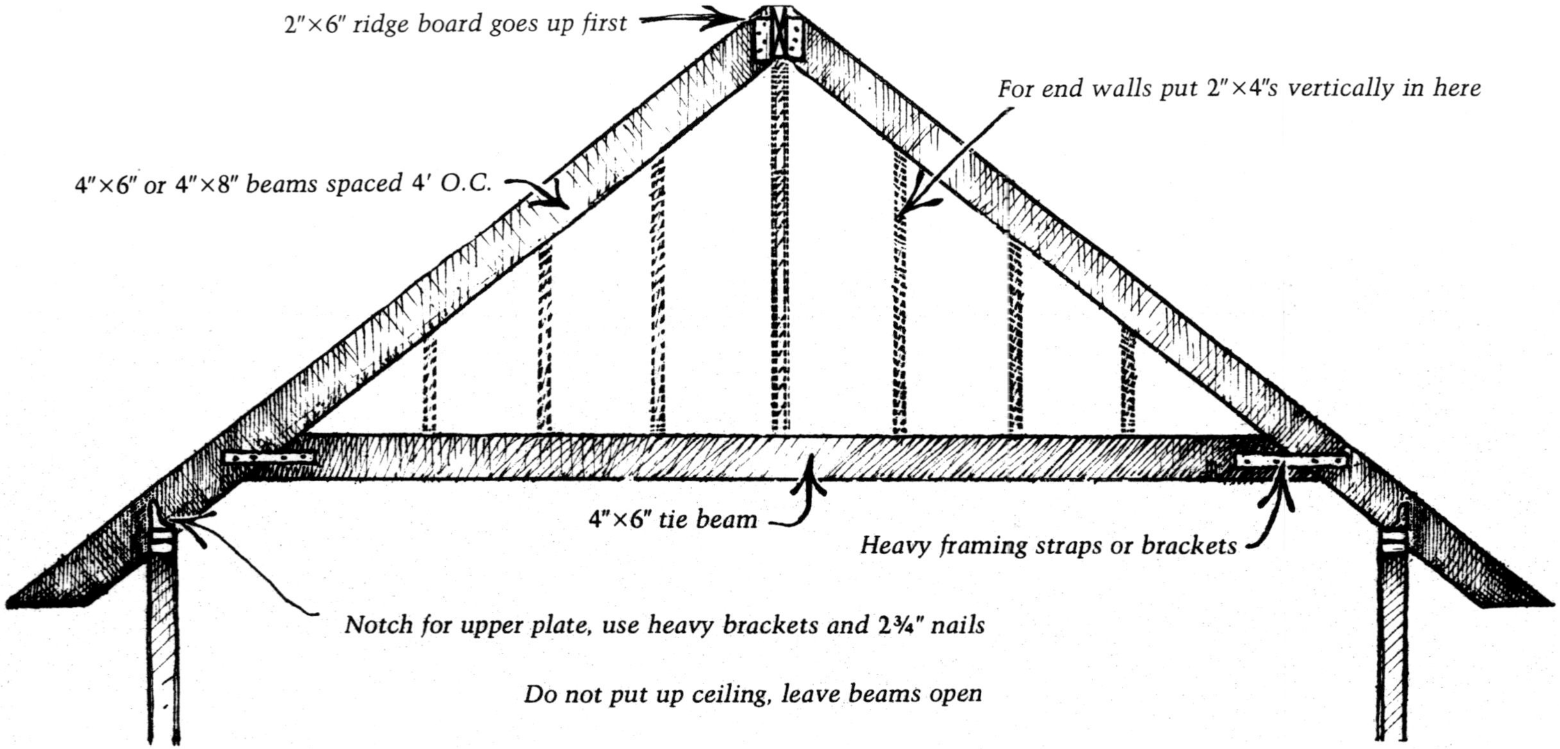

Fig. 6–B Example of a Modified A-Beam Rafter

ing department first. Ask them for a span sheet or information on the construction of rafters. "Tying in" the various members is fairly easy if you use plywood gussets (*see Fig. 6–A*) custom cut for each intersection. Metal fasteners are available, but sometimes they can be unnecessarily costly, especially if you have scrap ½-inch plywood you can use instead.

There are many types of rafter systems in use today. I have chosen to describe three types that combine the utmost simplicity with economic practicality.

MODIFIED A-BEAM SYSTEM

This first type is often associated with cavernous barns and

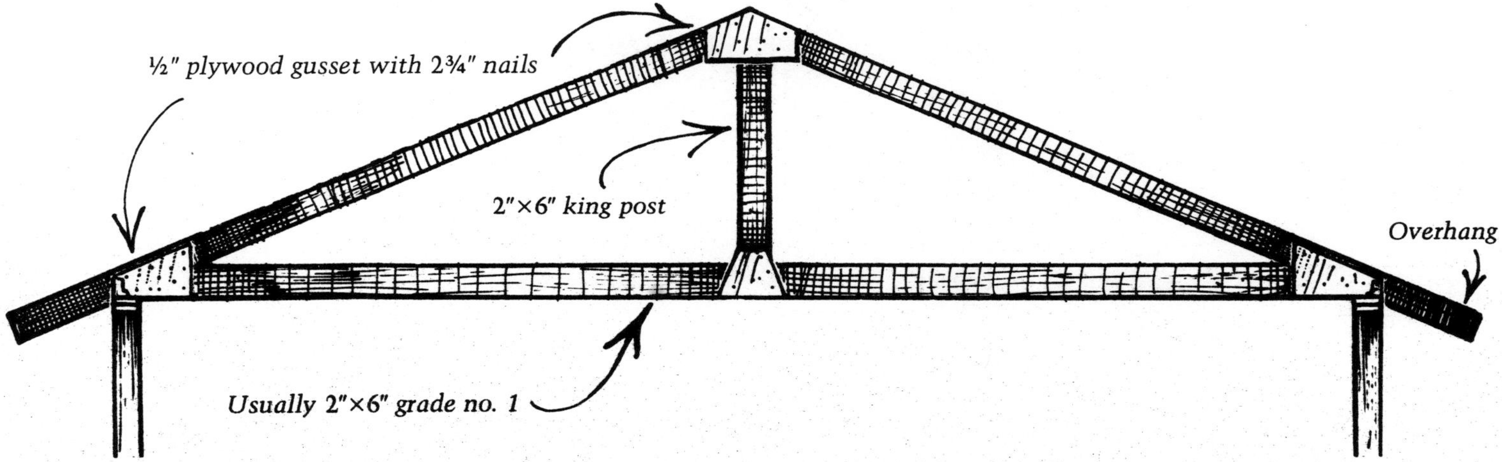

Fig. 6–C Example of a Common Rafter with a King Post

rustic mountain homes (*Fig. 6–B*). While not strictly a rafter roof, it does provide a high slope and a tie-in beam for rigidity. Heating can be a problem—but if you have a "back forty" full of oak, what's the worry?

When putting up the 4×6 or 4×8 beams you must construct the end walls first, and then erect the ridge beam, which is usually a 2×6. Next, lift up and nail the beams, first one side then the other. Sometimes a winch or coffin hoist is necessary for lifting the beams.

For this roof system be sure your ridge cuts (angles for the ridges) and seat cuts are dead accurate and neat. Be sure to use the strongest metal brackets you can find, one on each side of the beam. There are some cheapies out there that will scarcely hold a book case together, so look for thickness of metal rather than a shiny finish.

Next, *be careful.* A fall from the peak of this roof means you'll be wheel chair bound for many days. Safety lines (don't laugh) can save your life . . . just don't forget to tie it to something like a friend of mine did.

COMMON RAFTER WITH A KING POST

See Fig. 6–C. When constructing these simple truss rafters you may find it necessary to predrill the nail holes to prevent the wood from splitting. Again use 2½-inch nails and brackets to attach the trusses to the upper plates. These trusses are suitable for medium slope roofs and give the best strength for the amount of construction time and materials used.

In a few major ways, these trusses differ from the rafter

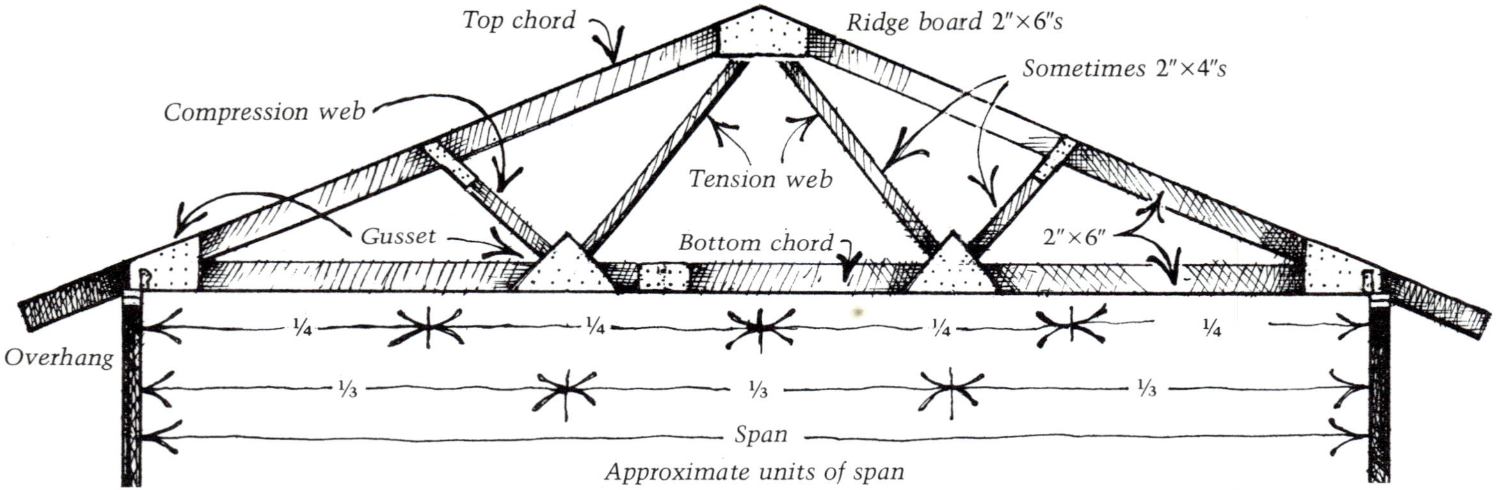

Fig. 6–D Example of a W-Truss Rafter With Plywood Gussets

beams discussed in the previous section. One difference is that these common truss rafters are nailed together *on the floor* rather than in place. Another difference is that one person can construct and position these trusses whereas the previous rafters are impossible for one person to do alone safely.

W-TYPE TRUSS

This third type of rafter system is a relatively modern innovation in the world of carpentry (*Fig. 6–D*). While these W-trusses share many of the features of the King Post Truss, especially in installation, there is one fundamental difference—strength. Since the internal W can distribute the compression and tension factors of the roof load more equally than a simple king post, the use of this system can virtually double the strength of your roof.

Notice the example of a W truss in *Figures 6–D & E* and note the various parts well. As you can imagine, the job of constructing these Pythagorean nightmares is tricky, but carpenters throughout the years have developed ingenious ways to solve the problem.

The first method of framing a truss involves constructing a big pattern on your floor or outside in the yard. Just go to the library, borrow a book of rafter tables, and determine your desired roof slope and span. Using the tables you will find out the length of your upper chords and the appropriate ridge cut angles. Using your new figures, make a paper sketch of your intended design on graph paper, then chalk this sketch blown up to full size on your floor. Match the member lengths to the

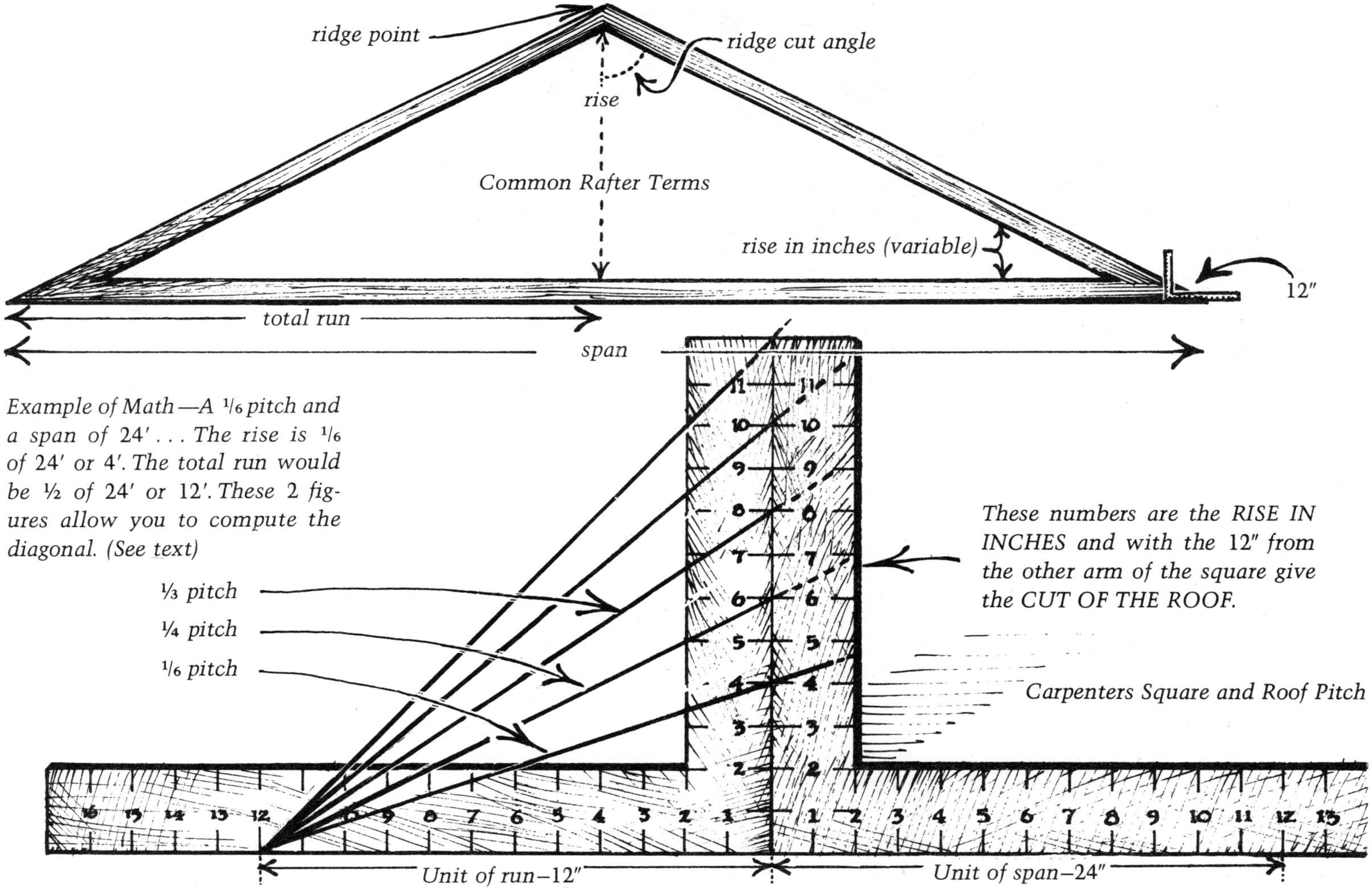

Fig. 6–E The Carpenters Square and Roof Terminology

pattern exactly and make all your cuts right on the spot. Nail together with ½-inch plywood gussets (one on each side) and 2½-inch long nails. Voilà, instant trusses—the easy way.

If, however, you don't have a handy place to construct a giant pattern, don't fear. The house builders' most classy tool—the *carpenter's square*—will rescue you. This L-shaped steel tool is actually a sophisticated computer capable of giving you all the figures and angles you will need to construct a roof system. *See Fig. 6–E.* However, like most computers you must speak the language. First, you must decide what *pitch* of roof you want. This is easy, since most modern houses seldom deviate from the simple 1/3, 1/4, 1/6 examples. Anything steeper presents radical roofing problems, and anything more shallow is hard to shingle or roof effectively.

After deciding what pitch suits your purposes, you can find the *rise* and *total run* by following the example of math in the illustration, substituting your figures for the hypothetical ones I used. If you did your math correctly, you should now know the rise and total run of your roof.

To determine the diagonal (the length of the upper chord), you will now need your trusty carpenter's square. This process of computation is called "stepping off the top chord." Proceed by placing a sufficiently long 2×6 on the floor and designating one edge as the crown or roof side of the member. As the illustration shows, place the square on the member and align the figure of 12 inches as shown. Align the proper figure of inches from the opposing arm (*Fig. 6–F*). For 1/4 pitch set it at 6 inches, for 1/3 pitch set it at 8 inches, for 1/6 pitch set it at 4 inches.

With the carpenter's square thus positioned, draw a line across the 2×6. Where the line intersects the crown edge, make a thin notch in the wood with a nail. Move the square to the next position and make sure the 12 inches and its corresponding number meet the edge. This is your first "step off."

Now as you continue stepping off the length, you'll ask yourself how many times do I do this? Simple. If there are 10 feet of run in your rafter, step ten times from the notch in the crown edge. If there are 12 feet of run, step 12 times, and so on. *See Fig. 6–F.* In essence, what you are doing is allowing the steel square to compute the correct hypotenuse and ridge cut angle as you step off. When you finish stepping off the correct number of times, draw a line on the 2×6 and that will be your ridge cut.

Before mass-producing your trusses however, complete one and measure it for accuracy. If you're curious to find out how accurate you were, double check your calculations with rafter tables found in any comprehensive roof framing book. Remember that the most important factors in truss construction are *perfect symmetry* and *exact duplication* from the first truss to the last.

To construct your trusses, cut out the gussets as shown and use plenty of Elmers Glue. Nail with 2-inch nails, about 10 per side. Pre-drilling may be necessary if your wood has a tendency to split. Allow your trusses to set undisturbed for 24 hours so the glue will dry thoroughly.

If you use the W-type truss, you must obviously make the exterior shape first and then complete the W. This is easy to do if you cut accurately and allow enough plywood for your gussets. The 1/3 and 1/4 *unit figures* showing the spacing of the W members are only simple examples. *Be sure to check with your building department for compliance with local codes* before you construct your trusses.

Nailing up the trusses on the walls is easier than it sounds. Just premark the upper plate at 16-inch or 24-inch intervals, whichever your design specifies. Next, lift the trusses up and hang them inverted. As you proceed, rotate them upward and nail the brackets on with 2¾-inch nails, one bracket on each

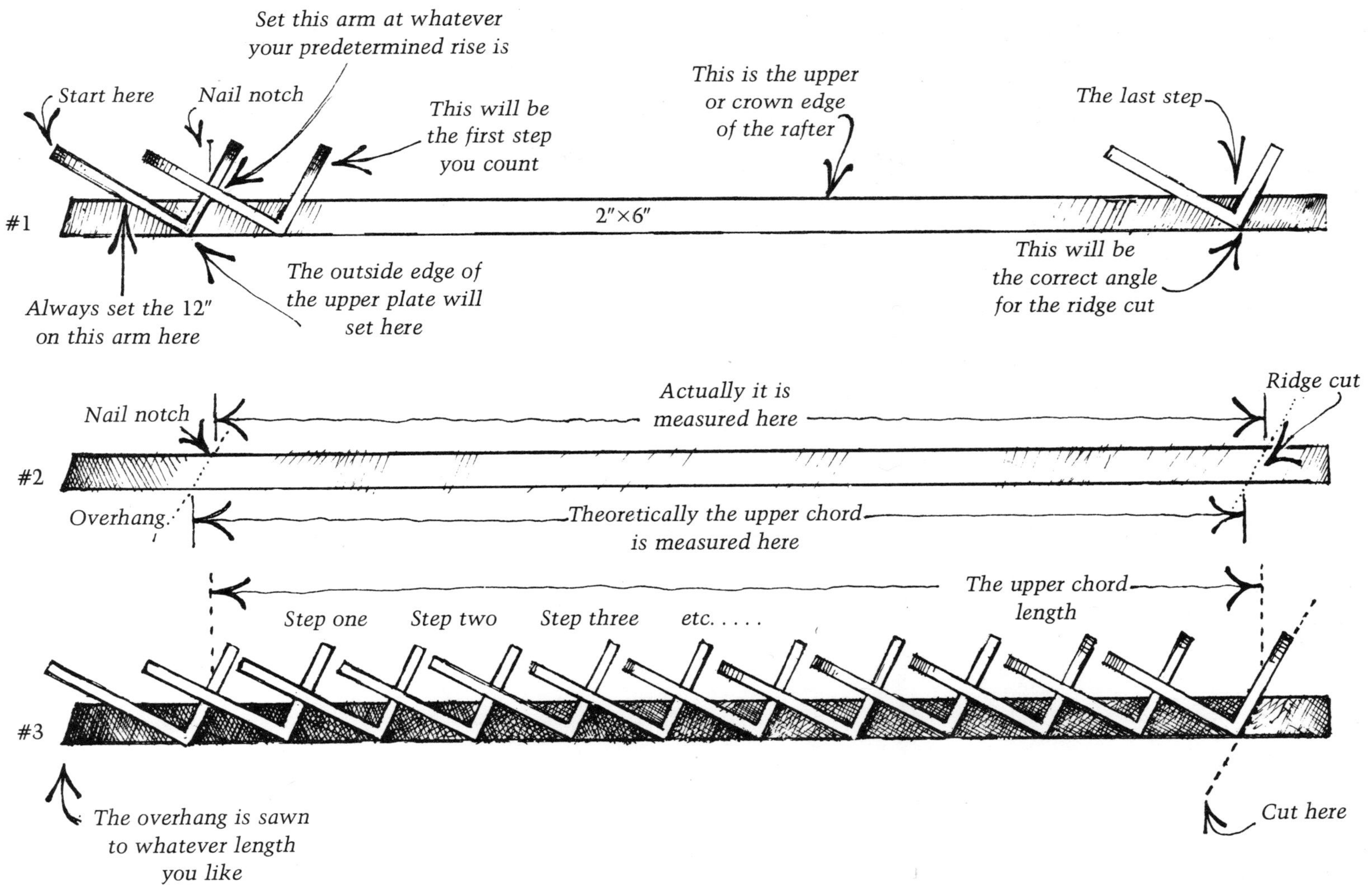

Fig. 6–F "Stepping Off" the Top Chord With a Carpenters Square

Fig. 6–G Use a T-Brace to Help Nail Up Sheetrock

side. For alignment use a level and tape measure. Temporary horizontal 2×4's can be used to steady and align the trusses prior to nailing and can even be left on 'till the ridge boards and the roofing plywood are up. For construction of the gable ends, see *Figure 6–A*.

The 2×6 ridge boards are usually toe-nailed at the top gusset with four 2¾-inch nails per joint. Allow the ridge board's top edge to be flush with the apex of the ridge peak of each truss.

The thickness of your roofing plywood is determined in part by the spacing of your rafters and in part by how much strength you'll need. Your building department will probably have noted on your blueprints the correct thickness and type plywood suitable for your area. Nail ½-inch or ¾-inch roofing plywood with 2¾-inch nails, but for thicker plywood use 3½-inch nails. Nail all edges every 6 inches O.C. and the intermediate points at 12 O.C. Now is the time to call the roofers or do it yourself. (See the roofing section in Chapter 5.)

Later, when it's time to panel or sheetrock your ceiling, you'll find the job is easier with the help of a T-brace (*Fig. 6–G*). Nail ½-inch ceiling sheetrock up with special 1⅝-inch sheetrock nails. Space the nails 6 inches to 8 inches O.C. and remember to dimple the nail heads into the sheetrock. (See special section on sheetrocking in Chapter 10.) Needless to say, two people working together make the hellish job of upside–down nailing easier by sharing the labor and by giving each other moral support.

Putting down roll insulation between the ceiling joists will seem like a holiday after your previous work. Whether you use *blown–in fiberglass* (*See Fig. 6–H*), *fiberglass roll* type, or *insulation batts*, you will find the work easy to do in one afternoon. Cutting insulation rolls is simple if you can get hold of a big pair of sharp scissors, but even hedge clippers will do in a pinch. (I don't know how you feel about fiberglass parti-

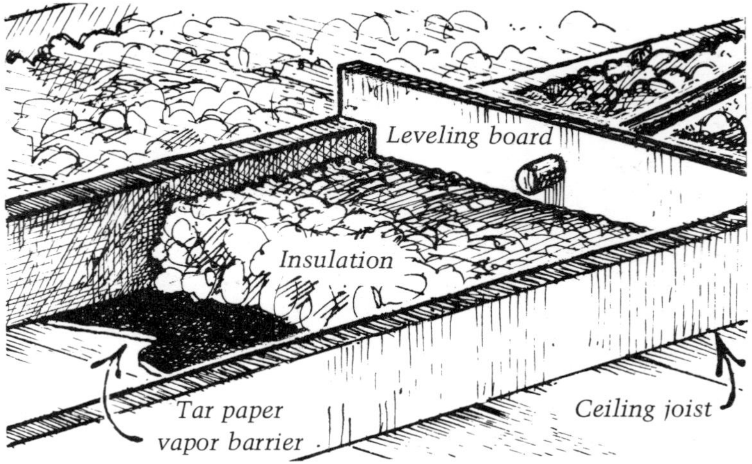

Fig. 6–H   Leveling Ceiling Insulation

cles, but I always use a mask when doing this type work.)

Most people allow some overhang in their rafter design, and when installed, this becomes the *eave section* of your roof. Since it is impractical to leave the spaces between the rafters open, you may nail up 1×6 boards with screened vents in them as shown in *Figure 6–I.* Screened vents are a necessity for proper attic ventilation—they improve the insulating qualities and deter the attraction of termites. Make sure though that the screen is no larger than 3/16-inch mesh to avoid hornets building nests in your attic. One screened vent every 10–12 feet should be sufficient. If you are the sort of person who enjoys seeing louvers in the gable ends, see the illustration just mentioned and remember that they can be made as half circles, rectangles, or even triangles.

As a final note to this chapter, I would like to add that the rooms you have created with the rafter roof system are cubic in nature—that is, they have flat ceilings. You will have to apply more thought in choosing your drapes and room paint than is necessary in rooms with a sloping ceiling. Small rooms with flat ceilings can get pretty tight if you lean toward dark colors, so plan everything as you go along, step by step. In other words, don't buy a case of dark navy blue paint—until you see how it looks on a small section first.

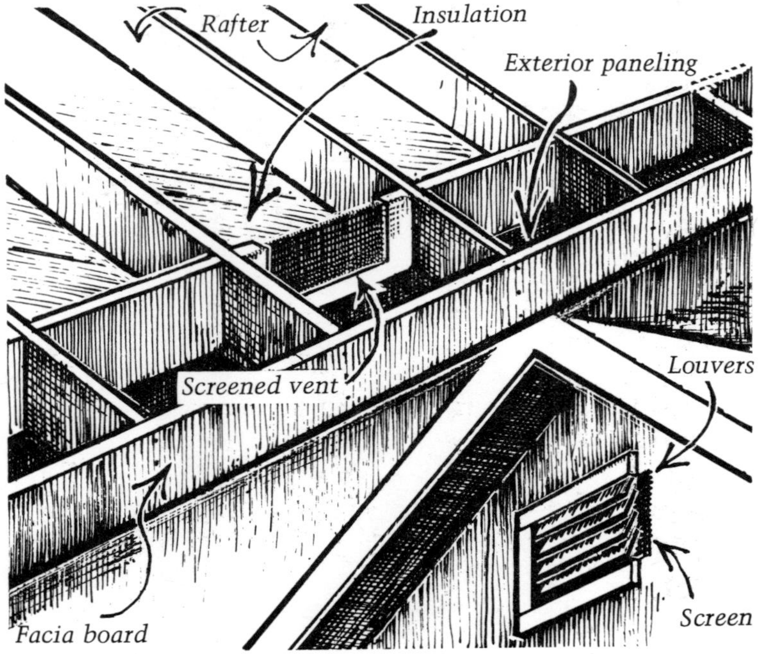

Fig. 6–I   Ventilating the Attic Space

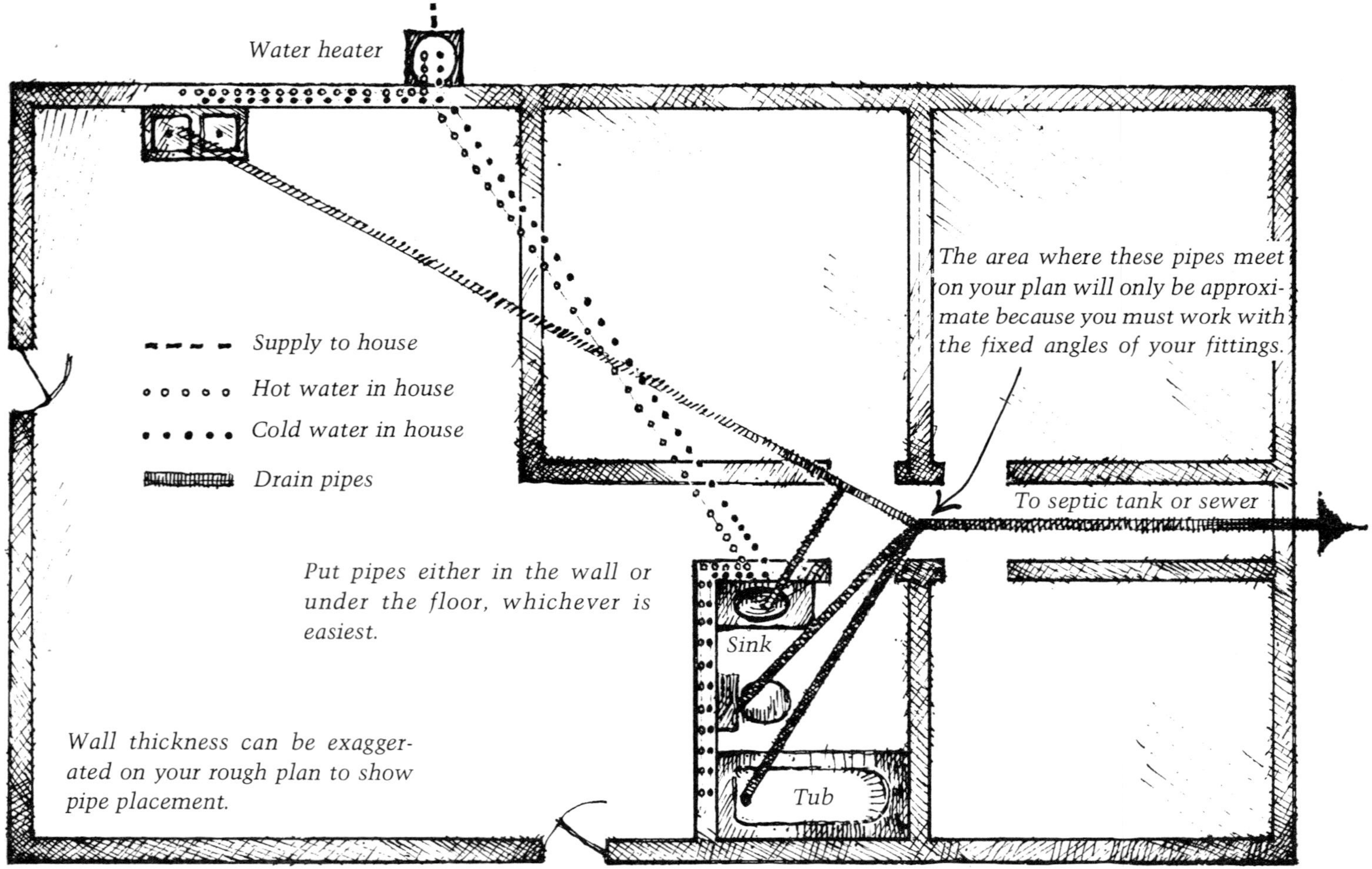

Fig. 7–A A Typical Rough Plumbing Plan

PLUMBING

CHAPTER 7

The job of plumbing a house is perhaps the most difficult the layperson encounters since it requires great attention to detail, such as measuring, cutting threads, and installing fixtures. If you live in the rare area that does not permit you to do your own plumbing, this will increase your costs. Sometimes by actually assisting the plumber you can save a little time and money.

If you do your own plumbing, you'll find that the houses I presented earlier have the plumbing designed fairly simply. The three major parts of the water system are *supply, drain,* and *septic tank* (or city sewer pipe). *See Fig. 7–A.*

PIPE TO THE HOUSE

However, before we get into the details of the plumbing system, let's discuss your supply source for a moment. Springs and wells were already mentioned in Chapter 2, but to get your water to where you can use it, you will need to know how to lay a pipe to your house. *See Fig. 7–B.* The pipe supplying the water to the house will have to be at least ¾ inch in diameter, and preferably 1 inch in most areas. Pipe run from a well or supply source to the house must be placed at such a depth that it will not freeze easily in cold weather. I was lucky, because in California I was required to bury the supply pipe only 1-foot deep. If you have to go really deep, have a tractor or caterpillar do it for you when you grade your house pad. Needless to say, use all galvanized pipe and fittings to insure long life. **WARNING:** If you cheat and lay your pipe on the surface, don't hook up your house's electrical ground to it because it could be dangerous. Drive a rod several feet into the ground to effectively ground your system.

Your tools for this plumbing job will be a vise-grip wrench or a plumber's wrench, a rented tripod and pipe threader, a hammer, nails, and *pipe dope* (gray paste used to seal threads).

Here is how you cut and install a simple underground pipe, or for that matter any type. Measure exactly the length you need, then correct the measurement by leaving ½ inch at each end for the pipe to go in each fitting. *See Fig. 7–C.* Measure very exactly and scratch the marking on the pipe. Cut the pipe with either a hacksaw or pipe cutter and tripod. If you use a pipe cutter, you will get a more perfect cut than is possible

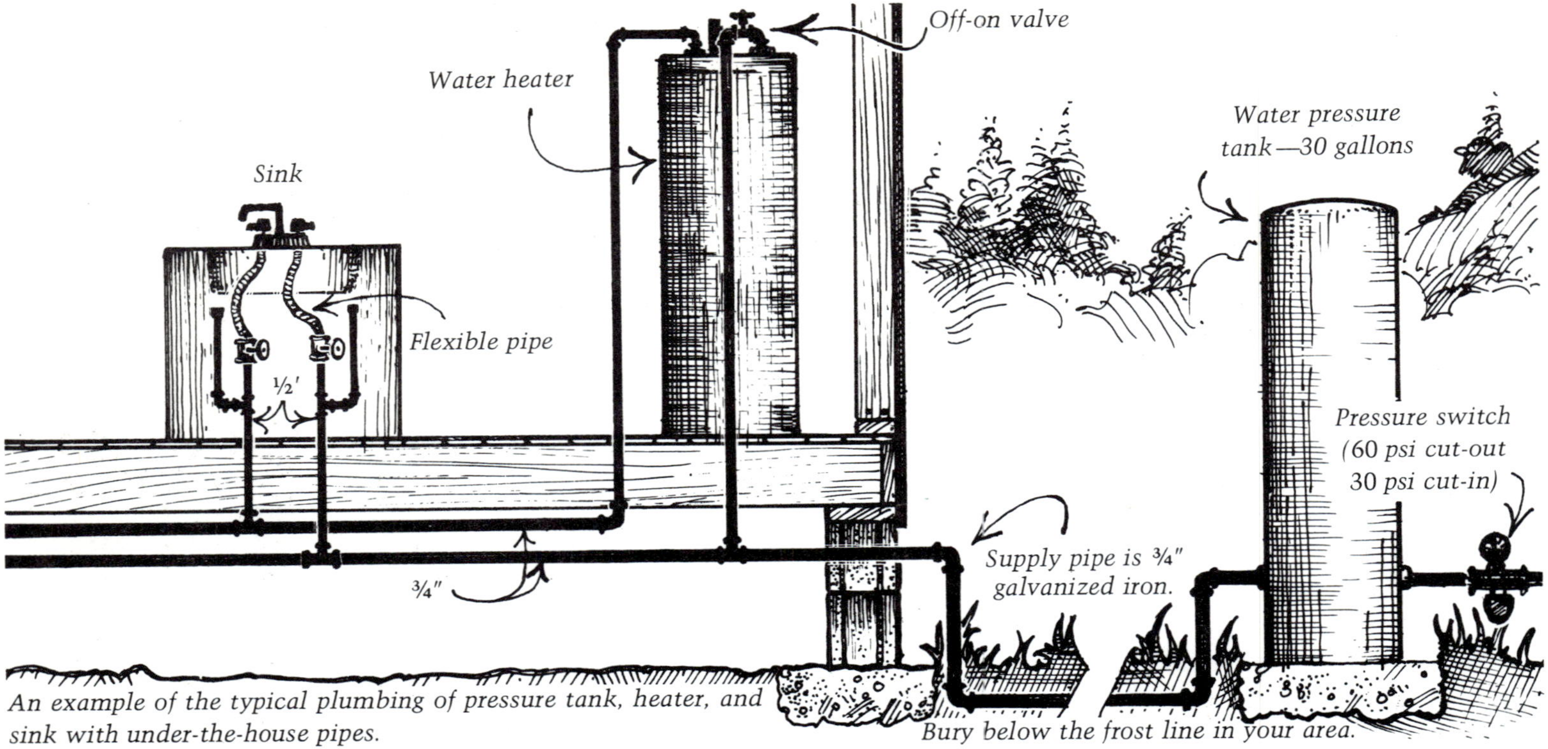

An example of the typical plumbing of pressure tank, heater, and sink with under-the-house pipes.

Fig. 7–B Under-the-House Plumbing

with the hacksaw, making it well worth the $2 or $3 in rental fee. The tripod and threader are approximately $10 for daily rental.

To thread a pipe, fit the proper size thread cutter in the handle of the pipe threader and oil the end that is to be threaded so it will cut smoothly and coolly. Make sure the tripod is firmly nailed down, and then rotate the handle in a clockwise direction until you've got approximately ¾ inch of thread on the pipe. File off the rough edges on the inside of the pipe and do the other end the same way. Smear plenty of pipe dope on the threads before fitting.

When laying the pipe, make sure you get the pipe and fitting screwed together tight so they won't leak, but don't overdo it by hammering the pipe wrench's handle. You can use a pipe

If you measure from the outside of the pipe fittings, allow an additional ½" at each end of the pipe to thread into the fitting.

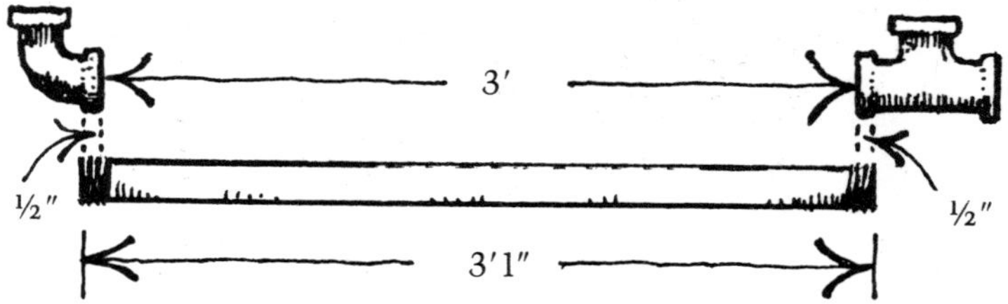

Fig. 7–C A Pipe Fitting and Its Threads

bender for bends, or you can use the proper fitting to achieve the same angle.

THE SUPPLY SYSTEM

Water supply pipes in the house are a bit more complicated since you must fit them all under the floor and in the walls. If you keep in mind these pointers, your house's water supply system should be efficient:

1. Always plan the drainage pipes and supply pipes in relation to each other beforehand, so that you won't be in the unfortunate position of having to cram them all in one spot.
2. Keep the hot water heater as close to the kitchen as possible, to reduce needless plumbing and having to wait an unnecessary amount of time for hot water at the tap.
3. If possible, keep the bathroom nearest the area of the house where supply pipes will enter.
4. For convenience, group together in one wall (called a *wet wall*) the plumbing for the bathroom and kitchen.
5. The farther that hot water has to travel, the more it will cost to heat it.

Your pipes will usually be ½ inch or ¾ inch, depending on the specifications of your building department. Most of the

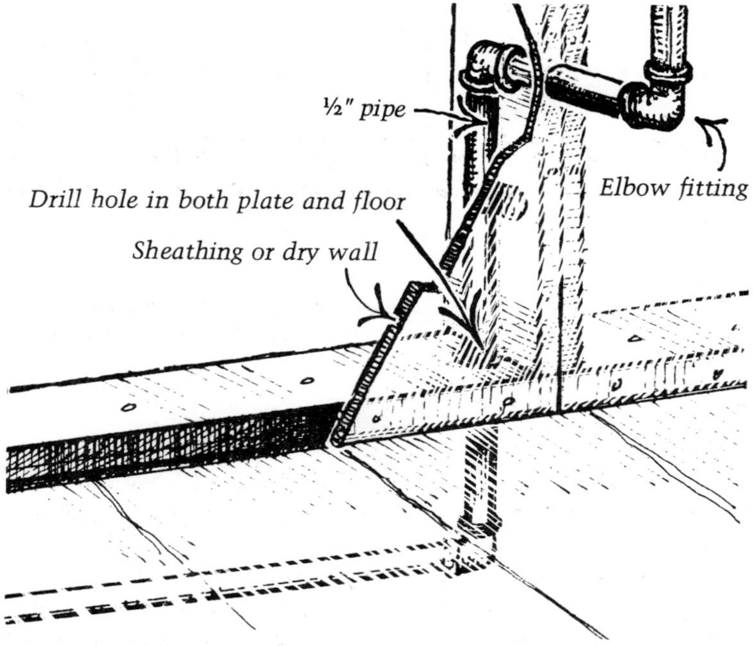

Fig. 7–D Snubbing Pipe Out of the Wall

common valves and stopcocks are available in both sizes at all hardware and plumbing supply stores. One-inch pipe and fittings are sometimes harder to find.

By referring back to your plumbing plan, you will see that it is quite easy to arrange the whole system, since most of the pipes run under the house. These pipes are nailed with brackets to the posts and beams. When bringing your pipes up through the bottom plate, just center the hole in the 2×4, and drill the hole larger than the pipe. *Snub-out* the end of the pipe so that it protrudes beyond where the *finished* wall will be by at least ½ inch or ¾ inch, depending on the fixture you attach. *See Fig. 7–D.*

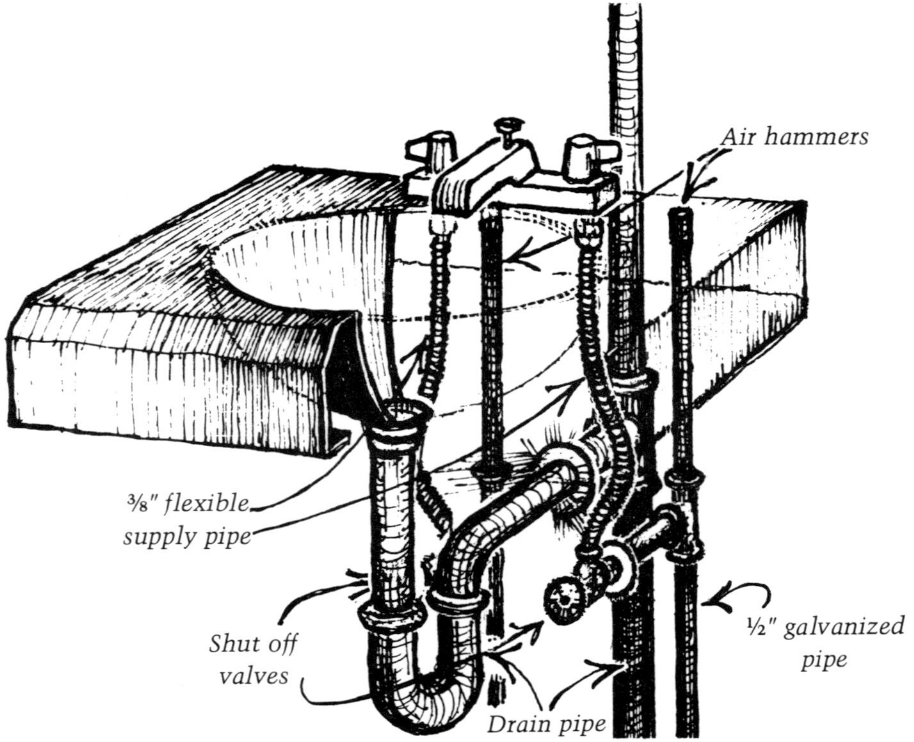

Fig. 7–E Hooking Up a Sink

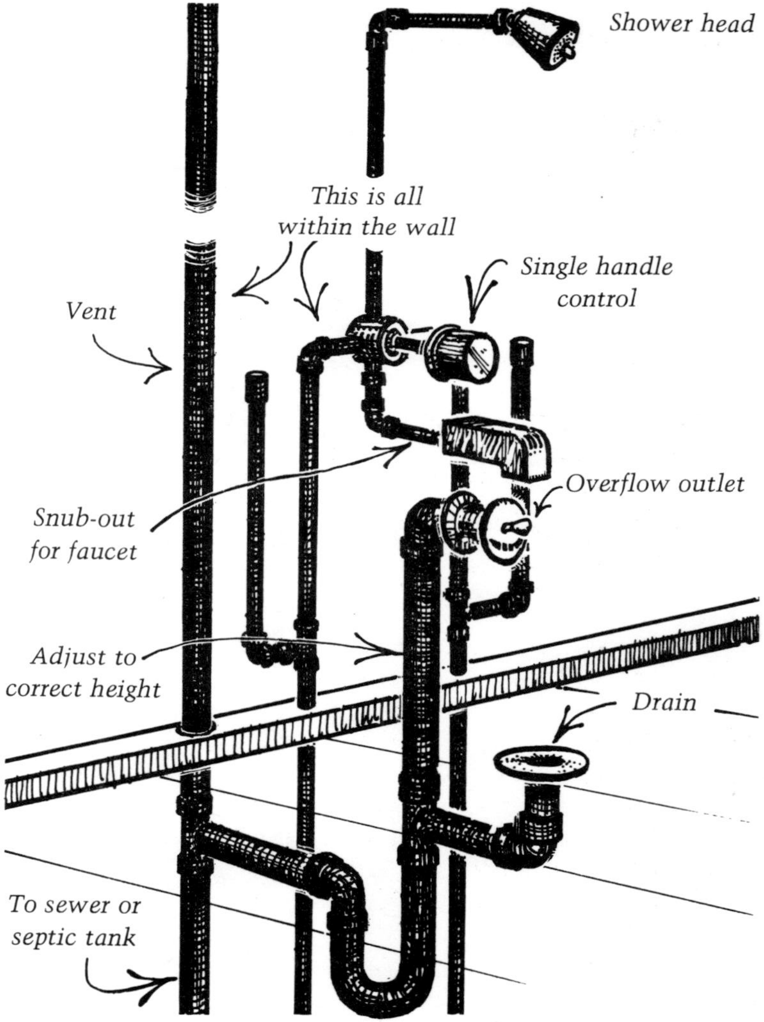

Fig. 7–F The Shower and Tub Hookup

When you plan a sink or bathtub, find out the manufacturer's recommended hook-up and make your pipe arrive exactly in the right spot. The usual method of sink and bathtub installation is shown in *Fig's. 7–E, F, & G.*

If the bathroom is 5 feet wide, you will be able to fit any standard tub in the space between the walls. Later you can use tile (see Chapter 11) or plastic-coated board to waterproof the installation.

THE DRAINAGE SYSTEM

The purpose of the drainage system is twofold. The first is to remove waste water and the second is to vent trapped gas from the sewer lines or septic tank. If you didn't build vent stacks to carry away the gas, you would have some very unpleasant odors bubbling up through your fixtures. *Fig's. 7–H & I* show the details of various venting techniques.

Plastic pipe and cast-iron hub-and-spigot pipe are commonly available for drainage pipe installation. Plastic pipe is the cheapest and easiest. I recommend it for the layperson, if the local building department allows it. Cast-iron hub-and-spigot pipe is soldered or packed and caulked together. This is excellent in terms of permanence, but it is difficult to install. See a professional to get it done right.

When installing plastic pipe, use the black plastic glue especially designed for that purpose. When you apply the glue, be sure your pipe is the right size and at the correct angle, because this glue sets so fast that you won't get a second chance. A tip for using the plastic glue and pipe: First put your pipe together with the fittings, not using glue. Then scratch a line on both the pipe and the fitting as reference marks. When everything is all ready to glue, you can disassemble the pipe and glue one piece at a time, using the marks to align them.

When you are ready to run the drainage sewer pipe under

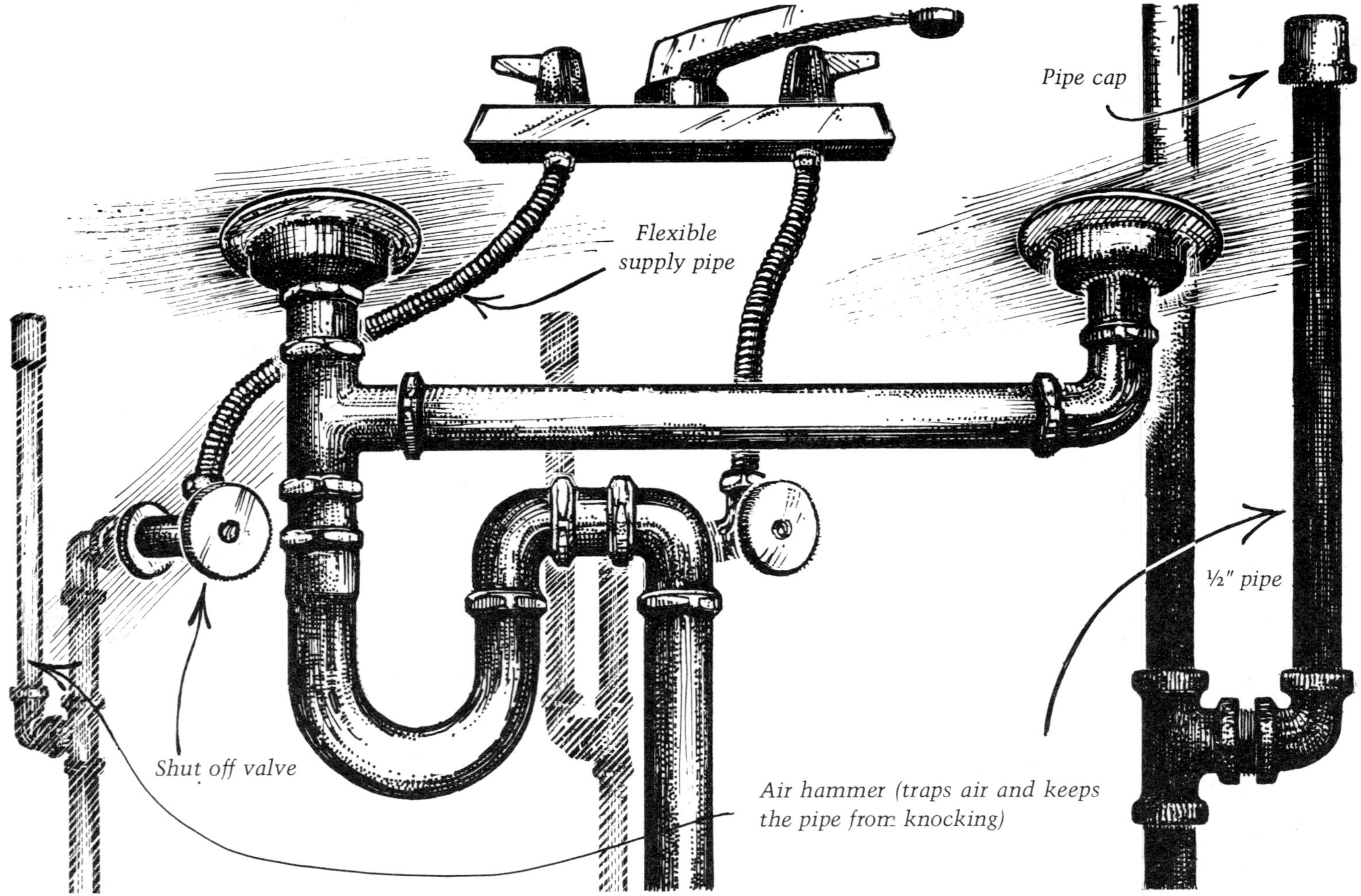

Fig. 7–G An Example of Plumbing Under a Large Sink

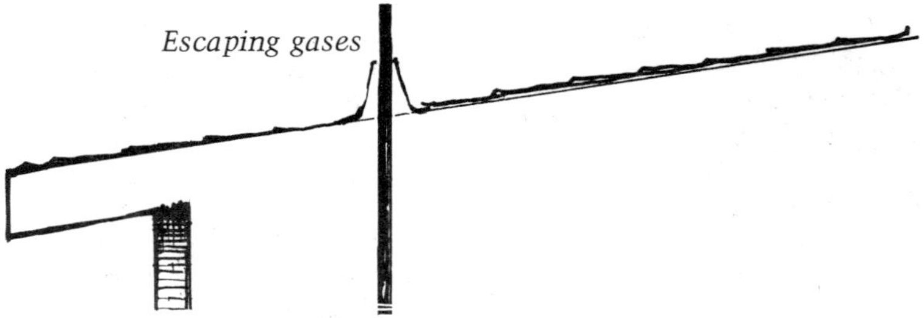

What a vent does is let the gases from the septic tank or sewer line escape from the system and not bubble up through the water traps in the facilities.

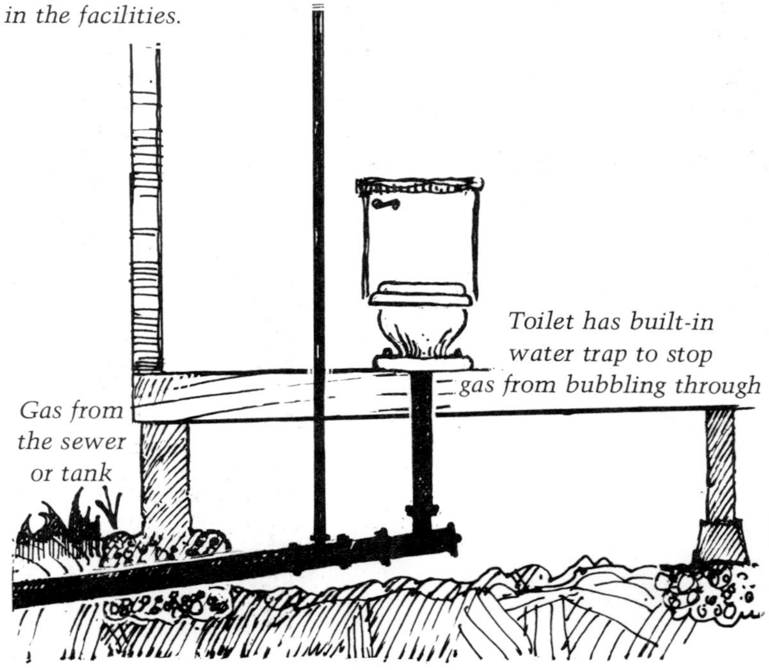

Fig. 7–H The Purpose of the Vent

the house, hang the assembled pipe with the metal straps specially made for the job. Nail straps every 8 feet to support the pipe.

For continuing the main drainage sewer pipe out of the *closet bend* (the fitting the toilet is connected to) to the septic tank, you will probably want to follow my suggested layout. A clean out plug is always included where the closet bend turns.

The drain pipe comes down through the floor and then travels on the ground several feet. After that the pipe sinks into a trench until it reaches the house foundation. Then it proceeds under the foundation and underground until it reaches the nearby tank. Given the depth of the pipe (2–3 feet), you should be able to dig the trench by hand. Maintain a fall of at least ½ inch per foot, but don't make it too steep, or it will clog.

The vents at the roof level must be made permanently watertight, and the best method I have found is to use a premade metal flashing of the correct size. *See Fig. 7–J.* Seal around it with plenty of thick asphalt sealant, and be sure you leave several feet of pipe extended above the roof. You don't need to cover the pipe, because rainwater running into it will simply run into the drain pipe.

The drainage pipe connection and the septic tank are discussed in the appendix.

Should you run into problems, your local plumber will help you install difficult parts, or he may even give you free advice. Call him.

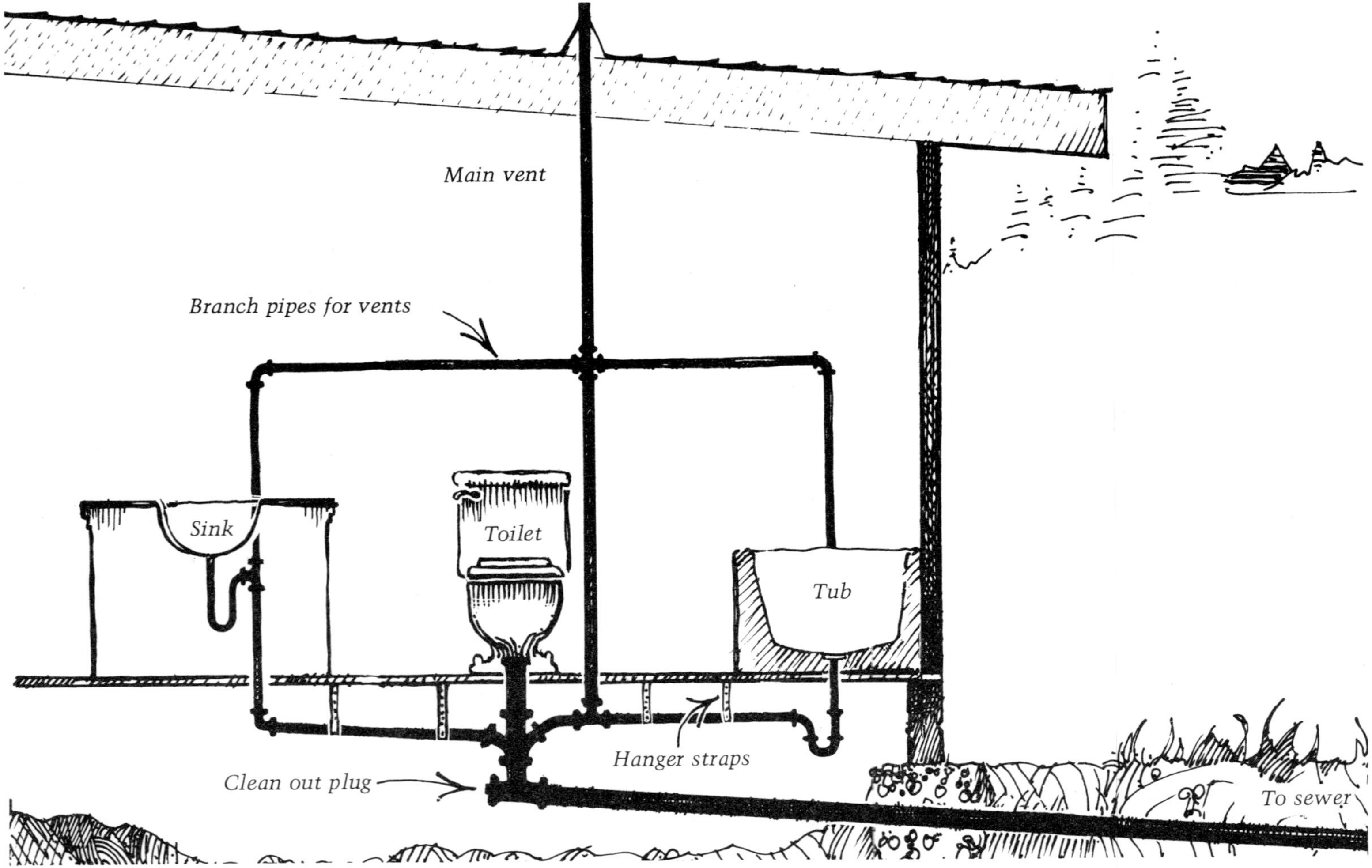

Fig. 7–I Cross Section of the Plumbing and Vent System

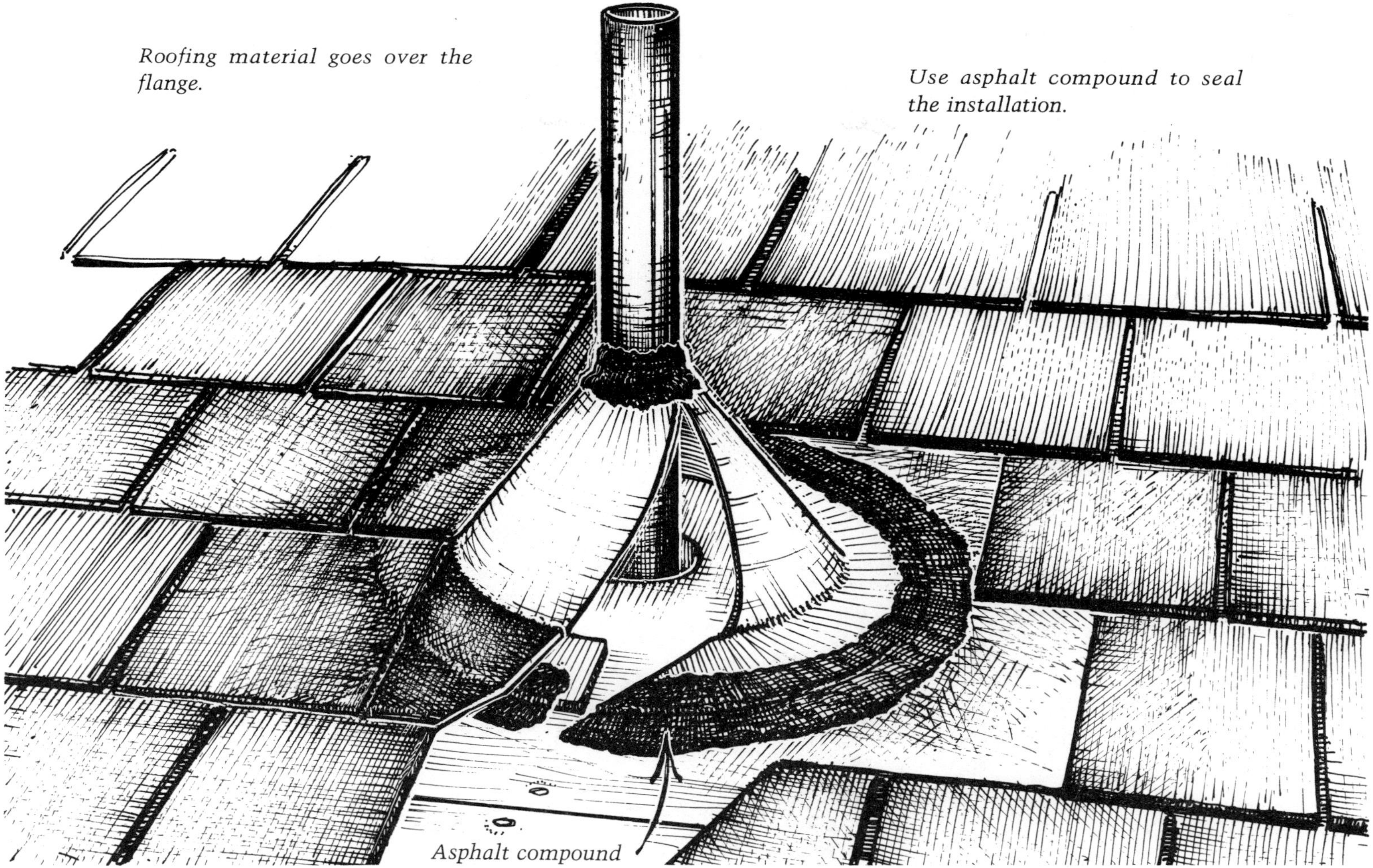

Fig. 7–J The Flashing for Vents

Lumber Yard

EXTERIOR SHEATHING AND TRIM

CHAPTER 8

When you think about it a moment, you'll realize that sheathing is just about the most important feature on the exterior of your house. You'll want to take some time and find sheathing material you can live with. Basic sheathing, or *siding*, is Douglas fir plywood. The size of the 4×8 or 4×10 plywood panel greatly simplifies construction, and its other benefits are beauty, strength, and low maintenance. I recommend using 4×10 sheets on your house, if financially possible, so that you won't have to add sashes or trim boards later. The extra foot or two of panel will cover the top of the foundation.

SHOPPING FOR SHEATHING

When you buy sheathing it pays to look around. As I mentioned in Chapter 2, you might want to consider renting a truck and going to the big sales often held in large metropolitan lumber stores. I scouted around for sheathing for a month or so before I found some brand-new 4×8 redwood siding panels at $8.95 each. This compares extremely favorably with the $15–$20 prices I had found earlier—I saved a couple of hundred dollars. A word to the wise, though: Be cautious about the quality of the sheathing you buy. Here's a small check list I would take along for reference:

1. Check for signs of extensive delamination, especially on wood left outdoors too long.
2. Stay away from siding with too many loose knots. If there are just a few knots or blemishes, you can probably use the panel if it's structurally sound.
3. Be cautious of shop-graded sheathing (see Chapter 4). I used a few pieces, and it was passed by the building department. Ask some local builders how severe the inspectors are about siding grades.
4. Measure the wood for correct size *before* you buy it.
5. Don't pay redwood prices for rough-sawn Douglas fir with red stain on it.

NOTE: Don't be afraid to bargain, even for wood already on sale.

Once I went to a small lumber company outside of Santa Cruz, and while purchasing a load of redwood posts I mentioned that I was building my own house. The old man in charge chatted with me awhile, and he finally ended up giving me almost a 50 percent discount on what I bought. By no means do you encounter this overwhelming generosity very often, but it's nice to know some people will bend over backward to help you out!

OLD WOOD SIDING

Earlier in the book I mentioned old wood, but the subject deserves a little more discussion. Here are some possible ways to get it, and later in the chapter some beautiful ways to use it. Almost everyone has heard of the old barn trick. You walk up to the farmer and very kindly offer to disassemble his ramshackle barn or shed. Usually this elicits a response something like, "Yah . . . well . . . I'll let ya do it, son, for . . . let's see now, how about 25¢ a linear foot?" By this time you're in your car and down the road, wondering about farmers. They ain't dumb. You'll be lucky to get that barn wood free, because there are companies that are actually offering money to strip old barns for the wood.

You will soon find that it's getting harder to bargain for that old wood. Here are a few ideas. Prowl around in the cities, looking for old fences, wooden garages, and sheds. Make the same offer you did to the farmer. Also look for old buildings being torn down, bridges being demolished, and railway ties being discarded.

CUTTING YOUR OWN

It is possible to buy or rent planking devices that attach to chain saws. An Alaskan chain mill is one popular brand. You can buy logs or wood from a stand of trees and cut your own rough planking. A few months out in the sun and rain will age the wood beautifully into a silver rough finish. Nature's antiquing service.

One idea that is catching on is to put on plywood as sheathing, then cover it with wood shakes or shingles however you like (shakes are thicker). Cedar shakes lend the house a particularly rustic feel when you put them on randomly. (Shakes also look good in the interior if you want the rustic look.)

REDWOOD SIDING

Redwood sheathing is beautiful and quite maintenance free. I've used redwood sheathing outdoors several times, and I love the way it ages with time, from light and golden to gray and mellow—almost like people. Often you can find redwood siding on sale. The great virtue of this kind of siding is that it will outlast all other plywood siding by approximately three to one, therefore virtually eliminating the need for replacement.

Lots of Douglas fir siding is available for exterior use, but don't use interior grades for the exterior, as they'll fall apart with age. Often plywood is treated with chemicals to make it look like redwood or hardwood sheathing. By the time they fix it up to look like something other than Douglas fir, the cost is usually so high you can save money by staining it yourself.

OTHER EXTERIORS

For the people who like the solid look of plastered or stucco walls, I recommend having it done professionally, due to the difficult nature of the work. Bad work or mixing will leave an extremely ugly and permanent blemish on your house. In some places stucco prices plus labor compare favorably with the cost of wood siding.

Brick and natural stone exteriors are not included here because these materials are seldom suited for the wood frame houses described in this book (except for decorative purposes, such as planters and trim).

When deciding what materials to buy, you may find some helpful architectural ideas by looking through magazines and books.

Fig. 8–A Tacking Up the Tarred Building Paper

HOW TO SHEATH YOUR HOUSE

Before sheathing the house, you must tack building paper to the exterior of the studs, completely covering the house. This will provide a vapor barrier, helping to keep your house dry. You'll need a friend to help heft around the roll. *See Fig. 8–A.*

While you are waiting to put the sheathing on the house, protect it with plastic sheet covers. If you can, stack the sheathing inside the house and lock the doors. Just think of it as a couple of hundred-dollar bills lying around waiting to be stolen.

Two people are necessary to install exterior sheathing, and

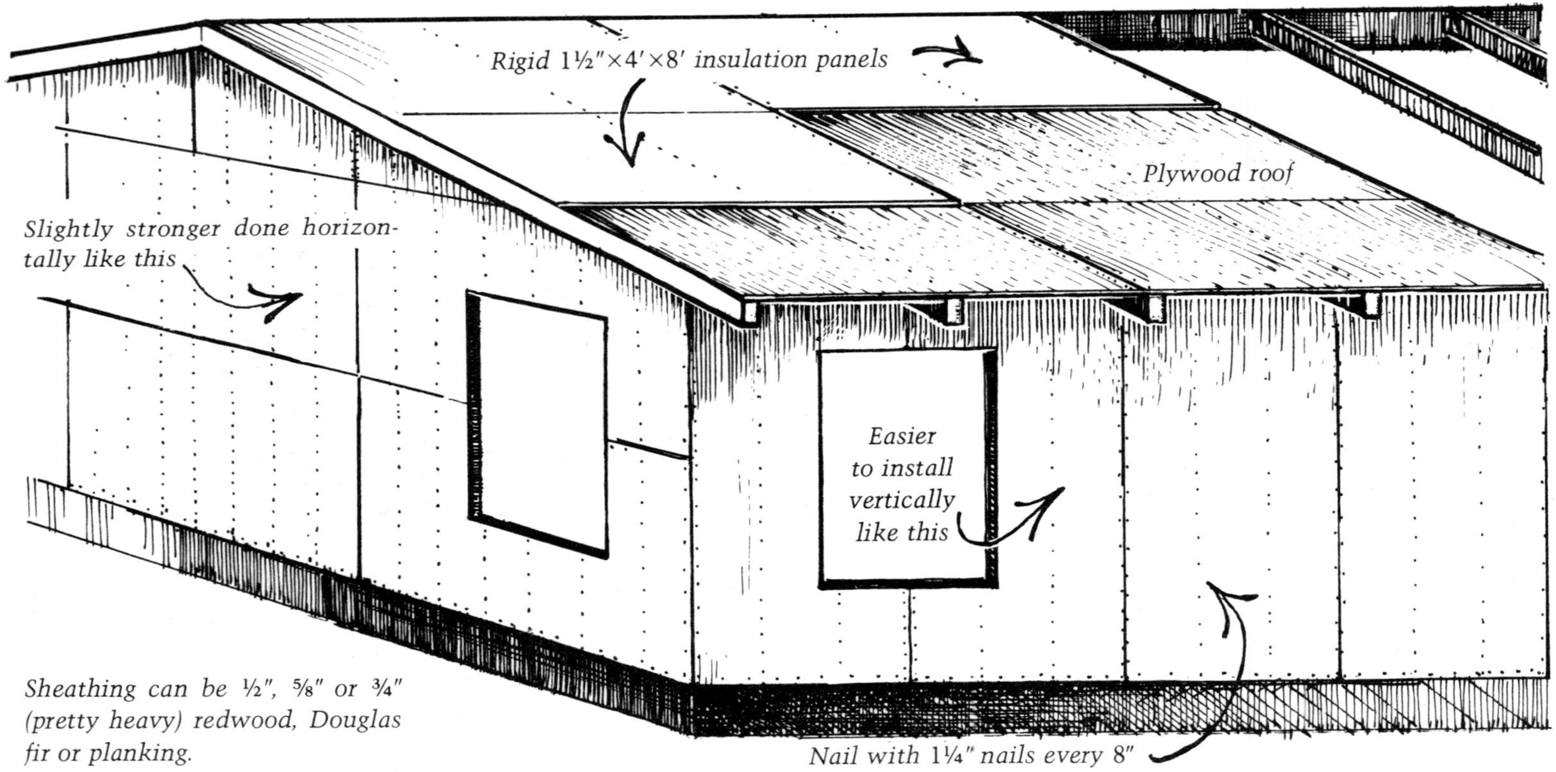

Fig. 8–B Sheathing with Plywood

three make it a lot easier, since one can run and fetch a hammer, nails and other supplies. *See Fig. 8–B.*

Start at the back of the house, and use your least preferable wood until you get the hang of it. Fill up your pockets with finishing nails (1½-inch long for ⅝-inch plywood), and grab your heavy framing hammer. At one corner place the panel edge flush with the edge of the studs, and adjust the panel so it fits on the studs. Drive in a nail every 6 inches on each stud and at the top and bottom.

When you have to cut out a piece of plywood for a window or door, measure against the studs it must span, getting your lines as exact as possible. Then transfer the exact measure-

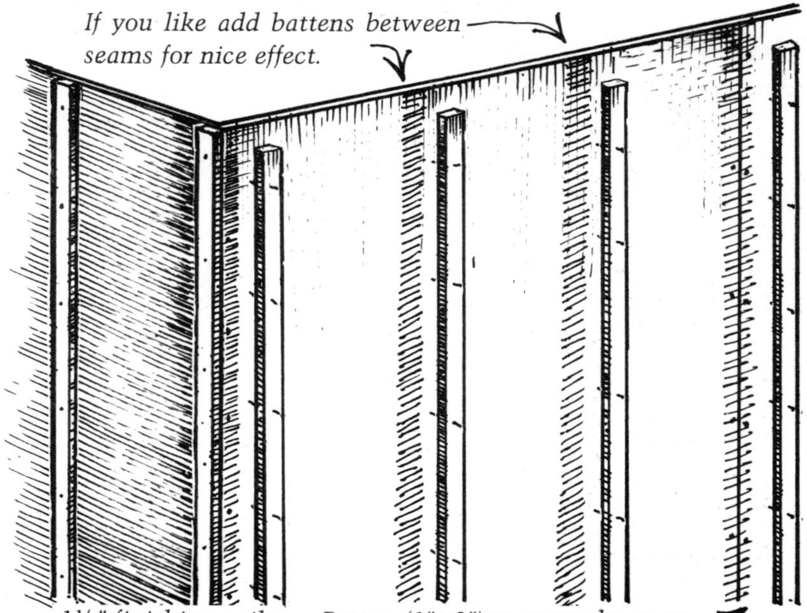

Fig. 8–C Example of Board and Batten Wall Sheathing

ments onto the plywood. Be sure to *double-check every time.* Use a power saw if one is available, and save all your cutouts, as they will come in handy later.

Each piece of plywood must be flush (tight) with the one next to it, unless you are going to use the *board and batten* technique. This siding method is well suited to the beginner who may not get all the sheets meshed perfectly everytime, or when using old or used siding sheets that don't have their edges planed accurately. *See Fig. 8–C.* The battens are usually

Fig. 8–D Countersinking Nail Heads ⅛"

1-inch by 2-inch wood nailed over the seams and at even intervals, thus hiding any gaps. But I say you can easily skip the battens. With reasonable care, the home builder can line up the panels accurately and save the cost of placing battens every four feet.

Since you planned your house in units of 2 feet, you will most likely not have to cut or waste much plywood. If you do have a lot left over, don't worry— as there'll be many odd jobs to do.

When you arrive at the next side of the house, you can pull out your choice pieces of plywood because you will have learned quite a bit by now. Proceed by working right around the house, but remember that you must cut a notch in the bottom of the plywood sheets to accommodate the openings for the foundation vents. Don't cover them up accidentally!

This work is tiring, so I recommend that you do only what you can do comfortably in one day. Your carpentry will get sloppy if you are too exhausted to concentrate.

If you are unlucky and happen to miss a stud with the edge of the plywood, don't worry. You can nail a "cheater stud" to the original and proceed. (See the illustration in Chapter 4.)

When you have finished nailing up the plywood, the next job is to countersink and fill all the nailhead holes with caulking compound. Buy the filler compound that's color matched to your wood. Uncountersunk nails in natural wood will stain and leave vertical streaks on the side of your house. *See Fig. 8–D.*

If you like the look of clapboard siding, you will have to apply it over plywood sheathing in most states. The clapboard is laid horizontally, and the bottom edge lies over the top of the last piece nailed up. It commonly comes in widths varying from 4½ inches to 12 inches. Naturally, this double siding will run up your costs. *See Fig. 8–E.* There are other styles of clapboard, so ask your lumber man to show you some choices.

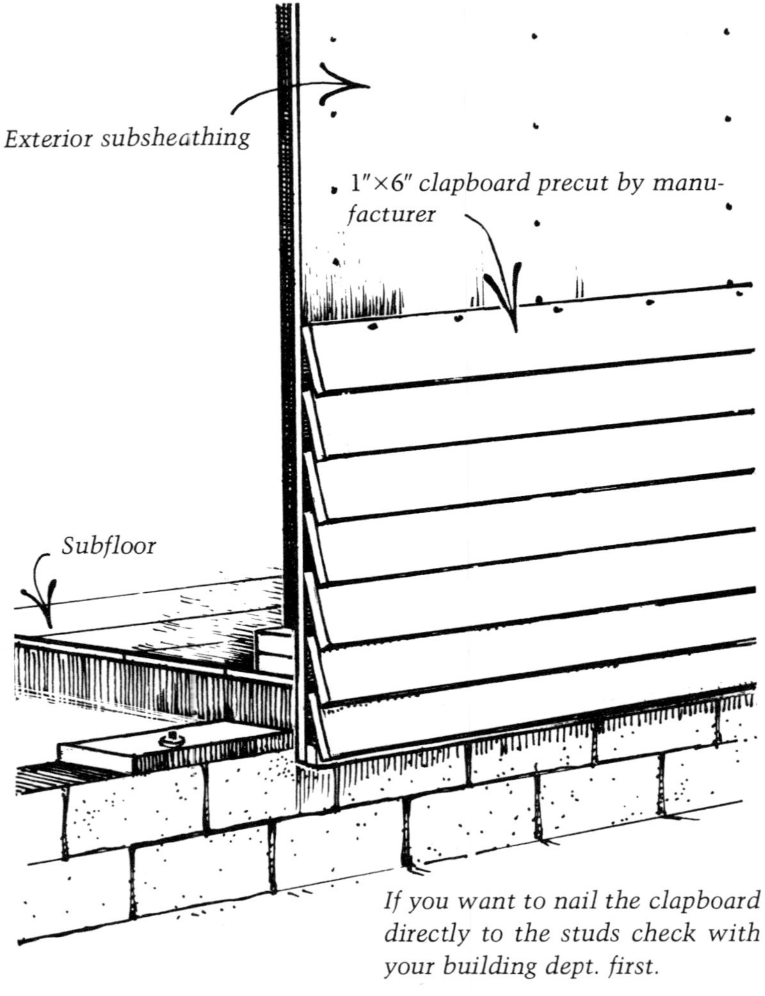

Fig. 8–E Clapboard Siding

But remember, plain exterior-grade plywood is just as strong and can be painted or stained easily to a multitude of finishes.

If you are building the open-beam roof design and you didn't extend the plywood up to the roof decking at the gable ends, you'll have to cut and fit pieces of plywood in the spaces between the ceiling beams. Nail some small blocks of 2×4's to the beam sides, and then nail in a piece of plywood cut to size. Use matching plywood if you like, and tack on a few battens to cover the seams. *See Fig. 8–F.*

If you're really pinching pennies, you can save $100 by making the roof flush with the walls. Then you can just nail a *fascia board* (see glossary) to the space, or you can extend your plywood siding to cover it. This type of roof, though, is pretty austere, even ugly, on most houses.

There is a way to keep water from running down the siding, collecting there, and ruining the bottom edges of the plywood sheathing. Nail a piece of wood or flashing, called a *watertable* or *dripcap,* on the bottom. *See Fig. 8–G.*

TRIM

You'll want to use one of two common methods to install corner trim on the house edges. *See Fig. 8–H.*

Nail ½-inch *quarter bead* down the seam for an L-shaped corner. If you are using aluminum or modern wooden windows, you can now put on the window trim. Use either a miter or oriental cut at corners for a little more class. *See Fig's. 8–I & J.* The oriental style is easiest and saves you the trouble of trying to get the miter cuts right. Should you want to try

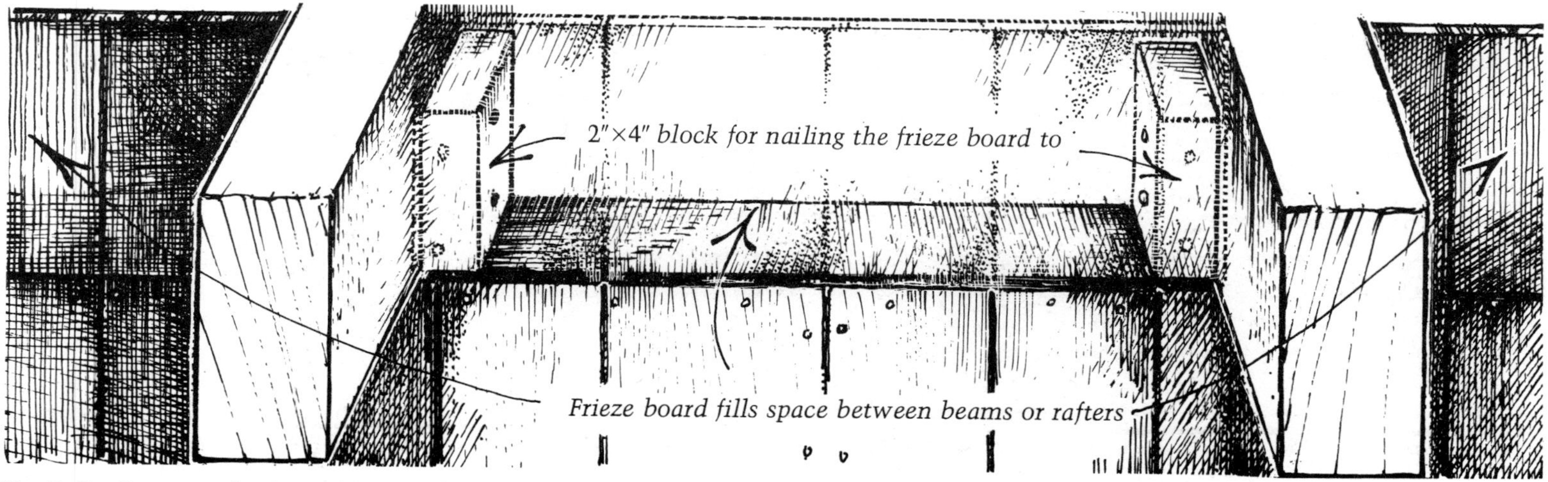

Fig. 8–F Covering the Spaces between the Ceiling Beams

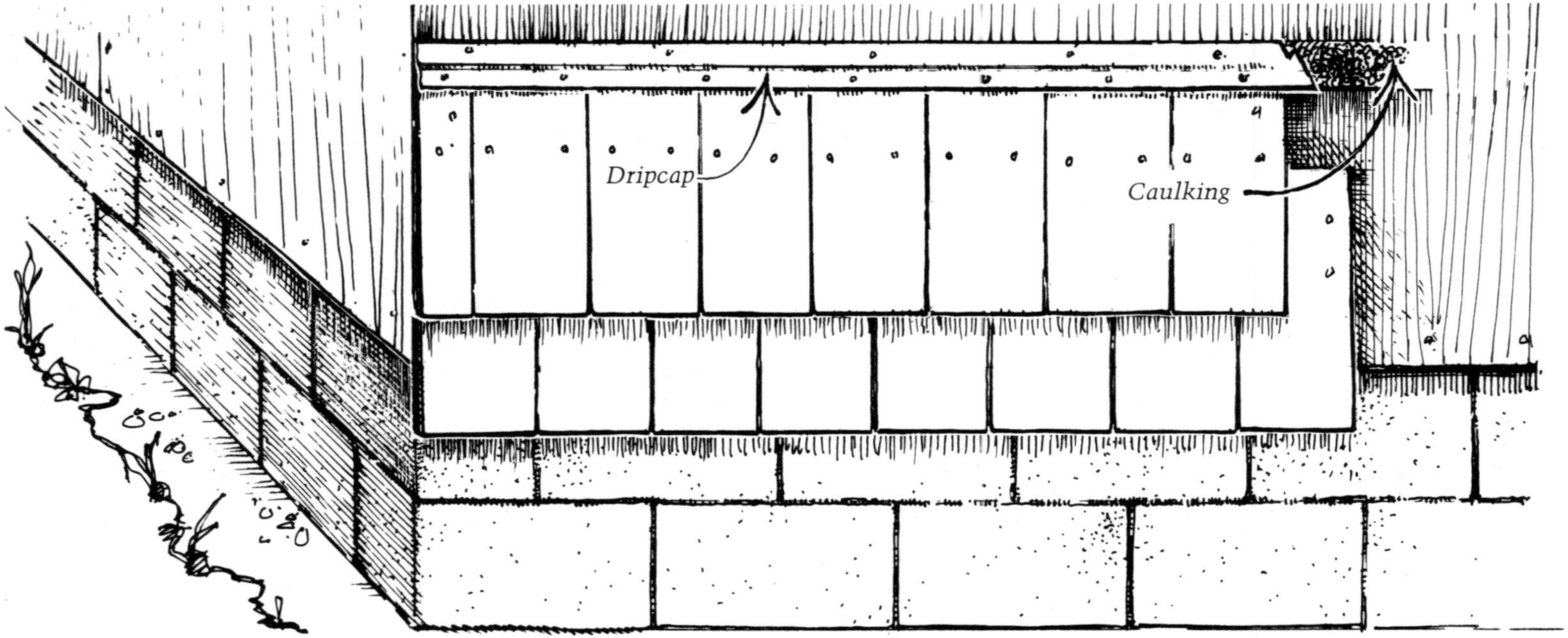

Fig. 8–G   Putting Up Wood Shingles on a Wall

the miter cuts, you'll need a miter box and a special saw. *See Fig. 8–K.*

Around the door you may want to put a little fancy scroll work as an elegant touch. Try to borrow or rent a jig saw; with a key hole saw, it gets tiresome. A wood chisel will add some dimension and shape if you'd like to try some carving.

If your hillside house built on a stepped foundation has a large expanse on one side, try covering the bottom part of that side with wooden shingles. Although this is a rather unconventional use of shingles, I have used it several times and am pleased with the way it looks. For some reason it always makes the house look lower and more solid.

If you use cedar shingles for the whole house, you might find that they make the house look a little too woodsy or that they clutter up the clean natural lines. If you want to make one side redwood sheathing and another entirely wood shingles, by all means try it. Often a simple idea like that can make an average house a truly beautiful creation to behold. *See Fig. 8–L.*

If you have a wall through which you plan to add a room

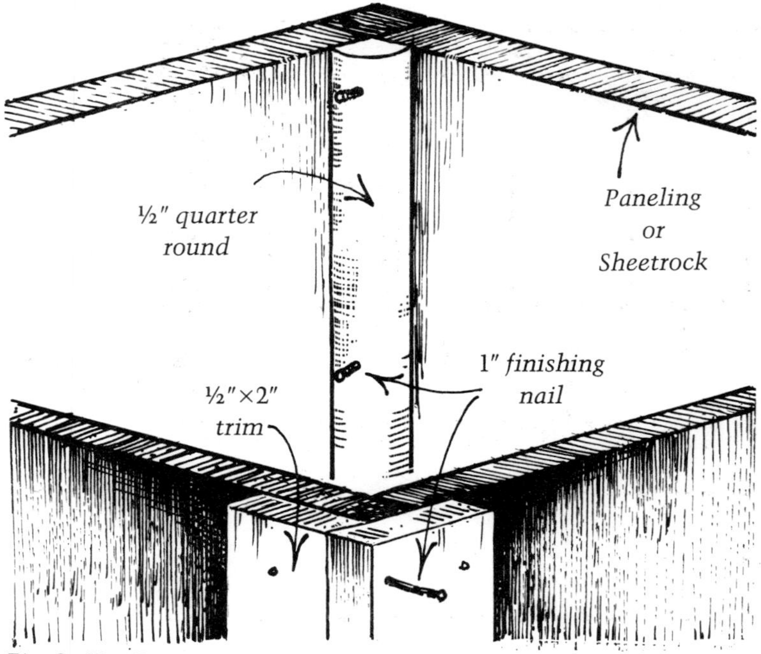

Fig. 8–H Corner Trim

in the foreseeable future, it might pay to leave off the wood shingles and stuff for the time being and just leave it plain plywood.

NATURAL WOOD OR STAIN

When new siding is plywood or redwood, it's wise to apply sealer stain or paint right away, particularly if the weather is bad. Douglas fir plywood can get rough and stained in one good stretch of bad weather, and it's a hellish job to refinish it to a light tone. Redwood holds up well, but the color it will turn when exposed to sun and moisture is almost impossible to predict. I've always been lucky when I've let redwood age naturally. Usually I get a darkish red-brown color with overtones of gray or silver. I feel this is largely because I use, whenever possible, deep overhanging eaves that protect the house.

Wood shingles require no finishing whatsoever, but be sure to nail them only where they overlap at the top, so that you won't see rust stains running down from the nails.

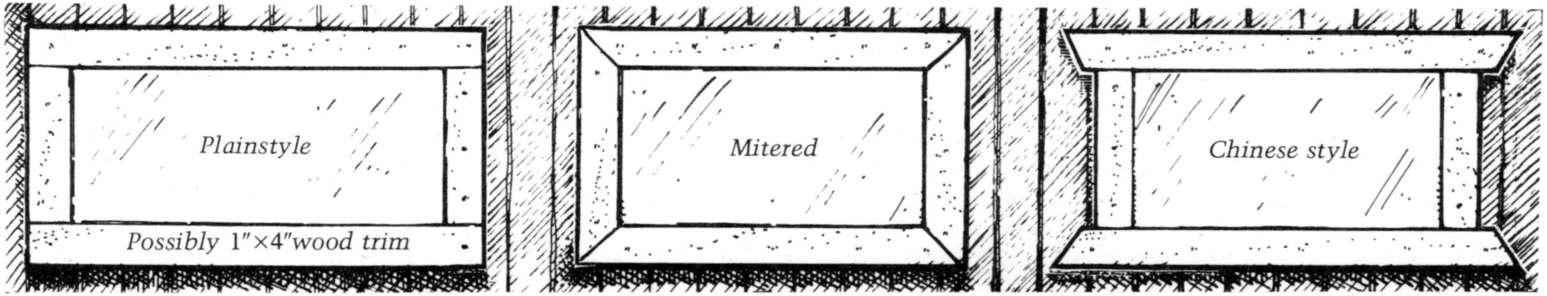

Fig. 8–I Exterior Window Trim Options

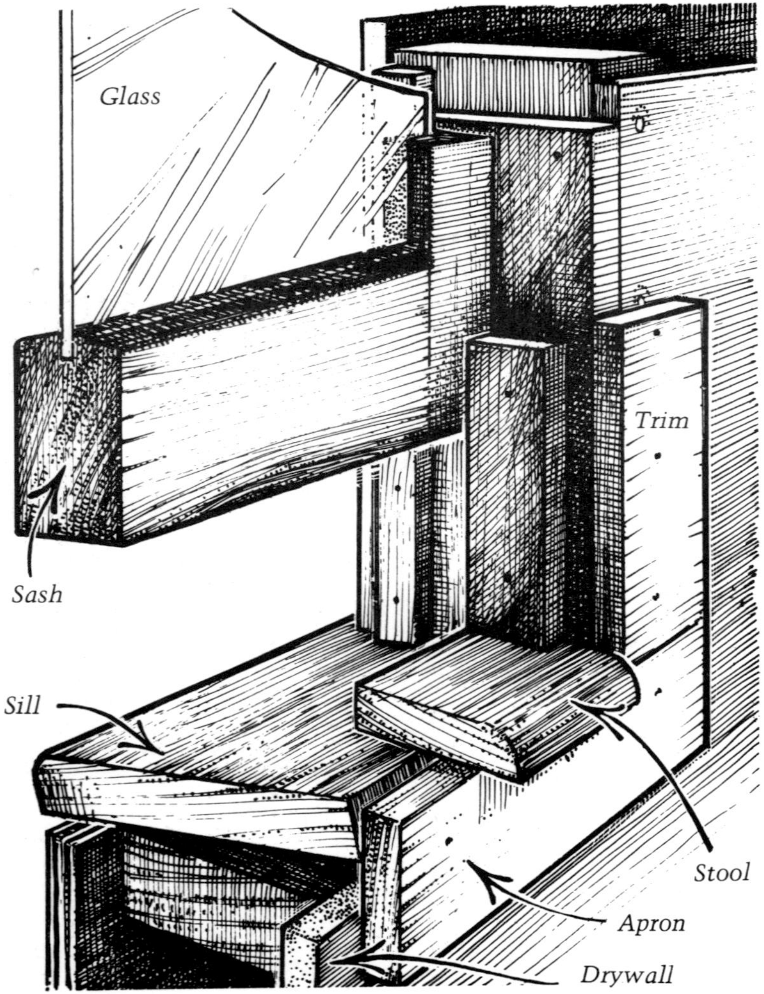

Fig. 8–J The Traditional Sash Window

Fig. 8–K The Miter Box and Saw for 45° and 90° cuts

Fig. 8–L Possible Use of Cedar Shingles

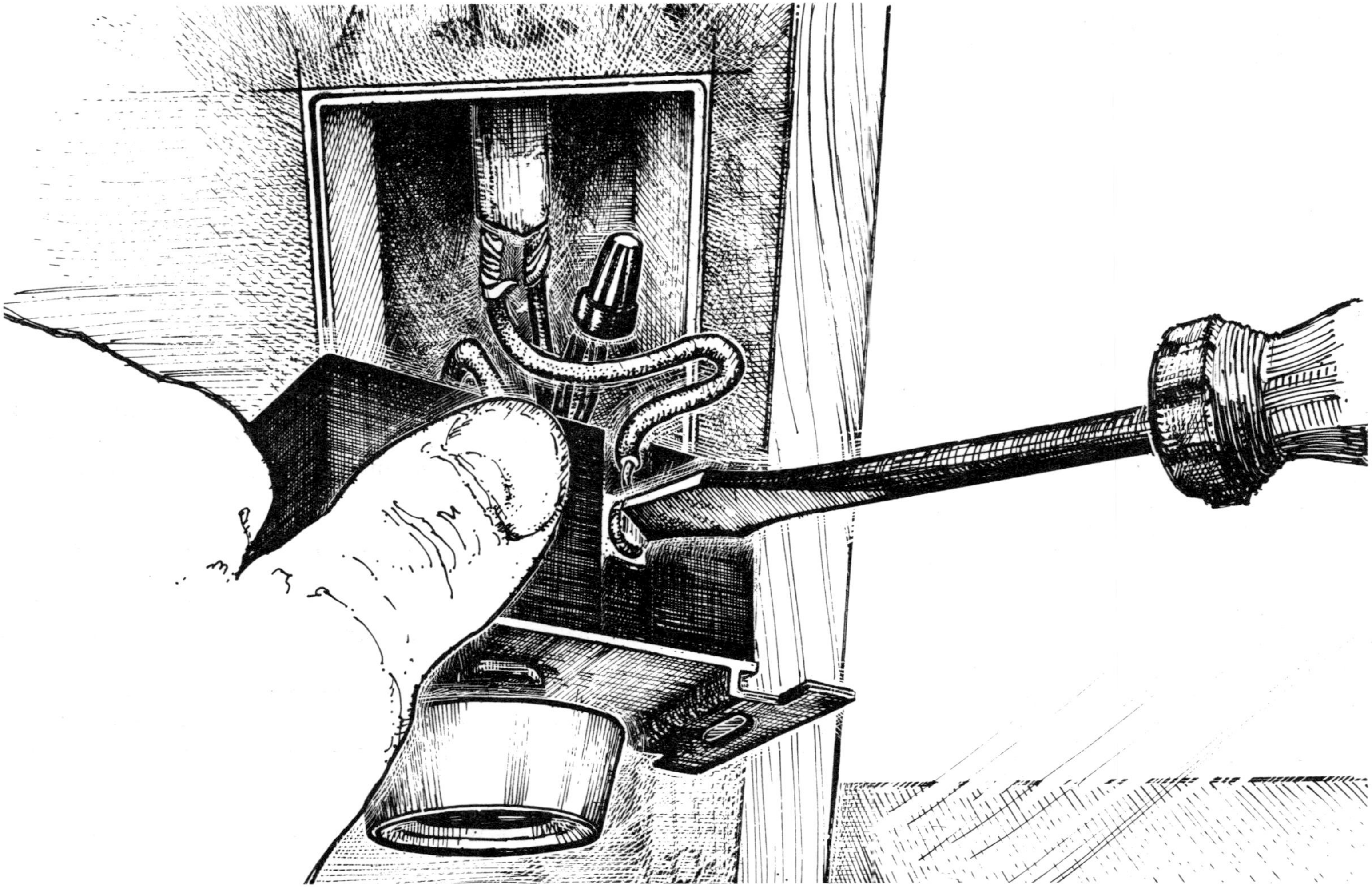

Installing and Wiring Receptacle

ELECTRICITY

CHAPTER 9

In the interest of safe grounding for your electrical system, it's well worth the $70 or so to have an electrician install your breaker box and help you design your basic wiring system. However, before we talk more about how an electrician can help you, at one-third the usual fee, we should discuss some basic principles of electricity and wiring.

At the outset you must decide whether you want all-gas, or an all-electric kitchen and water heater. An all-electric is what I chose; gas products are often unavailable in remote rural areas. When you use only electricity, you eliminate the need for a gas delivery every month (if you live in the country), and you have no fears about blowing up your house with a dangerous gas leak.

All your electrical supplies should be approved by "Underwriters Laboratories, Inc." Supplies that are so labeled have been inspected and tested for approved loads, and they will assure you of a safe system. You can pick up a list of approved electrical devices and a pamphlet that illustrates correct wiring at your local building department. What is approved for one state is not necessarily acceptable in another, since codes vary quite a lot. The illustrations and examples in this chapter reflect the current national codes, which in some instances may differ from local codes.

A separate permit is often necessary for installing wiring, at a fee of $10–$50. I know of no state that will not let you install your own wiring and thereby experience big savings.

PLANNING

When considering the number of circuits, plan more than you minimally need. Later on it would be exceedingly expensive to rip out a wall to put in heavier wiring. Also, install lots of receptacles, and you won't be tripping over extension cords later.

A *branch circuit* system protects your overall electrical system and ultimately your house itself. Imagine wiring your house on only one circuit, with one fuse to protect it. If that one fuse blew, the electricity for your whole house would go out needlessly. The solution is to use several separate circuits and to protect them with adequate breakers. Then if one blows, the others remain unaffected. How many outlets should go on each circuit? Usually no more than twelve, and ideally eight or ten. With more than a dozen, you may overload your circuit and blow too many fuses or start a fire.

Normally the wire size in the living room and bedrooms is #14. However, many people prefer the larger #12 wire with a 20-amp fuse, for cooler operation and less power waste. For the ceiling lights, swag lamps are decorative and speed up installation time as compared to ceiling fixtures. Cover plates and hanging chains are necessary for these lights. Wall switches are a convenient addition and add only a dollar or so to the overall lamp cost.

Plug receptacles are often required to be 8 feet apart all around the room. Any floor receptacles that take heavy-duty appliances or 120-volt heaters should be #12 wire with 20-amp breakers.

The dining room will take at least one 20-amp circuit with #12 wire. This supplies adequate power for things like toasters and electric frying pans.

It's a good idea to use #12 wire with 20-amp breakers for all the kitchen receptacles, including the one for the refrigerator. All the switches and pull chains should be terminated with thick plastic or insulators if they are within reach of a sink or stove.

Run the bathroom lights on a wall switch, and make sure you have plenty of light on both sides of the mirror, for even lighting. Have *NO* receptacle near the bathtub, and you'll save yourself worry when children are around.

Other places you'll need lights and receptacles: near stairs, outdoors, in large walk-in closets, and in garages or carports.

A few more tips: Some light fixtures are limited only to small bulbs; you may want to avoid these if you think the room will be used for reading or working.

Place ceiling and wall lights on opposing sides of the room to provide even illumination without harsh shadows. This will eliminate one of the major causes of eyestrain.

One large bulb is more efficient and less costly than two smaller ones of equal wattage.

A large light used with a light-colored or white ceiling will give excellent light dispersion throughout the room.

Fluorescent lights are cheaper to burn than regular incandescent bulbs, and they have the added benefit of being easier on the eyes. Follow the manufacturer's instructions when installing fluorescent fixtures.

SPEAKING THE LANGUAGE

Before you wire your house, you should have several basic electrical terms under your belt. If you imagine a water pipe with its contents under pressure, it'll help you visualize the dynamics of the process. When the faucet is turned on, let's say that the water pressure is 20 pounds per square inch. In electricity the "pressure" is measured in *volts.* Suppose the water in the pipe is flowing at a rate of thirty gallons per minute. This flow rate in electricity is comparable to the current, called *amperage.* Getting back to the pipe, we know that under a certain pressure, the flowing water from the pipe could turn a water wheel to do work at, say, 5 horsepower. In electrical terms the standard units of work are called *watts* or *kilowatts.* With the voltage "pushing" the amperage through a wire circuit including a light bulb, the "work" done by the light bulb might amount to 100 watts. This can be expressed in a mathematical formula: volts × amperes = watts.

In practical terms, you can say that a lamp that draws ½ amp from a 120-volt line consumes 60 watts. Since watts are a measure of work done, just as horsepower is the measure of the work an engine does, we can correlate the two measures and say 746 watts are equal to 1 horsepower (1 hp) if the watts are consumed by a motor or appliance. Kilo means 1,000, so kilowatts means 1,000 watts.

The electric company determines how much electricity you use by measuring the watts by hours; you're billed for kilowatt hours used over a certain time period.

WATTS CONSUMED BY AVERAGE APPLIANCES

Incandescent lamps	10 upward
Television	200–400
Portable heater	1,000–1,500
Sewing machine	60–90
Clock	2–3
Razor	8–12
Room-type air conditioner	800–1,500
Refrigerator	150–300
Freezer	300–500
Toaster	500–1,200
Clothes dryer	4,000–5,000
Stove	8,000–14,000
Washing machine	350–550
Water heater	2,000–5,000

You can easily tell how long any device must be used to consume 1 kilowatt hour. Just divide 1,000 by the wattage of the appliance. For example, a 600–watt toaster may be used 1,000 ÷ 600, or 1.67 hours, (1 hour and 40 minutes). An electric clock uses 2 watts and runs 500 hours to consume 1 kilowatt hour.

TYPES OF WIRE

Always use the correct size wire: If a wire is too small in size, it can overheat when too much current or amperage is passed through it, thus creating the potential for fire and doing serious damage to your house. The building department can help you determine what size is appropriate for particular items, such as pumps, ranges, or water heaters.

Overhead wire. Certain cables are designed for overhead hanging only, and they must be large enough to support their own weight plus that of ice when they are hung outside. This overhead cable is used for wiring barns and garages when you do not want to run wire underground. Size #10 is the usual for distances of not more than 50 feet, and #8 for longer. For more than 150 feet, it's recommended you use an additional pole.

Interior wiring. This wire is run through walls and ceiling, and it can be solid or stranded, depending on the size. (Stranded wire consists of thinner wires twisted together.) A flexible plastic insulation covers this type of wire, allowing it to bend easily and handle smoothly. The usual sizes for houses are #12 and #14.

Type T wire. This is covered with a single layer of plastic and is suitable in walls. *Type TW* is the same, except it is moisture resistant and is very good for wet locations (under houses and porches). Neither T or TW can be buried in the ground.

Rubber covered wire. This wire is used little today, so I will not discuss it.

Cables. Cables are groups of wires encased in armored or nonmetallic sheathing. Cable that consists of two #14 wires is called *fourteen-two cable,* of three #12's, *twelve-three cable.*

Nonmetallic sheathed cable. This cable often contains two or three Type T wires. It's less expensive than most wires and excellently suited to a frame house. There are two types, and they are available in various sizes. With *Type NM,* each wire is wrapped in paper and then fabric. The fabric is impregnated with moisture- and fire-resistant compounds. Some types of NM cable have plastic sheathing. The second, *Type NMC,* is designed to resist corrosion in wet locations, such as barns, sheds, and porches.

Underground wires. These cables are fine for underground

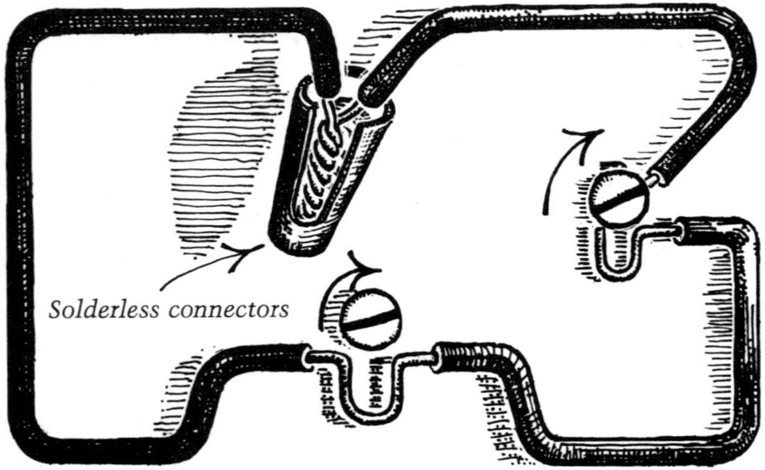

Fig. 9–A Wiring Examples

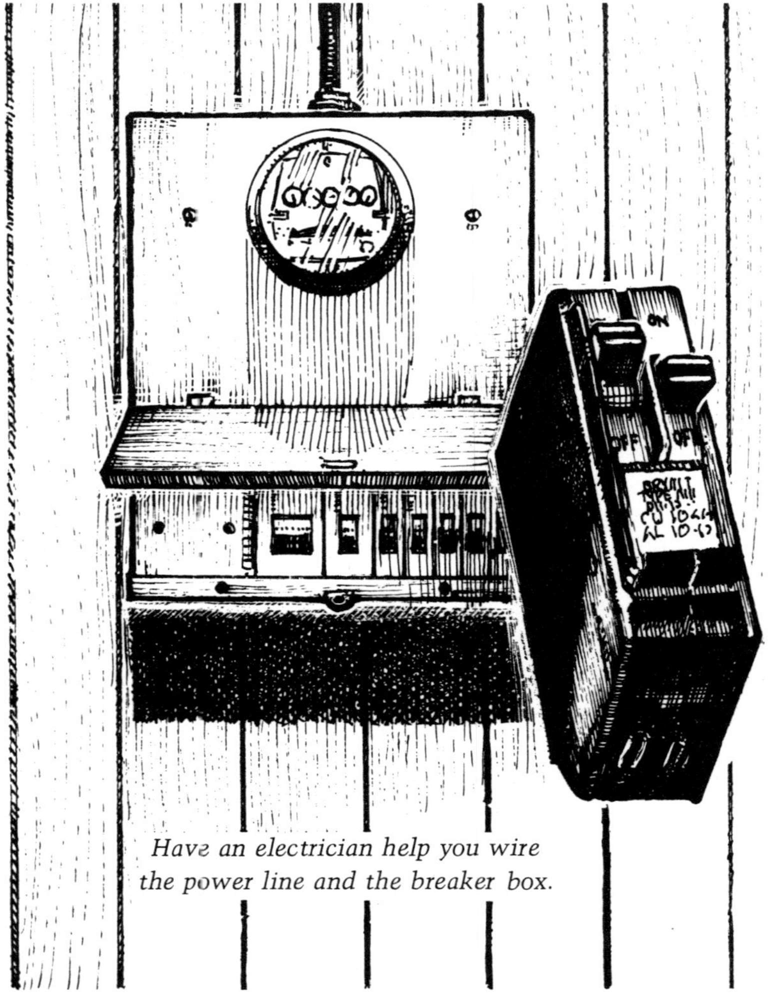

Have an electrician help you wire the power line and the breaker box.

Fig. 9–B An Example of Breaker and Box

installations and produce neat and permanent work. Designed with tough protective coverings, they are classed in two types: *Code Type USE* and *Type UF.* Code type USE (Underground Service Entrance) is designed to be buried in the ground with no conduit necessary. Only where the cable enters or exits the ground are you required to protect it with a metal conduit. Type UF is much like USE, except it must be protected with fuses or breakers at the starting point and therefore may not be used as a 220-v service cable to your breaker box.

Flexible Cord. Used for small appliances, toys, lamps and tools, this wire usually supplies power from the outlet. Materials vary, with combinations of rubber, plastic, and fabric insulations.

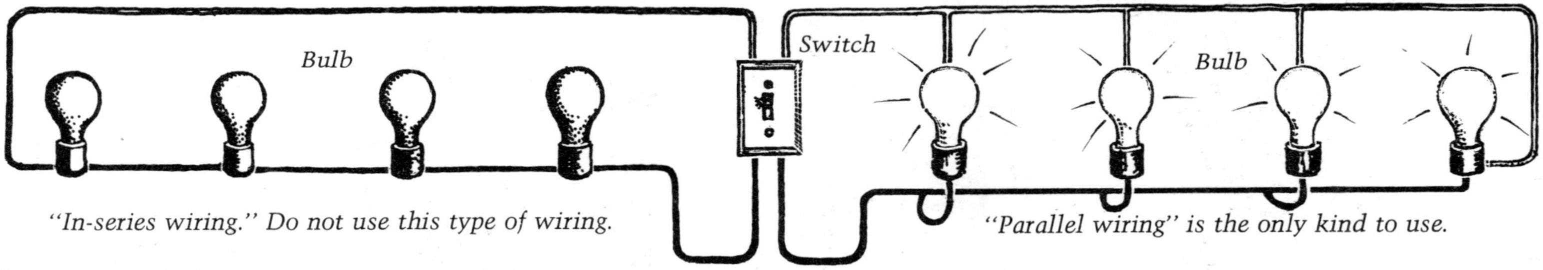

Fig. 9–C Circuits

WIRING FUNDAMENTALS

When you remove the insulation, be careful not to cut off wire strands, and be sure to taper the cut in the insulation towards the connection. Bend the wire in the same direction that the screw turns. *See Fig. 9–A.*

Solderless connectors work efficiently and save time. They should always be tightened down with pliers. Use the appropriate-size tool for the work. After screwing down a solderless connector, you should wrap electrical tape around the connector as a safety precaution. When there's a possibility that a wire other than ground wire will come in contact with another piece of metal, that wire should be taped also. Never use friction tape. *See Fig. 9–A.*

I prefer breakers to fuses for all overcurrent protection. These look like toggle switches and will provide excellent protection against wires overloading and heating. When the breaker trips off, you merely flip it back up. If it flips off again, you must locate the overload or short in that circuit. The breakers fit in a metal box that resembles a fuse box. However, inside the breaker box are two rows of metal ridges that the breakers snap onto in order to make contact. *See Fig. 9–B.*

CIRCUITS

The average-size house should have two or three branch circuits for its 120-volt outlets. This is essential; if one circuit goes out, you can still use the others. Even if you are permitted to install more in your area, use no more than 12 outlets on one circuit. The rule of thumb for the number of circuits to install in a house is one per 500 square feet of interior space.

For special high-wattage appliances, such as heaters, toasters, and small motors, it is advisable to use #12 wire with 20-amp breakers. Provide individual circuits for the following appliances and make them 220-volt in most cases: stove, washer, dryer, water pump, large heaters and water heater.

MECHANICS OF WIRING

Before you start wiring, there are a few more essentials you must know. We'll start with the most important safety factor in the electrical system: *ground connections.* For protection

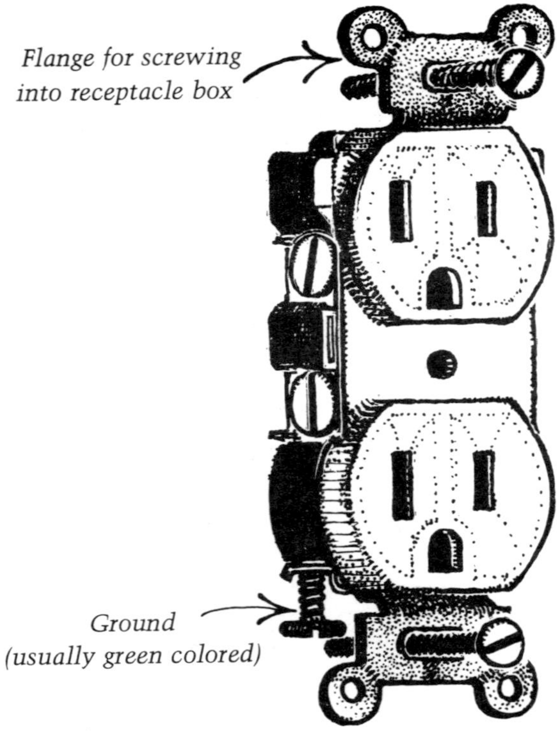

Fig. 9–D Fixture

from shocks and fire, you must include a *ground wire* in any 120-volt or 220-volt wiring you do. The ground wire is connected to a pipe or rod driven or buried in the ground; all other wires are known as *hot wires.*

Four things must be remembered about grounded wires:

1. They are always either bare or white in color.

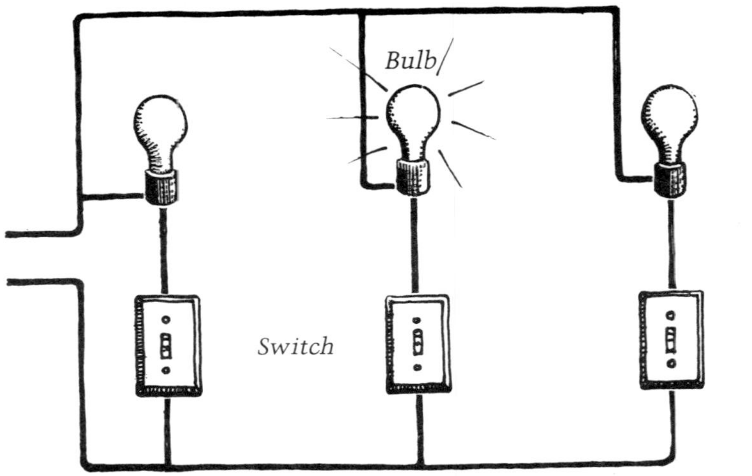

Fig. 9–E Example of a Wiring System Using Several Switches and Lights in One Room

2. They must always run to every outlet and electrical device.
3. There must never be fuses on the line.
4. They must never be switched or interrupted in any way.

NOTE: Always connect the white ground wire to the white or green terminal, which is usually light-colored nickel or tin-plated and painted green.

When hooking up a series of lights, you have two methods from which to choose. The first is almost never used, and it is called *wired in series.* As you can see, if one light goes out, all the lights go out, creating a great inconvenience.

The second method is the best all-around system. It's called parallel wiring, and one light going out will not affect any of the other lights. *See Fig. 9–C.*

The wiring of a receptacle is easy. There is a white wire, a black wire and a bare wire between them. Hook the black and the white to opposite sides of the receptacle, and hook the bare wire to the ground terminal, which is usually green and marked with a (⏚) symbol. *See Fig. 9–D.*

When there is more than one receptacle to be wired, wire them parallel, just as you do the lights. The plugs have two terminals on each side to make parallel wiring convenient.

IMPORTANT: The white wire may be extended at any point to the next outlet. The black wire can be extended too, but you have to be able to trace it all the way back to the source without interruption by switches. *See Fig. 9–E.*

GROUNDING WIRES SAFELY

The most important safety factor in the electrical system you wire will be the ground connections. A good ground will send the energy from a shorted wire or motor harmlessly into the ground, rather than through the more painful route of your body.

When the power company wires electricity to your breaker box it comes by three wires. Two are 120 volt carrying *hot lines* and the other one is a grounded neutral wire. Usually the grounded wire is insulated just like the hot wires and if so will be white colored. *See Fig. 9–F.*

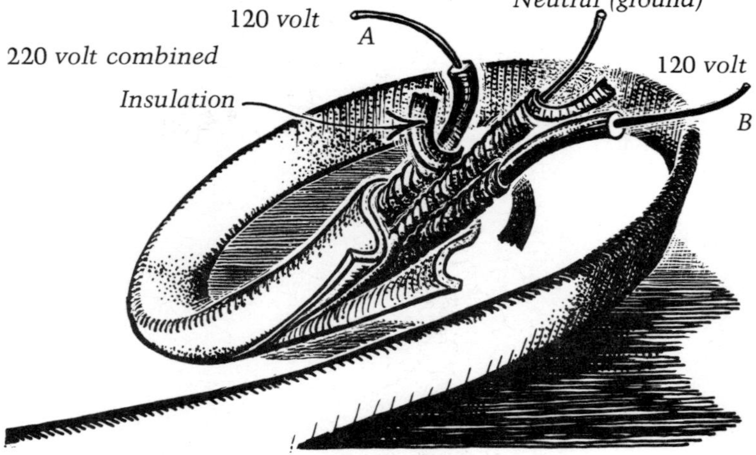

Fig. 9–F An Example of a 220 Volt Wire

AN ELECTRICIAN'S HELP

Safe grounding is the best argument going for hiring an electrician to plan and install the basics of your system. For $70 or so, you will assure yourself a safe and efficient system.

The electrician will put in the circuit breaker cabinet and wire the house with the proper circuits. Installing a breaker cabinet is a little beyond the ability of most people. If you have several complex problems of installation, let him wire them for you too. You'll save money by not having to bring him back later to correct your mistakes.

Also ask the electrician what types of materials you need to run wire to a pump or outside light, and ask him to explain how to do the job. When he tells you, write it down and have him draw a diagram. The electrician will explain which circuits are for what, and he'll tell you the size of the breakers you'll need.

If you write above each breaker its specific purpose, you'll save yourself headaches later in trying to sort out all the circuits.

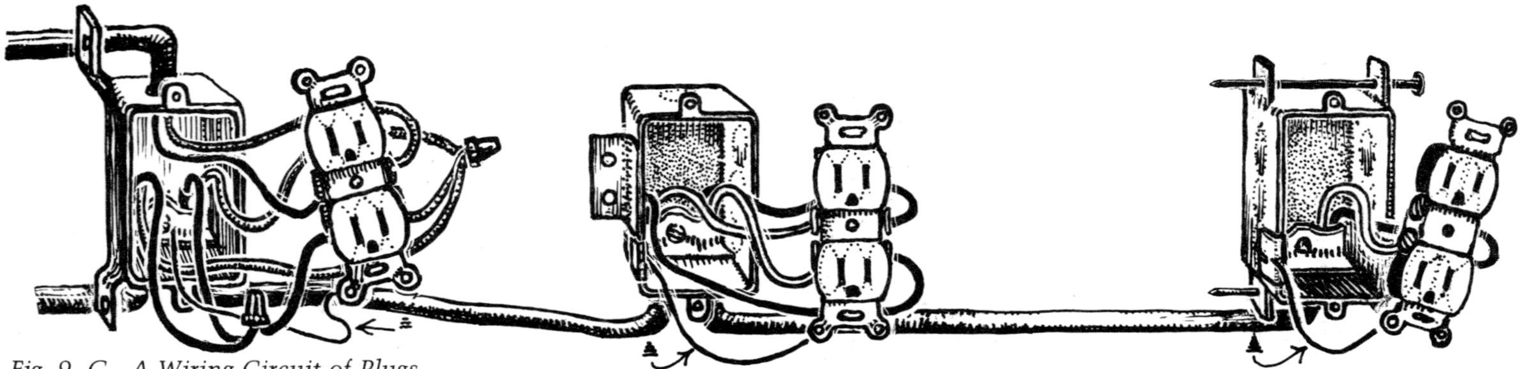

Fig. 9–G A Wiring Circuit of Plugs

WIRING THE RECEPTACLES

Now that the electrician has run the proper-size wire through the walls and has set up the circuit breaker box, you can wire up the more simple outlets he left for you to do.

Your most common situation will be the receptacle near the baseboard. There will be basically three installations you will encounter. *See Fig. 9–G.* Switches are a bit more difficult, but two simple ones are easily handled by the layperson, (*Fig's. 9–H & I*).

Connect all grounded wires to the green terminals on all outlets. When the outlet is in a metal receptacle box and is near a sink, water heater, or similar grounded appliance, ground the box as shown in *Figure 9–J.*

Usually a metal conduit is unnecessary if all wiring is under the floor or in the walls. If outdoor wiring is required, have the electrician install the proper conduits and wires. It probably won't take him very long, since he'll have the tools and materials on hand.

When you use an electric water heater, you must use flexible armor cable to protect the wiring to the heater. Have the electrician do this also, because it doesn't take long *if* you know what you're doing.

When using the water heater, consider turning it on only in the evenings for half an hour. Or possibly every other day, if you don't cook much and don't have lots of dishes to wash. This procedure can cut your water heating bill by three-fifths.

TESTING CIRCUITS

To test the circuits you wired, use two large dry cell batteries and a simple doorbell.

FINISHING UP

When you have screwed in the receptacles and switches, you may find that the switch sticks too far in or out. Correct this now. When the wall covering is up, you cannot change it. If you are using wood paneling, remember it is usually only ¼ inch thick and sheetrock is ½ inch thick. Plan accordingly for the thickness.

For a doorbell or buzzer you will need a 120-volt transformer,

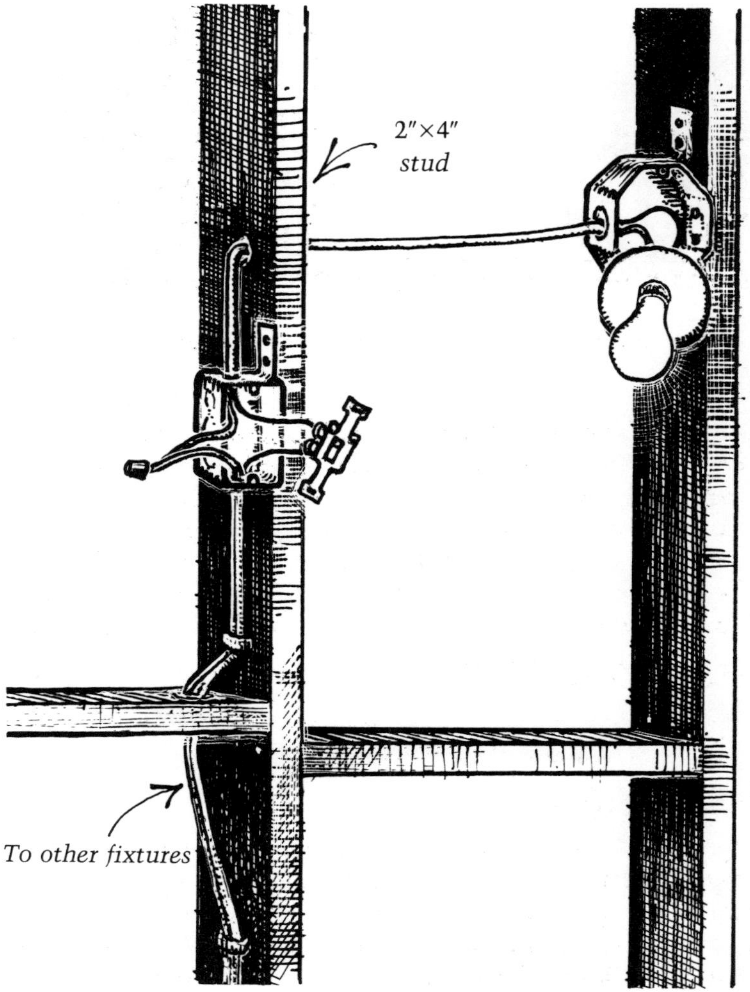

Fig. 9–H A Switch and Overhead Light

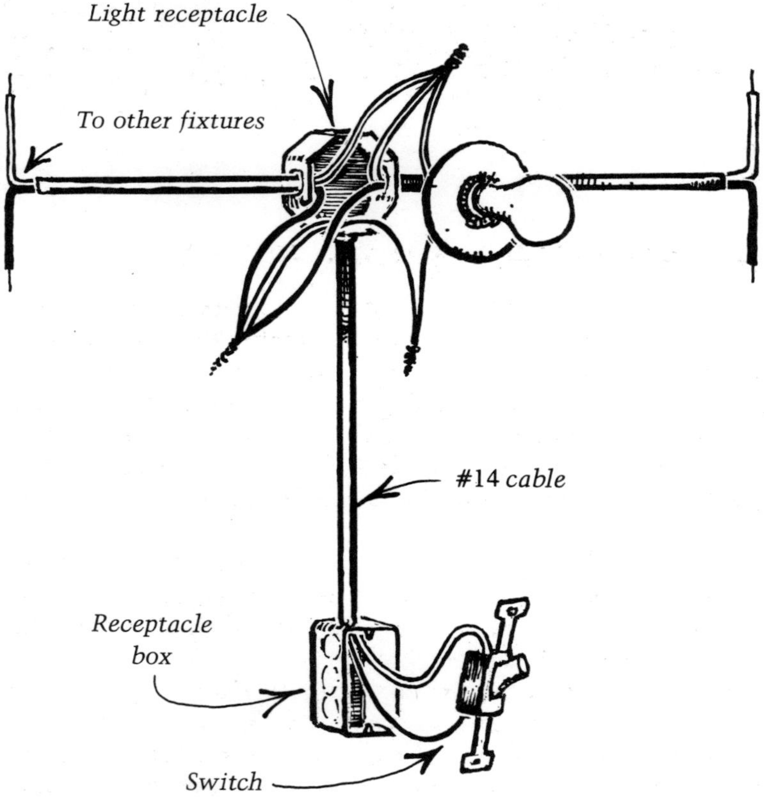

Fig. 9–I Another Type of Switch and Light

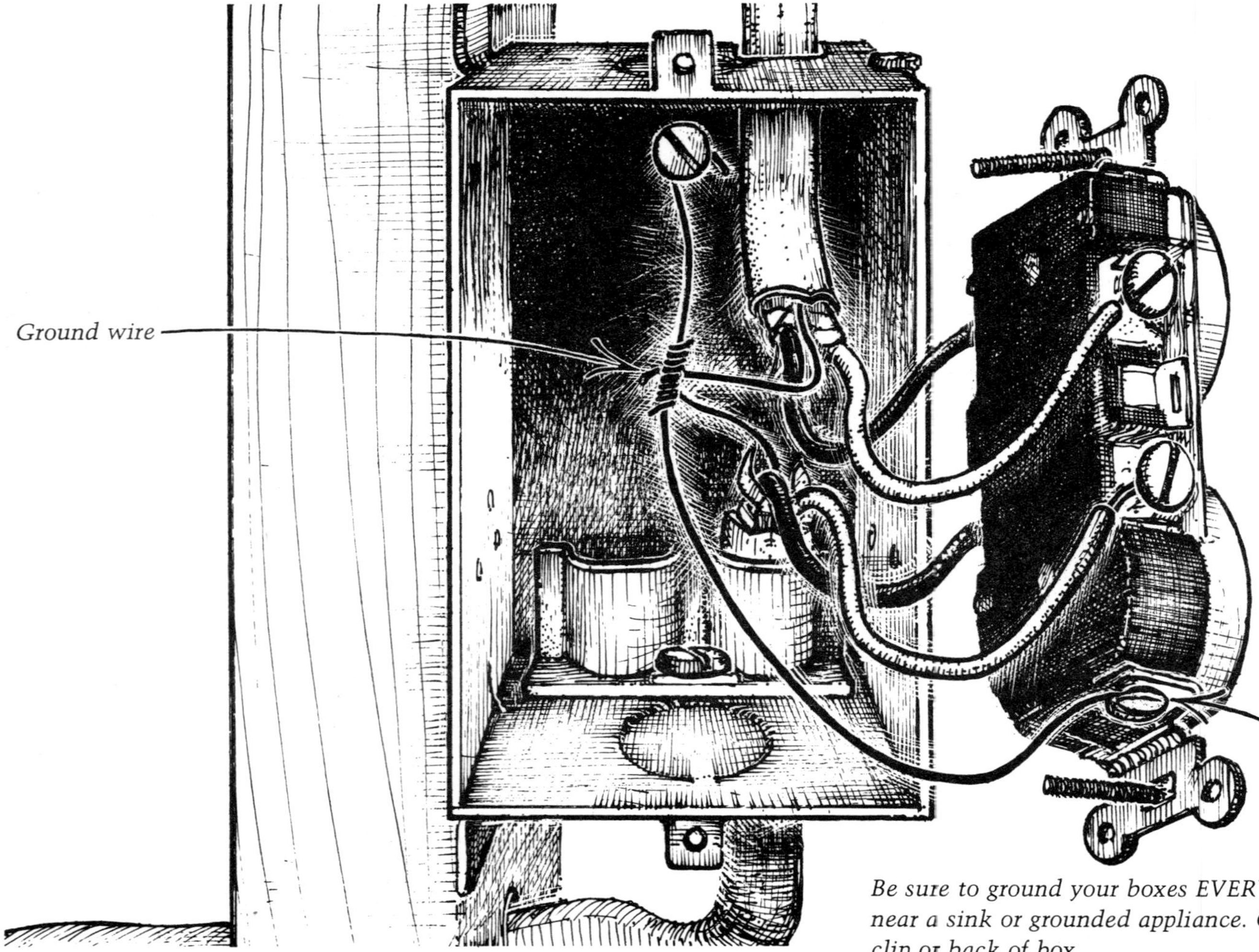

Be sure to ground your boxes EVERY TIME you wire one near a sink or grounded appliance. Ground either to clip or back of box.

Fig 9–J The Grounding of a Receptacle Box

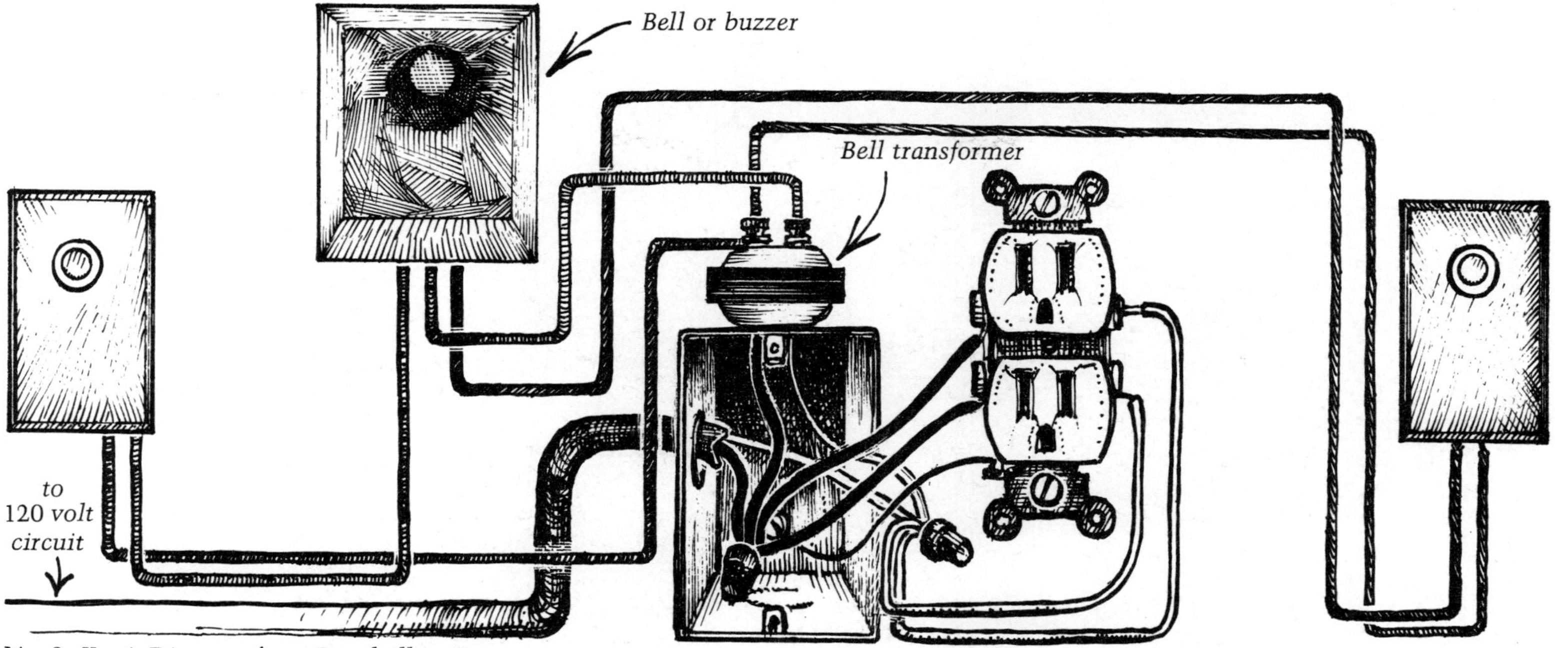

Fig. 9–K A Diagram for a Doorbell or Buzzer

if one does not come built in. Stop at a local electrical supply house for the transformer. *See Fig. 9–K.*

Many different cover plates for switches and receptacles are available, in materials ranging from copper and plastic to wood and porcelain, so match them any way you like. But I recommend you buy them last, since your ideas of room decor often change before the house is completed.

Installing Sheetrock

INSULATING AND COVERING INTERIOR WALLS

CHAPTER 10

WALL INSULATION

In insulating the walls of your house, you are really restricted to one method: using roll-type insulation. You can buy it with foil backing, which provides extra vapor barrier protection. Use the extra-thickness insulation (4 inch) if you think it necessary, and follow the manufacturer's instructions. *See Fig. 10–A.*

PANELING

For the interior paneling of your house, you have a multitude of choices at a wide range of prices. Most people choose more than one type of wall covering, and they use different materials to complement each other. Some combinations are:

—Rough redwood and sheetrock (often called *drywall*)
—Brick and painted walls
—Sheetrock with areas wall-papered
—Shingles and old beams

You could continue this list toward infinity without exhausting all the possibilities. My personal tastes run to rather simple bright-colored rooms with an accent wall of wood or trim. For instance, I would recommend a wall of dark oak paneling to create a closed-in, secure den feeling, which goes well with massive fireplaces and rough-hewn beams. You might also consider covering the bottom half of your walls in wood or any other material you choose, and the top half with plain painted sheetrock. Not only is this attractive, it's economical. *See Fig. 10–B.*

SHEETROCK

Unless you luck into a cheap source of old wood, the cheapest wall sheathing is without a doubt sheetrock. Sometimes it is called *plasterboard, gypsum board,* or *drywall.* It is made of gypsum rock, a chalk-like material that can be molded and compressed and covered with heavy paper on each side. It comes in sheets of 4×8, 4×10, and 4×12, and you also find it in various thicknesses. Use the ½-inch sheets for a more sturdy wall with less noise transfer and more insulation.

The seam edges of the sheetrock are tapered so that the finisher can apply joint compound and paper tape over the seams. For corners of the room exposed to banging or chipping, you can buy metal reinforcing strips to go under the spackle

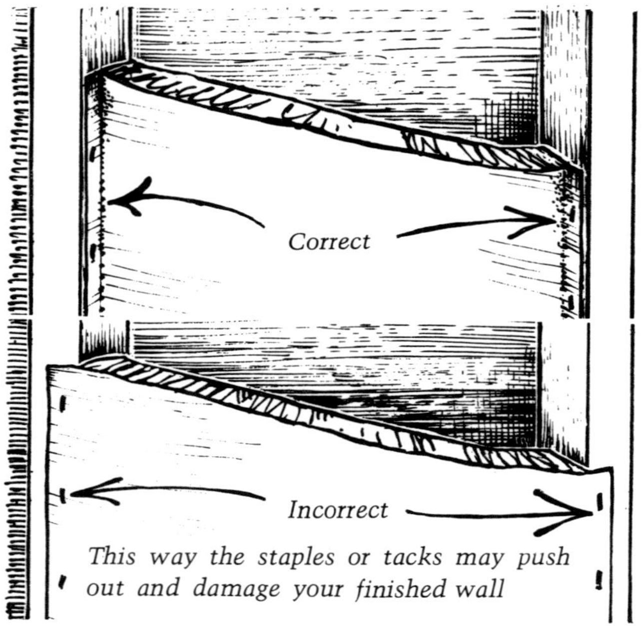

Fig. 10–A Installing Roll Insulation between Studs

and tape you would then apply. Special drywall nails are available to secure the sheetrock seams. Be sure to buy plenty when you purchase your sheetrock. *See Fig. 10–C.*

The first step in using sheetrock is to measure your walls and figure out how you want to hang the sheetrock, horizontally or vertically. Choose the way that gives the least joints and seams. Get a sketch pad and note how many sheets are needed for each wall, then do your shopping.

When you move your load of newly purchased sheetrock into the house, don't bend it or knock it around—it's not very sturdy until it's nailed up.

To cut a piece, lay it down and mark it off with a straight 2×4 and a pencil. Using a razor knife, score the sheetrock on the pencil line approximately ⅛ inch deep, then snap the board back and cut through the rest of the depth. With the ceiling you'll need another person's help holding up the sheetrock while you nail. Nail every 6 inches, wherever you can sink a nail in wood firmly.

Check the following diagram for three basic steps in nailing sheetrock. *See Fig. 10–D.*

Before nailing the sheetrock to ceiling and walls, cut out small holes for fixtures, keeping the cuts close in to the places where the fixtures will go. Later, after the sheets are up, you can cut the holes to fit your receptacle boxes exactly. *See Fig. 10–E.*

Seams must be spackled and taped when you've finished nailing. The spackle compound (a plaster-like material) is smoothed on with a putty knife, and you'll need both a large wide putty knife and a smaller narrow one. First spread a layer of spackle on the entire joint, using the smaller knife, then press the tape down over the filled seam. Spread more spackle over the whole seam and tape, then use a broad putty knife to feather out the edges.

After the spackle has dried for at least twenty-four hours, sand the joints smooth with 100 grit sandpaper so that the seams are undetectable when you sight along the wall. Where you have cut out a small hole for a pipe snub-out, apply tape around the opening and build it up. Spackle it, then feather out until smooth.

The inside corners are a little more difficult to do, but if you fold the tape before you press it to the seam, it will be much easier.

Fig. 10–B An Example of Half-Wall Paneling

For doing your ceilings with sheetrock, see the end of Chapter 6.

In finishing this type of sheetrock construction, you can make it rough, smooth, or wall-papered. You can texture the sheetrock by buying a special plaster compound in powder form, mixing it according to the directions and smearing it on with your hands (using gloves of course). You can create any texture you wish, from rough to smooth. Some people like to add fine, clean sand to the mixture for a rough texture reminiscent of plaster walls. *See Fig. 10–F.*

Sundry tips for sheetrocking:

—Save all your odd pieces of sheetrock because you can

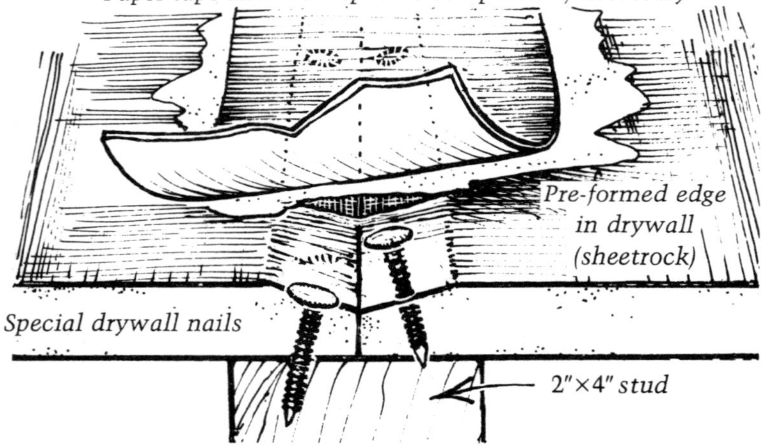

Fig. 10–C Tacking a Sheetrock Seam

tack a layer of these pieces under your rugs for extra insulation and noise reduction.

—Paint manufacturers often recommend that you apply a primer coat to plain sheetrock before you paint it. Ask your paint supplier for it.

—Sheetrock is not as strong as plaster. After it's up, treat it with greater care when pounding nails or hanging things.

PLYWOOD

Plywood paneling is available in a truly bewildering array, and prices seem to fluctuate wildly. Real wood paneling may be on sale for $5 a sheet in one store, and in another store you may find a higher price for imitation wood. Shop for a good deal.

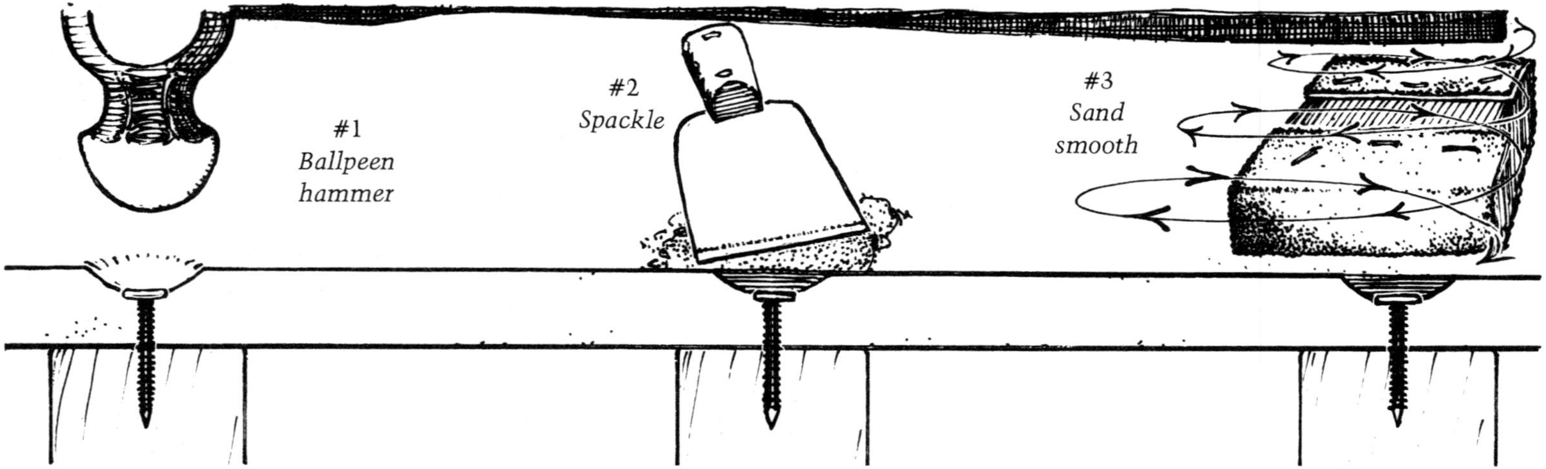

Fig. 10–D The Three Steps to Nailing Drywall

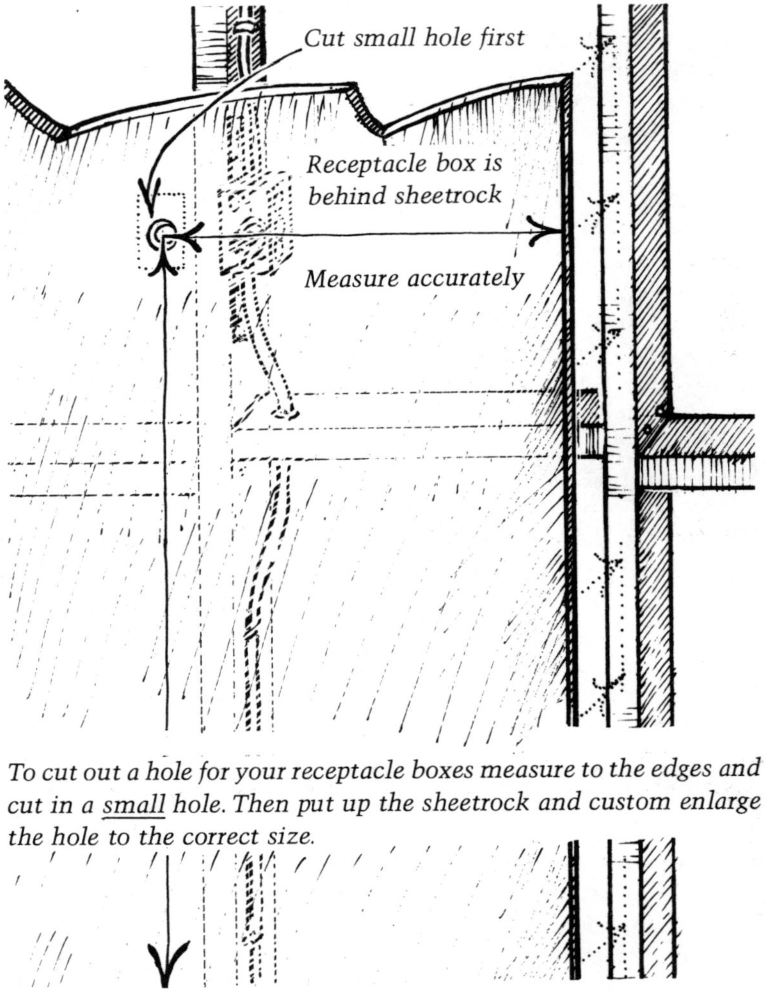

To cut out a hole for your receptacle boxes measure to the edges and cut in a small hole. Then put up the sheetrock and custom enlarge the hole to the correct size.

Fig. 10–E   Cutting Holes for Receptacle Box and Switches

If you find some inexpensive paneling that's being discontinued, be sure they have enough to let you do the whole job. Otherwise you'll be looking all over town for something that matches.

It's a bit tricky to decide what to buy right in the store, because showrooms are usually brightly lit with fluorescent lights. Take the piece you like and move it to a darker corner of the room or shade it from the light. This will give a more realistic picture of how your paneling will look once it's up. Even so, paneling almost always turns out darker than you guessed.

Nailing up paneling is usually simple, but be careful not to bang it hard, since the veneer is often fragile.

You can get by with ¼-inch thickness if your studs are 16 inches on center, but ⅜ inch or even ½ inch is preferable for durability and solidity.

Drive finishing nails approximately 1 inch long approximately every foot, and countersink them 1/16 inch into the wood. Next take a little scrap of your paneling, go to the lumber store, and pick out a countersink hole-filler that matches it closely. Use this precolored plastic filler, and you won't have to touch up all the filled holes with stain later.

HINT: If you find a deep scratch or make a mistake while cutting wood paneling, there is an easy solution to patching the flaw, providing it's redwood, Douglas fir, or other wood paneling. Saw through a piece of similar scrap wood and collect the sawdust. Then mix it up with white glue and make a paste. Pack the hole or notch with the wood-and-glue paste and let it dry. Then gently sand it smooth until you have hidden the blemish.

PLASTERING

Plastering is expensive and requires a lot of skill. When pro-

Fig. 10–F Hands Make Excellent Texturing Tools

fessionally done, it is one of the most attractive and permanent wall finishes you can have. Consult a professional.

HEAVY WOOD

Heavy wood paneling also requires a great deal of skill, and it is beyond the pocketbooks of 95 percent of the population anyway. Better leave the King George carved panels to the experts, or else take a class in advanced wood carving!

OLD WOOD

Old wood from barns or other structures is very elegant if it is used conservatively and with taste. Make sure all the wood ants and termites have abandoned it, or they might turn your house into their next meal!

Consider applying the old wood horizontally for a change. The effect will be unusual and will tend to make the room appear longer and wider. Also running the wood diagonally

Install the molding or trim after you face the interiors of your windows with sheetrock strips. You must measure each strip of sheetrock, one at a time, to insure accuracy.

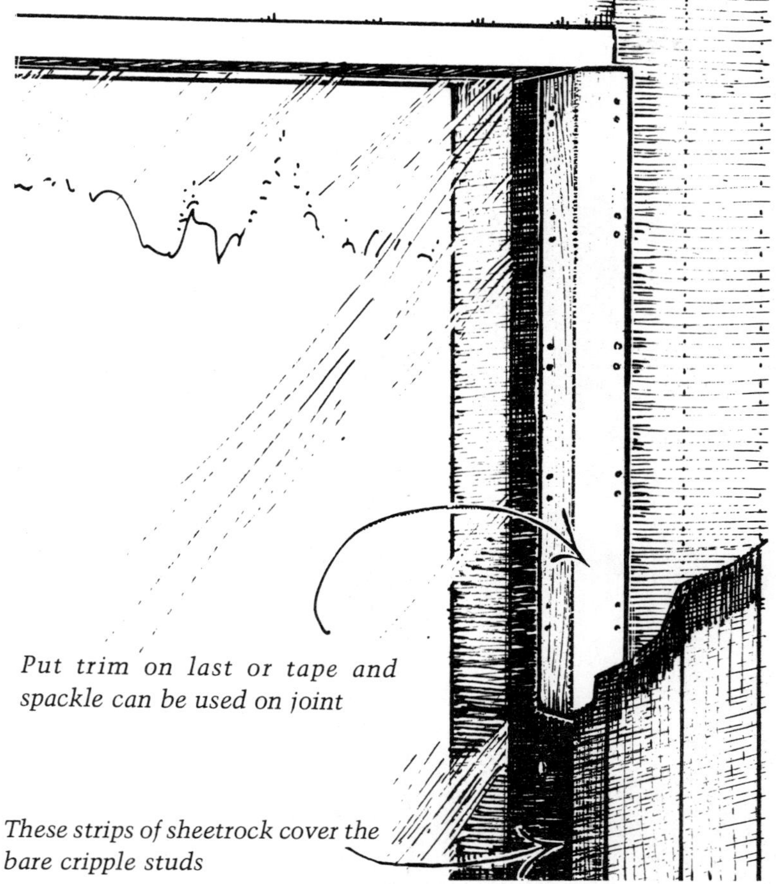

Fig. 10–G   Finishing the Windows with Sheetrock

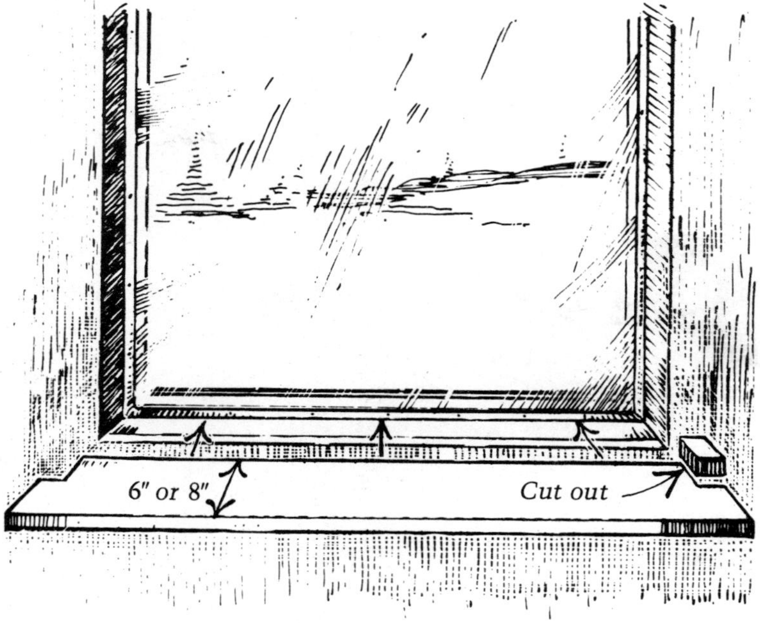

Fig. 10–H   Window Sill Being Fitted

is very tasteful.

If your wood is not too thick, you might try using a quick-drying adhesive to glue up your wall. This adhesive will give you a nice surface without protruding nails. Ask your hardware supply what products are available.

WINDOW TRIM

Around the windows on the interior you will need to apply some type of finish material. Whether sheetrock or plywood is used, the technique is the same. Measure the spaces to be covered, cut out the right size pieces, and use finish nails to tack them up. Keep the seam edge on the outside. *See Fig. 10–G.* On the exposed edge nail some molding that goes well with the surrounding area. If you use sheetrock, spackle and tape the seam.

Window sills can be made of different materials for different rooms. Use tile in the bathroom and kitchen, where water may collect and cause damage. Wooden window sills and ledges are practical in the living room. Use extra-wide ones if you want to put plants on the window sills for sunlight. I like to use 1×6 Douglas fir nailed to the window as shown in *Fig. 10–H.* Even wider wood can be used to create window seats, which liven up a room when they are strewn with pillows. *See Fig. 10–I.*

Be sure to paint or varnish raw wood trim because sun coming in the window will discolor it rapidly.

If you have the more traditional casement type window, or if you wish to line the inside edges of a more modern window with trim, you can refer to the illustration on page 116 in Chapter 8. Around the doors you will nail trim to the wall and jamb with finishing nails. Use wide or narrow trim depending on the effect you want to achieve. *See Fig. 10–J.*

OTHER TRIM

If you have a seam where sheetrock stops and natural wood begins, you might want to put a strip of ½-inch half-round bead over it. This will make any seam, even a sloppy one, look professional.

If you used my beam-and-bracket roof support idea, metal brackets are exposed where the beam meets the center supporting wall. Nail trim around the brackets to hide the metal and give it a harmonious effect. *See Fig. 10–K.*

This is a possible window seat using store-bought wooden legs and a piece of leftover plywood.

Fig. 10–I Homemade Window Seat

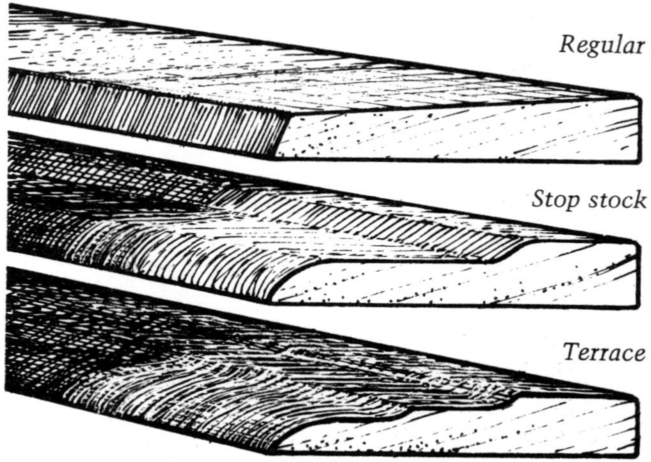

Fig. 10–J   Types of Molding

If you have a seam where wood ceiling meets a sheetrock wall, you can put a ½-inch quarter-bead strip around the ceiling to hide the seam.

Don't worry about the floor and wall joint, because your carpet or finished wood floor will cover the rough wood and come up against the wall tightly.

NOTE: It's easier to stain the trim before you put it up. That way you won't have to tape the wall when you stain it later. Patch up all the countersunk holes with matching colored filler, and you're ready for the next chapter.

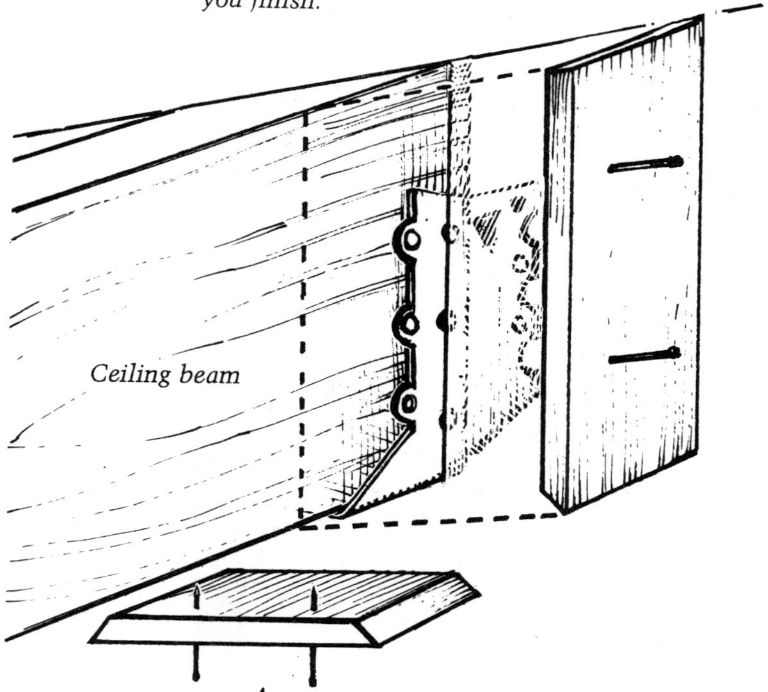

Fig. 10–K   Covering the Exposed Brackets on the Interior Wall

Considering the Possibilities

FINISHING OFF THE ELECTRICAL SYSTEM, PLUMBING, AND KITCHEN

CHAPTER 11

This is a catch-all chapter, because at this point a lot of loose ends and leftover jobs must be done.

ELECTRICAL FIXTURES AND APPLIANCES

If you haven't installed all of your electrical fixtures, this is the time to finish putting in the wall lights, swag lamps, and switches. Swag lamps are easy to install and fit in virtually any decor. *See Fig. 11–A.* I prefer the silent type of switches for all rooms, and they only cost a few cents more. Dimmer switches are also excellent in the bedrooms and living rooms, and they provide money-saving lighting possibilities.

For electric heaters along the floor boards, you can often just bring the wire directly out of the wall and connect it to the heater without use of a receptacle box.

The water heater, if electric, will need a special receptacle box cover plate and armor cable that reaches to the top of the heater. Ask the building department or electrical supply house what is recommended locally for this type of installation. *See Fig. 11–B.*

If the electrician helped you rough in the house's electrical system and hooked up the stove's electrical connection, then you are all set. If he just brought the wires up to the receptacle box near the stove and left them loose, then you will have to hook them to the proper receptacle. Usually the plug and receptacle look like the ones in *Fig. 11–C.*

BATHROOM

When you have finished your electrical work and have installed all the fixtures, you will want to put in the bathroom's finished plumbing, i.e. the plumbing for the bathtub, toilet, and sink.

You already nailed the bathtub to the studs, as explained in the framing section of Chapter 5. With the finished wall up, you can put in whatever type of bath or shower arrangements you happen to like. I prefer single-lever type faucets with an outside shower attachment, since they are simple to install and operate.

TILE

Providing you have a good smooth wall, tile is easy to work with. If the wall is plywood or sheetrock, you should smooth a continuous layer of *rubber cement mastic* (a rubbery adhesive) to the surface. The mastic forms a water-tight seal. Smear some more mastic on each piece of tile and stick the tile to the wall. Start at the bottom corners of the wall and work up and out. On the top and sides put *cap tiles,* which look like this (*Fig. 11–D*).

After all your tile is up, mix a paste of *grout,* (a plaster-like mixture) and push it into the spaces between the tiles. Wipe off any extra grout, let the walls harden, and you've got a tiled bathtub enclosure in one easy afternoon! **NOTE:** To chip a hole for a pipe to stick out, you need a tile chipper that costs only a dollar or so. The tile chipper also usually has a glass or tile cutting device on it should you need to cut a tile.

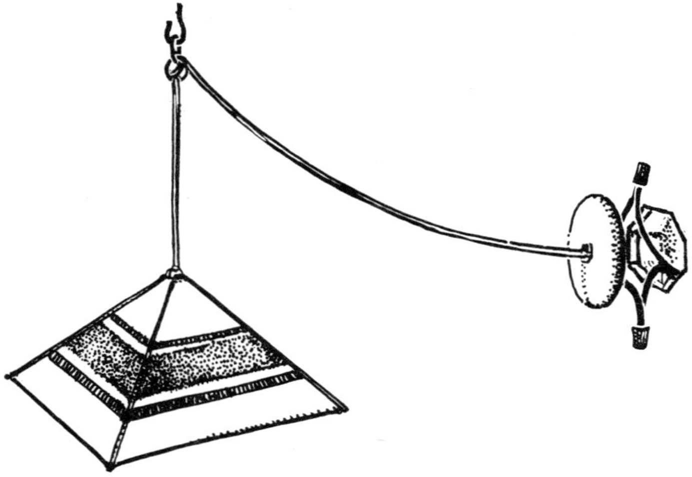

Fig. 11–A Wiring a Swag Lamp and Overhead Receptacle Box

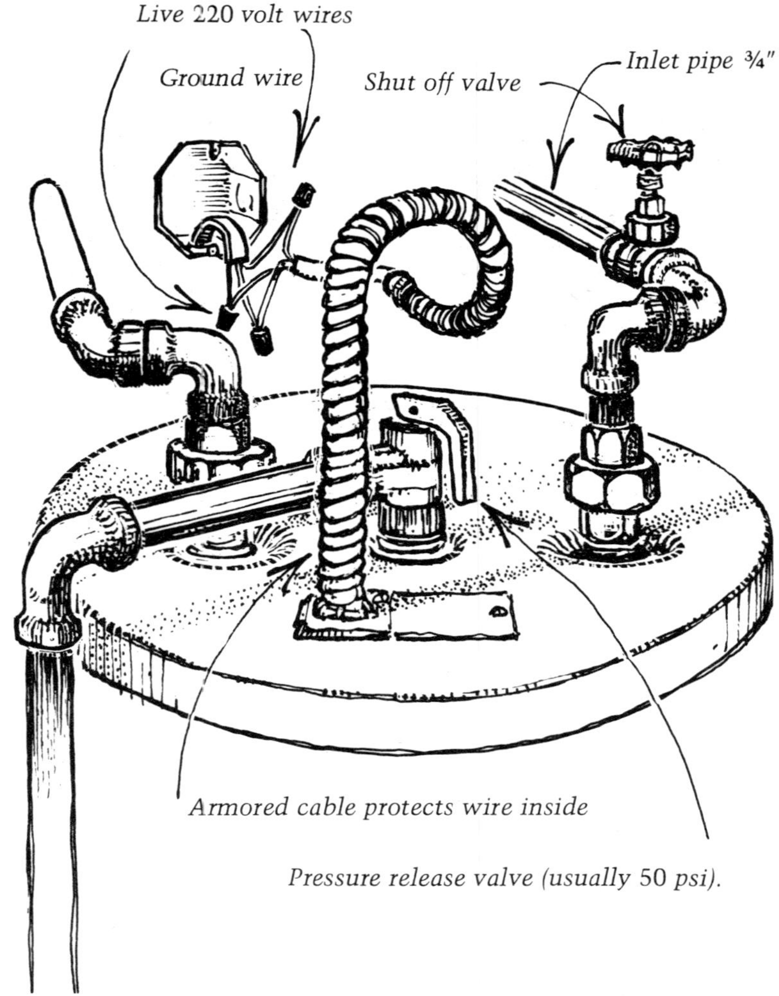

Fig. 11–B Installing a 220 Volt Electric Water Heater

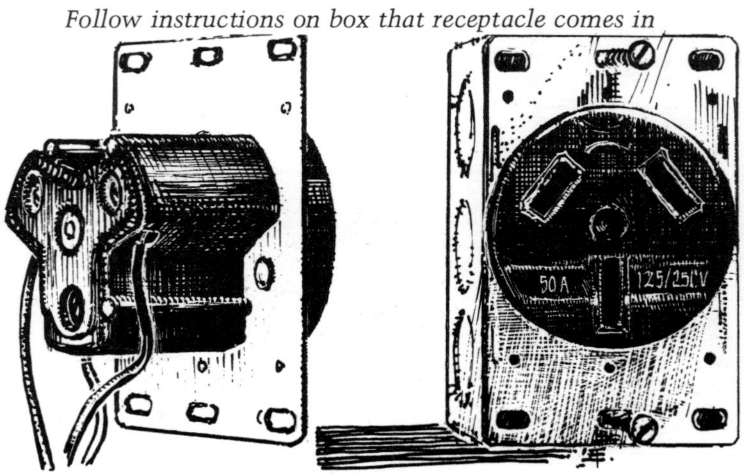

Fig. 11–C Stove Receptacle and Plug

BATHROOM SINK

The sink for your bathroom must be mounted to the wall or set into a cabinet of some sort. Usually a wall-mounted sink comes with a bracket that secures to the wall. The sink then slips onto the bracket. It's a good idea to buy a wall-mounted sink with legs for extra support if it's likely the sink will be leaned on very heavily. If you choose the cabinet-style sink you can build one from scratch or buy one ready-made.

In hooking up your sink, use a flexible connection hose rather than regular pipe. The flexible hose has a flow adjustment valve right on it, so you'll save money and can easily adapt it to any sink position. Next you'll need a U-bend drain pipe. Set the drain in plumber's caulking putty, then adjust

Fig. 11–D Tiling a tub, Starting with a Pyramid and Working Outward

the movable U-bend to the height of the drain snub-out. Smear the whole connection with pipe dope, and tighten it up with a vise-grip or plumber's wrench. *See Chapter 7.*

TOILET CONNECTION

For the toilet connection, the drain pipe (or closet bend) must be topped off at floor level with a special fitting that contains a wax gasket. The toilet is then slowly lowered onto the gasket for a water-tight seal. *See Fig. 11–E.*

Once the toilet is in place, you can bolt it to the floor with the supplied bolts. If the floor is rough and you're going to carpet it, bolt the toilet base directly to the rough floor. If the floor will be covered with tile or linoleum, install that first and then bolt down the toilet over the finished floor. Complete the plumbing job with a flexible connector, the same type you used under the sink.

Install whatever towel racks, cabinets, shelves, mirrors, and curtains you like, and your bathroom is finished.

KITCHEN

The kitchen is probably the area of your house that requires the most exacting work, specifically the counters and cabinets. The cabinets themselves are difficult to build according to professional standards. However, if you wish to build your own, several easy short cuts can speed up the work.

CABINETS

First you will want to draw a diagram of proposed counters and storage space in your kitchen. Hypothetically, it could look like the example shown below. *See Fig. 11–F.*

Old shutters or aged wood are good for cabinet doors, or make some nice cloth curtains to cover the shelves. Be sure

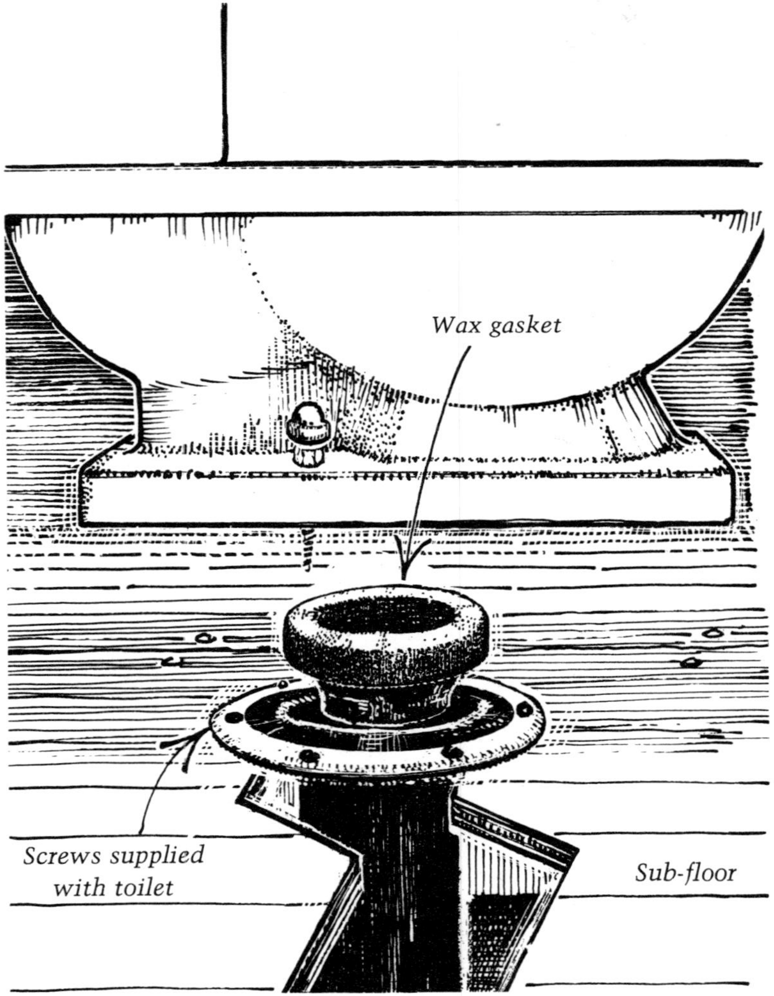

Fig. 11–E Installing the Toilet

to leave one unit free of shelves, so that cleaning supplies can fit in easily. *See Fig. 11–G.*

When you design the cupboards above the counter, don't get them too high. Remember that some people will probably have to stand on a chair to reach them.

If you are cramped for storage space, you can build a cupboard from floor to ceiling. That should stock enough food to supply a small army. *See Fig. 11–H.*

Here's a tip for making cabinet doors that will save you frustration. Instead of trying to build cabinets with doors that fit into the openings, build units with doors that close *over* the openings. This simplifies your job considerably when you have perhaps a dozen doors to fit. *See Fig. 11–I.*

Once the cabinet frame is built, you can use plywood to cover the sides. Then nail small wood blocks inside to hold your shelves. Use a level to get the blocks even. Next put on the doors and be sure to chisel out the wood underneath the hinges so that the hinges set flush with the surface. *See Fig. 11–J.*

COUNTERS

With all your bottom framing done now, you can consider your countertops. Many commercial tops are available made of formica and modern plastics, so see what's around at what price. If you can't afford the contractors' bids, consider making your own formica countertop. It will cost you approximately $85 if you use scrap plywood.

Across the top of the cabinet frames, place either one 1⅛-inch piece of plywood or two pieces of ⅝-inch plywood glued together. Then use a ruler to pencil a line all around the counter, 1 inch from the cabinets.

Place the countertop foundation on the floor and saw exactly on the line. Next use a file to knock off the splinters along the

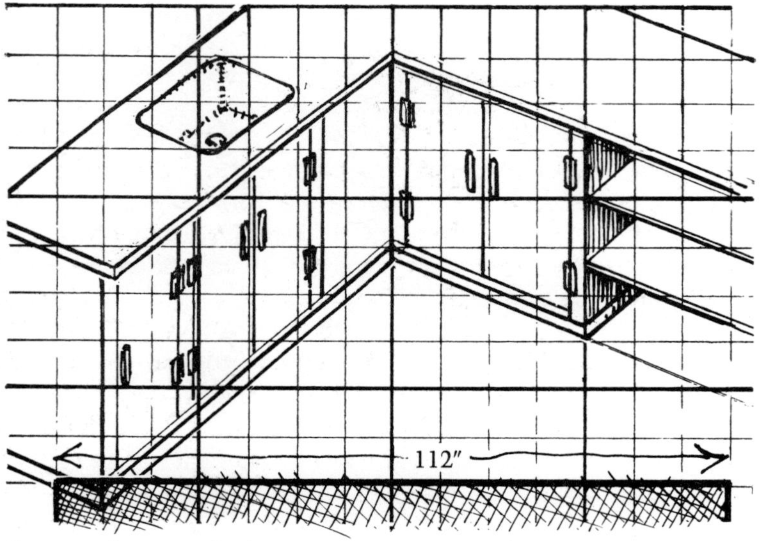

Start with a rough diagram (use graph paper) then develop a 3-dimensional drawing for better accuracy.

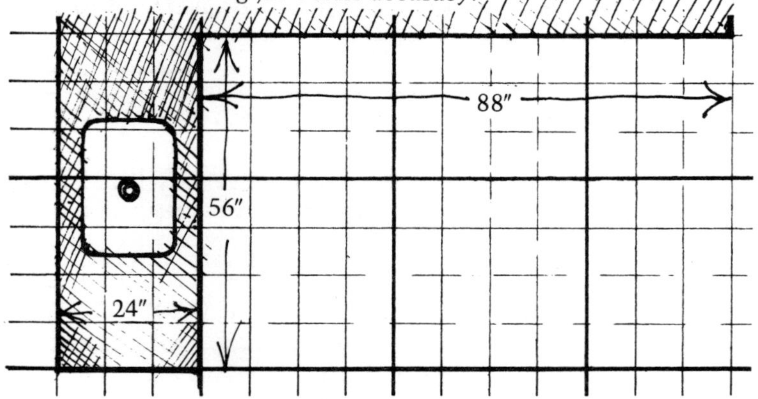

Fig. 11–F Designing Your Counterspace

rough edges. Nail on this plywood with 1½-inch nails and check to be sure it's solid.

In the drawing you will note that the width of this top should be no greater than 24 inches. If the top is wider, the overhanging lip of a formica counter will not fit over the plywood.

Now is the time to go to the nearest lumber or hardware supply store and get your pre-molded formica tops. Should you want an L-shaped top for a kitchen corner, have the dealer make the 45-degree miter seam especially for you, but this will cost an extra $20. If you want a simple, straight piece, the costs are fairly reasonable, usually in the neighborhood of $25, $35, and $45 for the 6-, 8-, and 10-foot lengths respectively.

Gluing on the formica sections is easy if you use a contact cement like Weldwood, but go through a dry run first to see if everything looks good. If everything fits, take off the counter and smear the cement on the plywood foundation with an old paint brush. Do likewise to the bottom of the formica and press into place. Next put down some cardboard or heavy paper and load up the counter with building blocks, books or objects equally heavy. Dry overnight. *See Fig. 11–K.*

Your counter will probably butt up to a wall somewhere. If so, you may want to ask the formica dealer for an end splash ($10) and glue this on with contact cement. For the end of the counter that barely sticks out, glue on end caps ($5) of matching color. Use a jig saw to cut out the hole for the sink, or if

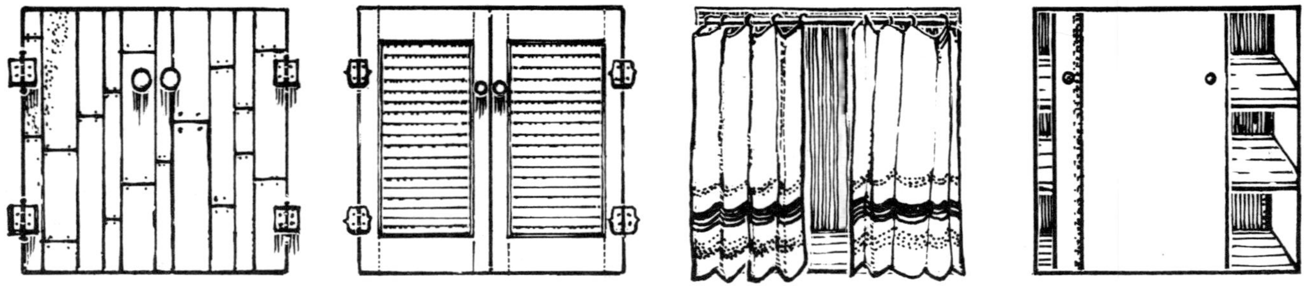

Fig. 11–G Ideas for Covering the Shelves

Fig. 11–H Storage Shelves with Doors

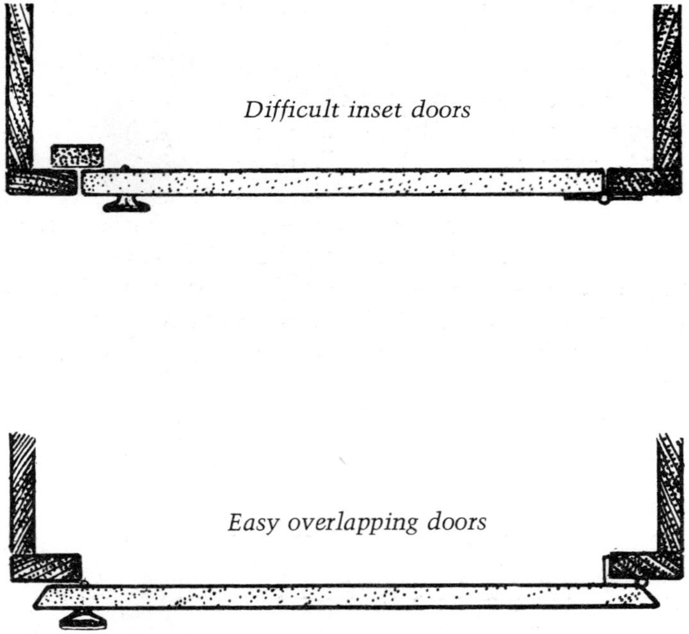

Fig. 11–I Cabinet Doors

you have no electric power you can settle for a keyhole saw.

Remember also to ask the dealer for suggestions and guidance—for that much money you've got it coming.

KITCHEN SINK

For your kitchen sink you will probably want the double sink made of stainless steel. I recommend stainless steel as the best, but it generally costs a bit more.

Kitchen sinks are easy to install. The most important thing

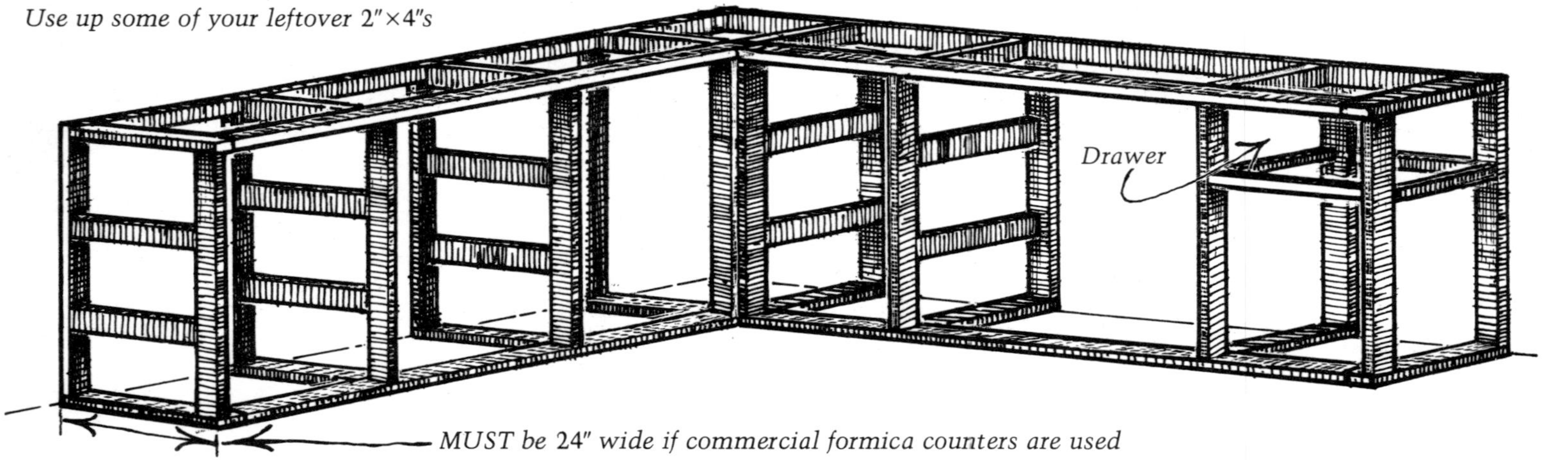

Fig. 11–J Typical Framing for Cabinets

that the home builder need remember is to use plenty of waterproof plumber's putty to seal the sink against leakage. Hook up the faucets to flexible supply hoses and connect the drains just as you did in the bathroom. (See Chapter 7.) Special double-sink drains are available, if you use that type of sink.

Now you can add whatever you like to make your kitchen suit your fancy. Some good ideas are snack-bar-type tables and counters and bookcase dividers. Some people like shelves in front of the windows for plants and herbs, if the kitchen receives good sunlight. The plants are easy to water in the kitchen window, and what could be nicer than growing and picking your own fresh herbs?

If the water heater stands in the corner of the kitchen, you might want to disguise it in some fashion. The easiest thing to do is to build a little wooden screen around it. Or use a bamboo fencing and put that around it to a height of 6 feet. (Arrange the bamboo so that it runs vertically.)

FLOOR COVERING

With the bathroom and the kitchen almost finished, you can decide now what you're going to do with the floors. Linoleum and tile are best suited for these utility areas, although some people do put in special indoor/outdoor carpets.

Laying floor tile is easy, but the cost is high—unless you find a sale on a discontinued style (but be sure you get enough).

If you want to put down linoleum, measure it exactly and double-check it before you cut, since it looks awful when patched together. Darker greens and blues will remain attrac-

Blocks to hold down formica countertop while adhesive drys. Use contact adhesive.

If you want to be creative with your cabinets and drawers study a book on the subject.

Fig. 11–K Detail of Finished Cabinet with Drawers

tive longer but will also make your kitchen seem smaller. Put down plywood first if the floor is a really rough subfloor.

After the linoleum is laid, you can use one of various styles of molding around the edge of the floor to cover any gaps left by uneven cutting.

Fig. 12–A The Basic House Addition with Either a Low Pitch Roof or a Shed Roof

ADDING-ON

CHAPTER 12

THE PORCH AND THE "ADDED-ON" ROOM

As time passes you may want to enlarge your house, for whatever reason, be they relatives, additional children, or just a crowded feeling.

One of the easiest and cheapest "add-on rooms" is the enclosed porch, which can be screened or partially walled in. Later the porch can serve as a breezeway to larger additions, should you have cause to expand further.

I particularly like the semi-enclosed and paneled room because it does not appreciably up your taxes, and it serves so many useful purposes. *See Fig. 12–A.*

By covering the windows with heavy drapes or by sealing them up with shutters in the winter, you can make the porch into an easy-to-heat room. In summer it then converts into a light and airy family room.

As I suggested before, it's wise to keep free of windows and wood shakes any exterior walls through which you may later add rooms. If you place a door in the wall, however, you will have easy access without having to cut open the wall.

For the new room's roof, you'll want to nail a joist hanger bracket to the side of the existing building. The ceiling beams or rafters are then connected to a ridge beam that in turn has been set in the bracket. *See Fig. 12–B.*

The porch or added room foundation and subsequent framing should follow the style and technique that you've already applied to your house. If you use extra-wide windows, be sure to get your lintel size large enough to accommodate them structurally. (See glossary and framing diagrams for *lintel.*) If you panel your porch, you can leave the house's exterior wall as an interior wall, or you can panel over it with any material you choose.

When attaching the roof of an addition to an existing structure, you must insure a watertight junction by using metal flashing. Flashing is a long sheet-metal strip folded in the center and tacked to the seam after a generous application of asphalt compound is laid down. For extra protection, smear more asphalt over the whole flashing, including all nail heads. *See Fig. 12–C.*

SEPARATE ROOM

Another house-expanding idea is the separate room concept.

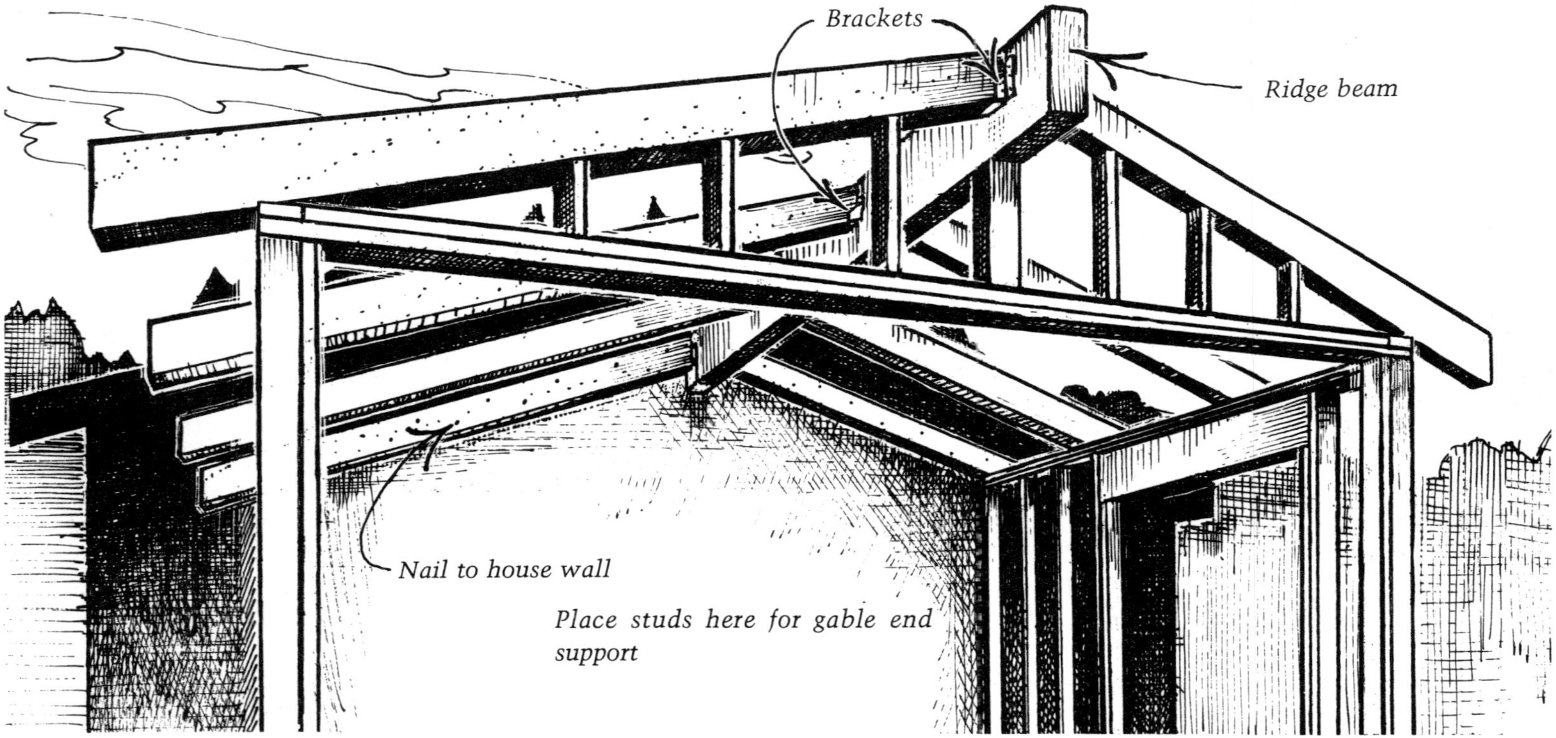

Fig. 12–B Roof Framing the Low Pitch Added-On Room/Porch

A separate room connected to the rest of the house by a breezeway or porch gives the advantages of seclusion and quiet for people who want to practice music or work. In a family set-up, it is also ideal as a utility room or recreation room, for it can be used to creatively release harsh feelings caused by too much activity in a crowded house. *See Fig. 12–D.*

You can plan a small bathroom for this new room, even if you're working in limited space. Instead of a big space-devouring tub, put in a shower stall and a corner-mounted basin. Your local building and plumbing supply will be able to help you plan your second "minibathroom."

When building a large breezeway, consider putting in it an

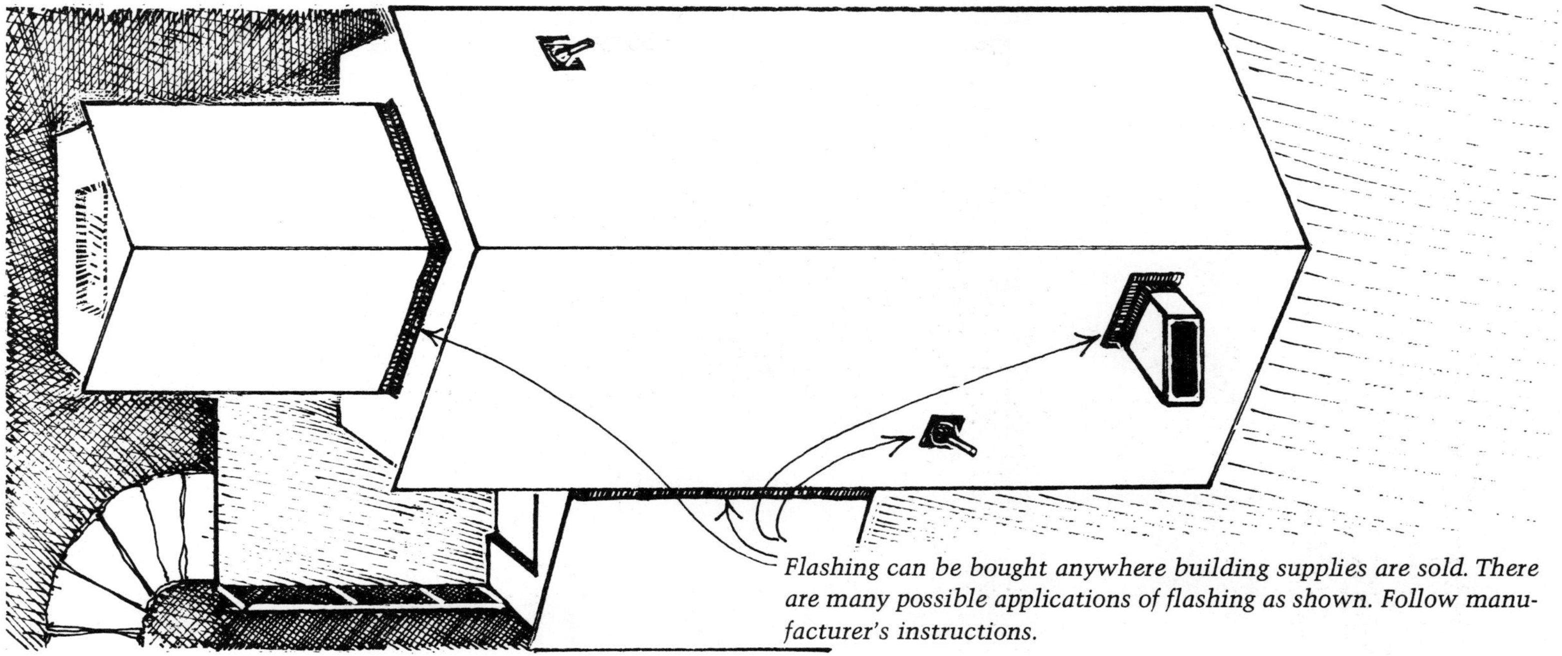

Flashing can be bought anywhere building supplies are sold. There are many possible applications of flashing as shown. Follow manufacturer's instructions.

Fig. 12–C Where to Use Flashing

outdoor barbecue pit or fireplace. Then on chilly autumn evenings you can sit around the fire and drink hot mulled apple cider. For the breezeway you can use cheap plastic roof panels nailed to 2×4 roof rafters, since most building departments don't consider this type of construction on a par with house framing.

TOWER ROOM

I have seen people build towerlike rooms on top of or next to their house, or even connected right to it. When your view is inspirational, these rooms are perfect for meditation or just plain thinking. This idea has been used successfully many times. *See Fig. 12–E.*

LOFT

If your house has a sloping open-beam ceiling, you can increase the living space by building a large loft. See *Fig. 12–E* for an example of a loft over a bedroom. The loft isn't high enough to

Fig. 12–D An Added Structure with a Connecting Breezeway

stand up in, but it's good for lounging around and just getting away for a while.

STORAGE IDEAS

With your house built, you may need a little more storage room for that extra junk you bought and didn't need, or for that stuff you bought and do need. Here are some ideas on conservation of space you can apply to the $9,000 home.

Like most people, I've saved up tons of junk and have often been at a loss as to what to do with it. Here is how I stash it away.

In your utility room or bedroom, you can use some space not otherwise used. How is that, you say? Look up . . . above your head is the best place for little-used and reasonably sized objects. Build cupboards and shelves up to the ceiling, you'll still be able to slide a chair or TV against the wall. *See Fig. 12–F.*

Given the nature of any room, some accommodation for

Fig. 12–E   Get-Away Spaces

storage can be made. How about under-the-bed storage? Don't just slide stuff under, build a captain's bunk with drawers. This is a fairly easy project for a weekend or two, and it will give you a chance to use up some of your scrap wood. Consult any of the fine woodworking periodicals for plans.

The parson's chair or bench is a good colonial American solution to storage problems. Under its wide seat cover lurks a giant chest that will successfully hold all your winter coats and jackets.

One of my all-time favorites is the bookcase room divider. It is especially useful as a dining room/living room divider, or even as a kitchen/living room divider. Old 2×4's nailed to-

Fig. 12–F Overhead Storage Using Otherwise Wasted Space

Fig. 12–G Bookcases Make Good Room Dividers

gether and stained walnut make attractive posts on which shelves can rest. Cut up your old plywood scraps and stain them, then use these pieces for shelves. *See Fig. 12–G.*

If you get stuck and can't find the right idea for your house, try searching through your public library's craft magazines. Remember that the library has all the back issues, which will supply you with a wealth of ideas. Furniture books are also widely available, and the handicraft magazines, such as *Woodworker,* will point you in the right direction.

While you're sweeping up the litter or crawling around on the floor looking for stray nails and bits of wire, you'll suddenly straighten up and say to yourself—MY GOD, I'M DONE! Your first feelings will be relief and euphoria. All the hard work and scraped knuckles are behind you. No more taking showers and lathering your whole body with Boraxo. No more buying two new pairs of jeans a month. No more cussing of that little screwdriver that is always at the bottom of the tool chest.

So close the door and check the latch, for tomorrow you move in. A house now lives where there was none, and as you walk down the driveway, you may feel a little sadness at knowing your home is now complete. And as you stand in the darkening shadows gazing at your house, you'll feel the finest of human emotions—pride.

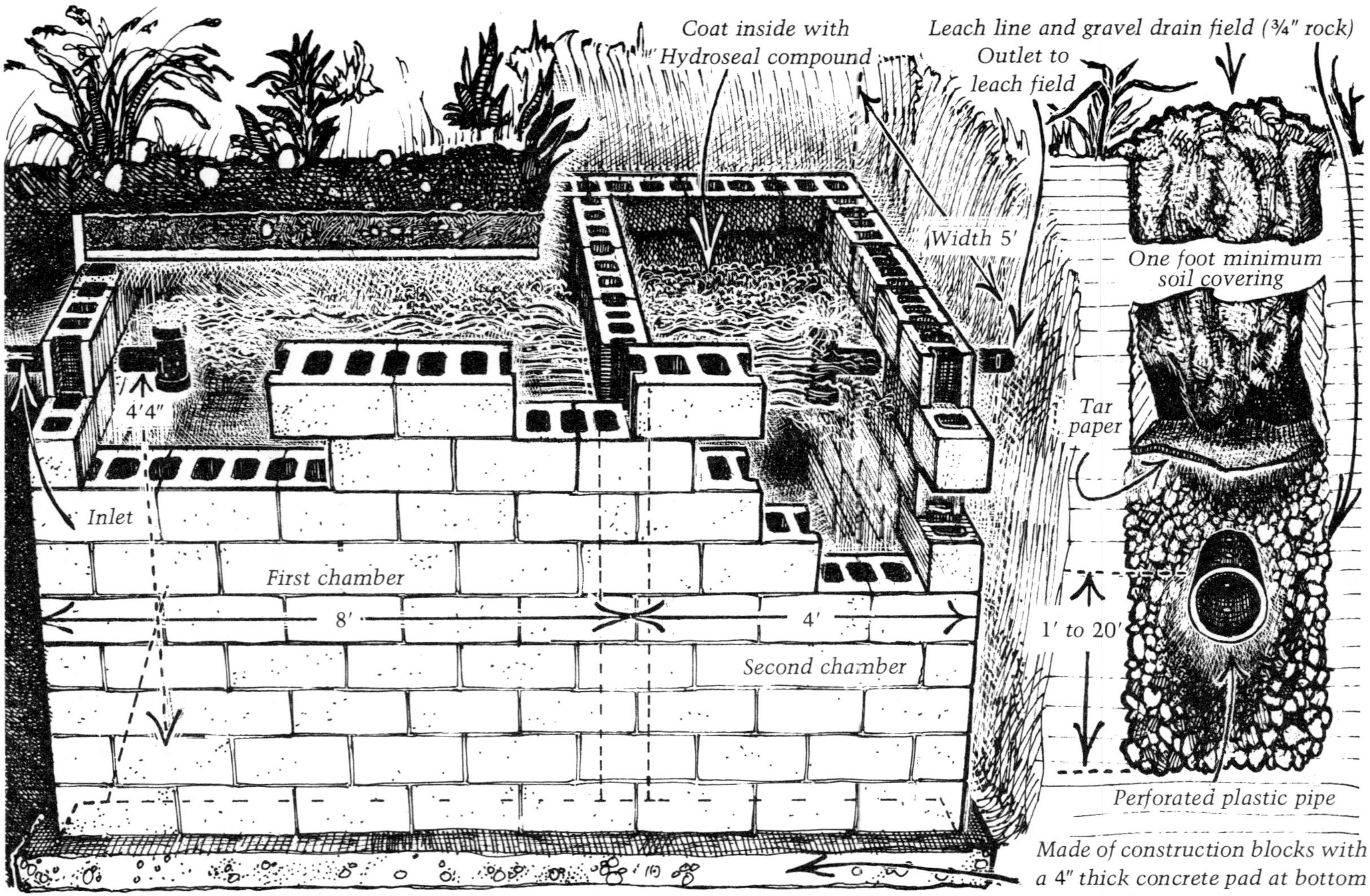

Fig. APP–A   A Septic Tank for $300

APPENDIX

SEPTIC TANKS

All a septic tank really is, is a large holding tank that separates waste matter into solids and liquids. Then it allows the liquid waste to drain away into the earth. Periodically the solids that sink to the bottom of the tank must be removed by a tank-pumping truck.

Premade concrete tanks are often available at large hardware stores. Wooden tanks are allowed only in some areas, so ask first. Finally, if you want to work with cement or wood, you can make your own septic tank. First you might want to consult the chart which shows the advantages and disadvantages of each type.

The building or sanitation department will explain what type of tank you can legally use. Ask also if they have a copy of sanitation codes or a fact sheet.

Since I am seldom in a big hurry for anything, I like to build my own. Here is how I do it:

The first step after you have located a safe spot for your system, hopefully at least 100 feet from your water system, is to have a backhoe tractor dig a hole for the tank. Then have it dig the proper-size trench. The trench will be filled with gravel later, and this will serve as a drain field for your septic tank.

The second step is to dump marble-size or ¾-inch round gravel into the trench, to within 1½ feet of the surface. When this is done, pour a 4-inch layer of concrete on the bottom of the tank hole. This is the foundation and floor of the tank, so get it fairly level.

The third step is to build up the sides of the tank with building blocks. Bed down the first course (row) in mortar, and make sure it is very level. Proceed to lay one course on another, leveling as you go. *See Fig. App.–A.* Following the diagrams, leave holes for the inlet and the outlet. When this is done, build out of blocks an interior partition wall (usually you are required to have this type; single-compartment tanks are sometimes allowed). Leave several blocks out near the top, as the diagram indicates, so the liquid can flow freely from section to section.

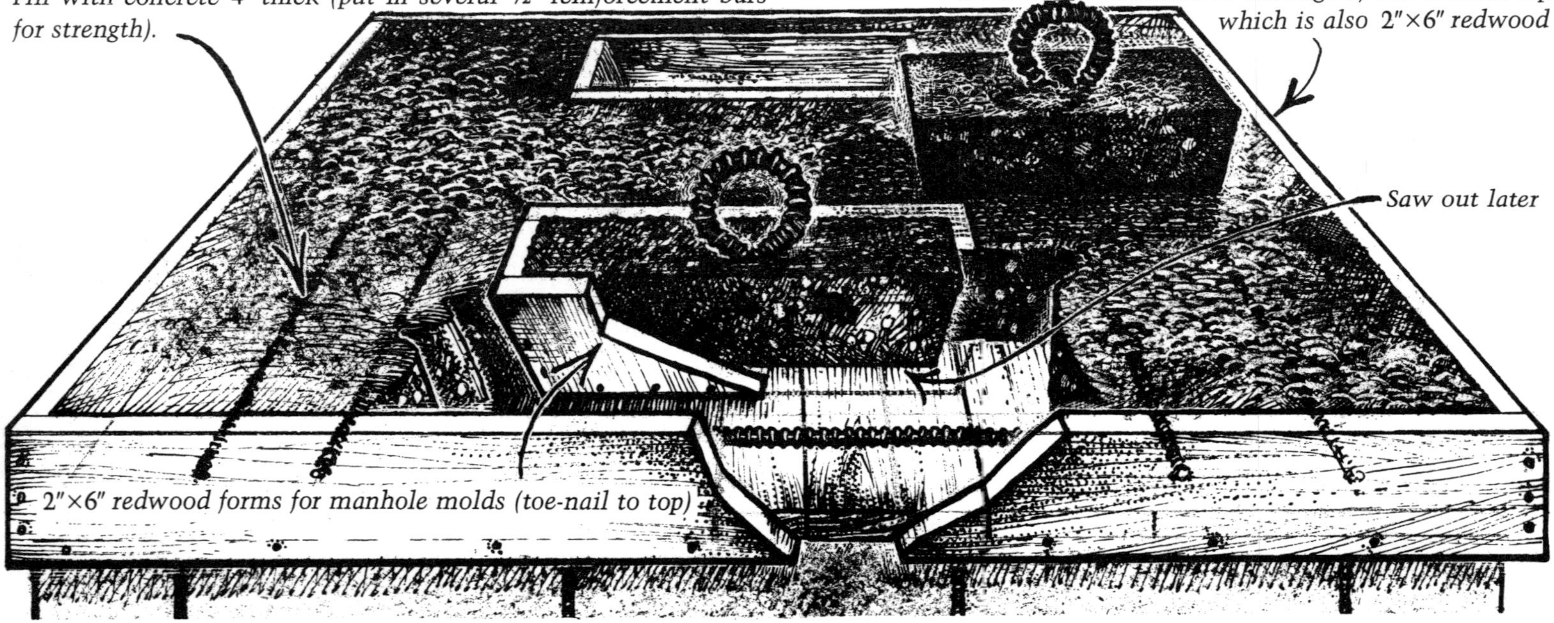

Fig. APP–B The Top of the Septic Tank

The fourth step is to lay 2×6 redwood planks over the top of the tank. The manhole molds, made of ½-inch plywood are then toe-nailed to the top of 2×6 planking. Put a 2×6 redwood plank on edge all around the exterior of the planking. After the top is 4 inches thick with concrete (*Fig. App.–B*), pour more concrete into the manhole molds. After the concrete has hardened for two days, pull out the manholes with a hoist. Saw out the planking underneath the manholes and then replace the concrete manholes with the hoist (they're really heavy!).

The fifth step is to cover up your leach line (*see Fig. App.–A*) with 6 inches to 1 foot of gravel, and then put a couple of layers of building paper on top of that to seal off the trench. Next, cover up the whole thing with the surplus dirt until the area is level again. *See Fig. App.–C.*

The sixth step is to coat the tank inside and out, whether it be redwood or concrete block, with a black bituminous or asphalt compound. This coating minimizes corrosion and

ADVANTAGES

Home-Built Concrete Block Tank	*Redwood Tank*	*Premade Concrete Tank*	*Premade Fiberglass Tank*
Cheap construction; $100–$300, depending on size	*Easy to build by hand*	*Virtually permanent*	*Light and easy to install (two people)*
Fairly watertight	*Medium long life (50–75 years if heartwood is used)*	*Watertight*	*Maintenance-free*
Strongest construction of all types		*Quick installation with a crane*	*Different sizes available*
		Suitable for all areas and occasions	

DISADVANTAGES

Home-Built Concrete Block Tank	*Redwood Tank*	*Premade Concrete Tank*	*Premade Fiberglass Tank*
A lot of hard work takes weeks of time	*Usually leaks in time*	*Must be installed with a large crane*	*Not allowed in some places*
Must be accurately masoned, or problems can occur	*Not often allowed by building department*	*Expensive*	*Expensive*
	Not as strong as concrete	*Not always readily available*	*Questionable life expectancy*

Comparison of Different Types of Septic Tanks

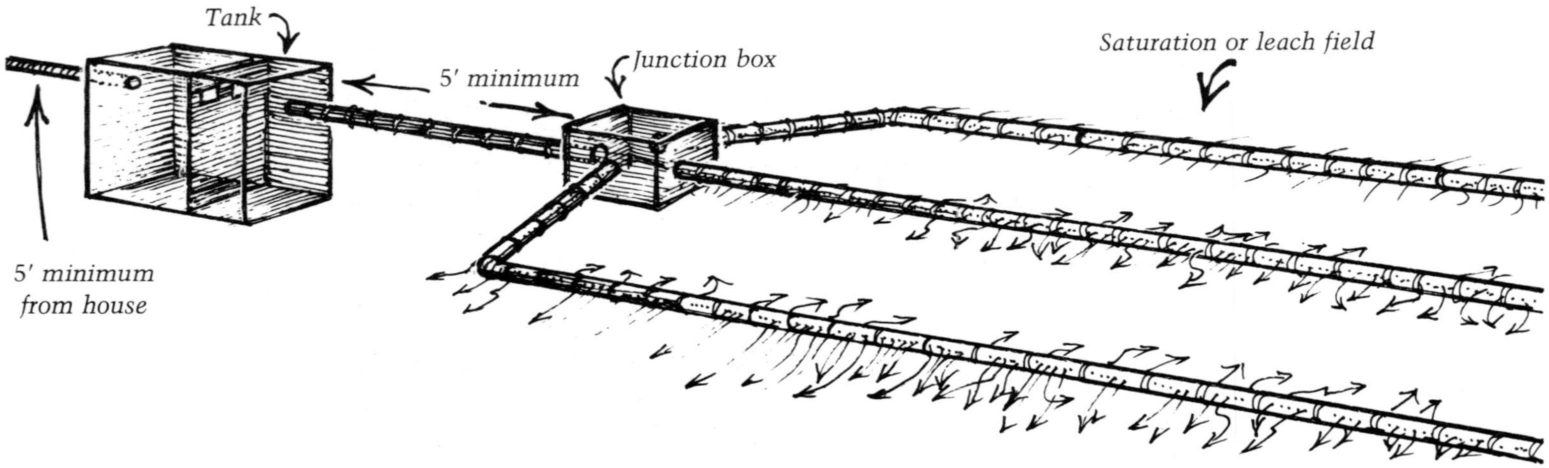

Fig. APP–C Looking Down on the Leach Field

helps seal the tank against moisture. A paint brush is all that's needed for application.

A septic tank often stinks for the first month or so because it is starting up the digesting process. Don't use any starters or enzyme helpers, because your waste contains everything it needs to digest itself.

If you opted for the redwood tank, use the same basic construction design, but be sure to use heavy galvanized nails, and lots of them! Choose only heart-grade redwood that has been dried out sufficiently.

HEATING SYSTEMS

Your choice of electric, gas, or wood heating will depend largely upon your preferences and your budget. While electricity is the most expensive in nearly every area, natural gas prices are soaring up closer to it every day. The time may come when all fuels for heating cost the same. I feel it's wise to have two sources available to heat your home, or parts of it. Different types of heating systems can supplement each other very well and can save you money in the long run by helping to conserve energy. One system that heats your whole house may not be practical when only one or two rooms are in use. Keep your system flexible around your life style. Some good combinations are:

—Several permanent electric baseboard heaters, either 220- or 110-volt, with one or two smaller portables for use in bathrooms, utility rooms, and other places.

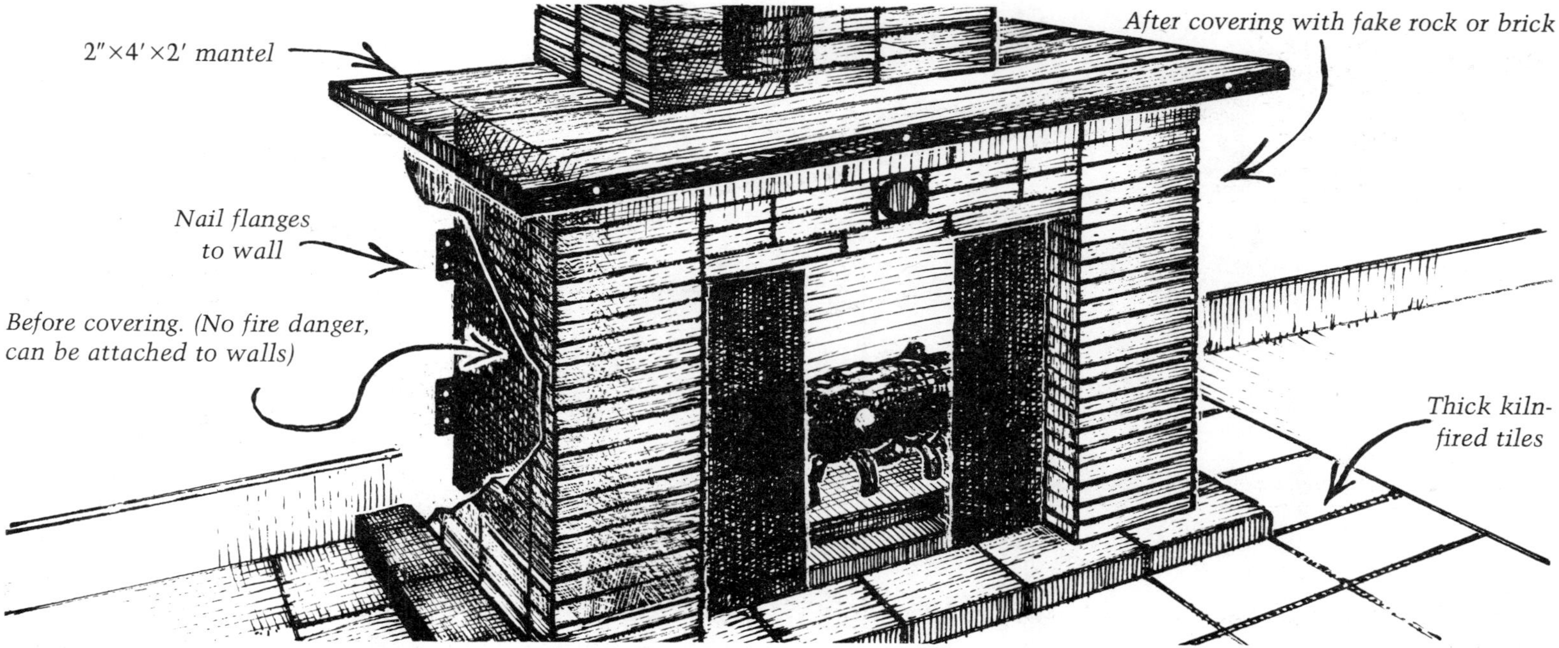

Fig. APP–D Using a Factory-Made Firebox to be Finished at Home

—Gas space heater mounted in the floor or wall, supplemented with small portable electric heaters.
—Central gas heater with a duct system, supplemented by a fireplace.

FIREPLACES

Fireplaces are popular, but I wager it won't be long before hardwood cords are selling for $150 each. For practical heating, fireplaces are usually wasteful, since much heat is lost up the flue.

Modern fireboxes are worth the couple of hundred dollars you have to spend for them. (*Fireboxes* are premade metal fireplaces designed to be covered.) They offer two big advantages. First, they maintain a high efficiency of heating, and second, proper draft and heat reflection in the box is insured. *See Fig. App.–D.*

Building a fireplace from scratch is a large and complex undertaking, and I recommend that you at least let a qualified designer draw up your plans. In the firebox flue, for instance, a difference of ¼ inch to ½ inch can spell disaster or success.

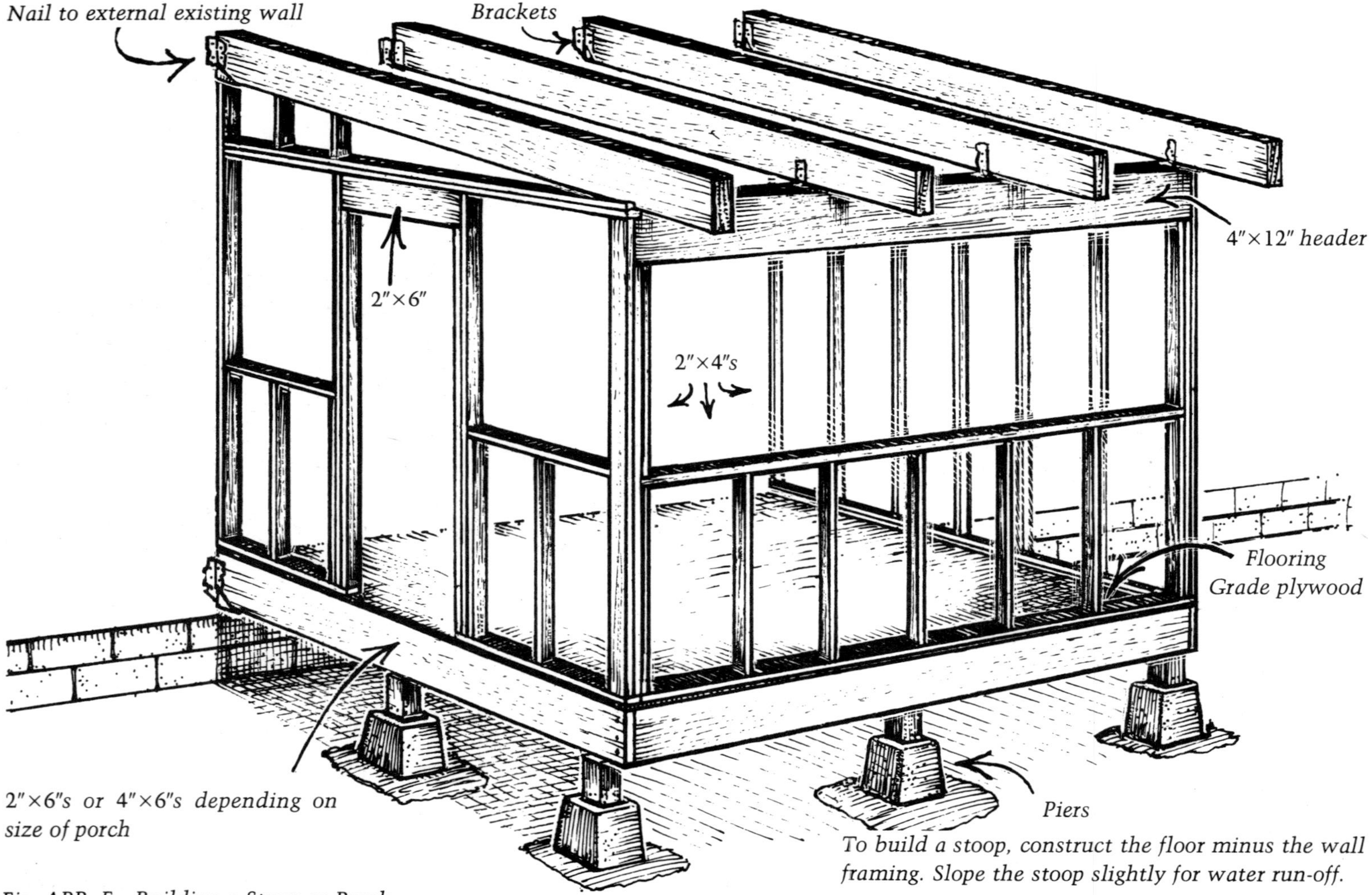

Fig. APP–E Building a Stoop or Porch

If you've never worked with concrete, stone, or bricks before, do something else first—masons consider fireplaces to be postgraduate work.

If I've scared you off sufficiently, remember, before you abandon all hope of a fireplace, that the trusty old cast-iron Franklin-type fireplace is time-tested and approved. I suggest that you not get the smaller model, though. Cords are usually cut in logs approximately 24 inches long, so with the smaller model you would have to go through the whole stack of wood and recut it to make it fit. All the larger Franklin types accept the standard-size piece of wood.

As a final note on fireplaces, there are several books and magazines on the subject. (*Sunset* and *Arco* for example). Refer to these before you decide what you want.

STOOPS

When you first built up your foundation a couple of months ago, you probably noticed that the building codes suggested you build your floor 1½–2 feet off the ground. In the event that you get tired of stepping up and down on building blocks, or whatever else you are using to enter your home, here is a simple and cheap solution.

A *stoop* can be an uncovered porch that is raised off the ground, or it may be a concrete pad in front of your door. Either way, it's essential to your house. When planning a stoop, remember to keep it as strong in construction as the floors in your house, so that later you can build it into a porch if you wish. *See Fig. App.–E.*

MIXING CONCRETE

There are basically three types of concrete you will have to mix:

Fig. APP–F Tools for Cement Working

1. *Mortar concrete,* for cementing blocks together.
2. *Grout concrete,* a runny type of concrete mixture poured into the spaces in the blocks. When hardened it makes the blocks solid.
3. *Small or large gravel-type concrete,* used for purposes such as house foundations, small walkways, and fireplace pads.

To mix and work the various types of concrete you will need

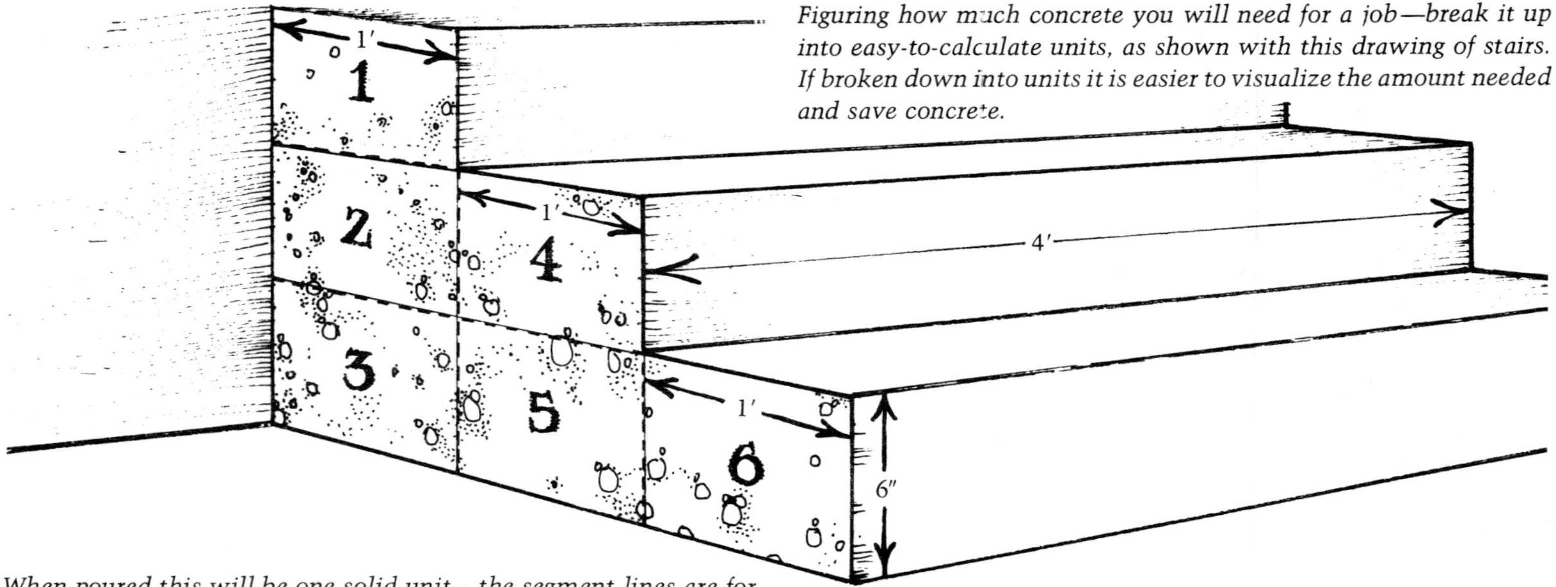

Figuring how much concrete you will need for a job—break it up into easy-to-calculate units, as shown with this drawing of stairs. If broken down into units it is easier to visualize the amount needed and save concrete.

When poured this will be one solid unit—the segment lines are for your ease of calculation only.

Fig. APP–G Making Concrete Porch Steps

the tools as shown in *Fig. App.–F.* There are some other specialized tools for driveways and other large areas that you can rent anywhere.

Remember, if you can't find someone to help you who has experience with concrete, stay away from big complex jobs. Most concrete mistakes are permanent.

Suppose you want to make a foundation footing or build some concrete steps; how do you go about it? First sketch out what you'd like to do. Next mark down the dimensions and multiply them to find out how many cubic feet of concrete you'll need. One cubic yard equals 27 *cubic feet. See Fig. App.–G.* In the example, there are 1-foot by 4-foot units, and each is 6 inches deep. For each long cube, multiply the depth by the length by the width: ½ foot × 4 feet × 1 foot = 2 cubic feet. There are six units, so multiply by six: 2 cubic feet × 6 units = 12 cubic feet of concrete needed.

After figuring out how much concrete you need, go to the cement supplier and buy the quantities he recommends of sack cement, small gravel, and sand. If you wish to pick up some lime, a shovelful in each batch will make your concrete more waterproof and durable.

Following the directions on the cement sack, mix all the portions dry, then add water. Use a flat-nosed shovel and wheelbarrow for small jobs; for larger jobs rent a mixer. Stir the concrete mixture until it is very thoroughly mixed, then pour it into whatever forms you have constructed for the job. Some jobs, such as walls and larger pads, require steel bar reinforcement and sometimes welded steel wire mesh. When getting into this sort of work, consult a book on concrete working.

It's not absolutely necessary, but if you want to do a good, professional job, you should cover your wet concrete with water-soaked strips of cloth (old sheets, burlap, or whatever's available). This helps it to cure properly without cracking. Be sure to re-soak them as they dry out.

For a different type of job, such as mortaring block, you mix only *sand* and *cement* to a rather thick consistency. Again, follow the directions supplied for the mixture.

When mixing grout, you can use a little more water and a little less gravel. But don't make it overly runny, because the concrete will lose some of its strength. Use a bucket to pour the grout in the block holes.

For smoothing a finished surface, use a smoothing trowel and push down on it to pack the gravel. This allows the sand and cement mixture to rise to the top, and you can then work it to whatever finish you like. For better traction on a walkway or driveway, create a rough texture by sweeping the partially hardened concrete with a broom.

As a final note, remember to work fast with concrete. On hot days it helps to get someone to lend you a hand.

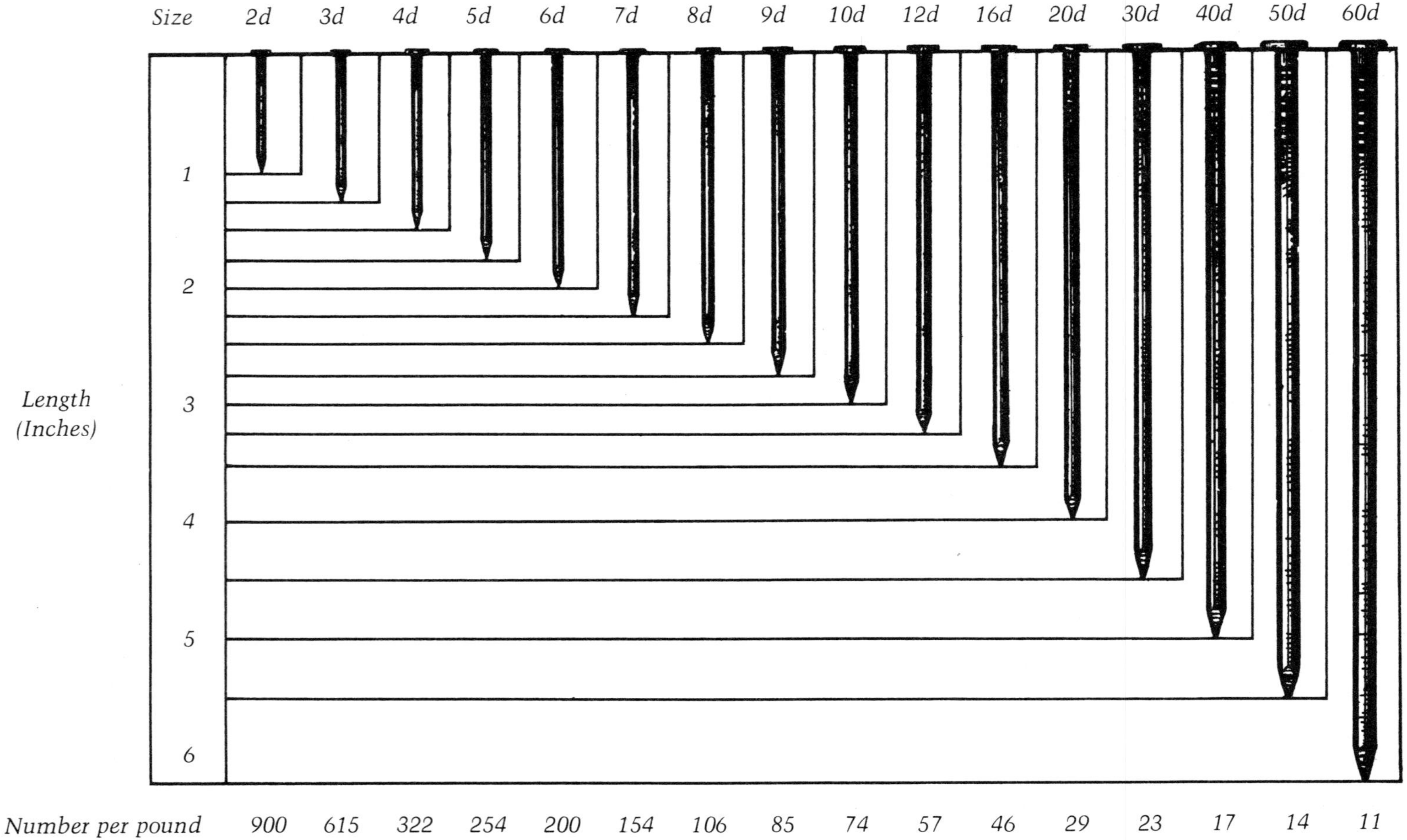
Size
2d
3d
4d
5d
6d
7d
8d
9d
10d
12d
16d
20d
30d
40d
50d
60d
Length (Inches)
1
2
3
4
5
6
Number per pound
900
615
322
254
200
154
106
85
74
57
46
29
23
17
14
11

Nail Chart

GLOSSARY

A-Beam A rafter system using a high pitched roof and a tie-in beam. (See example in Chapter 6.)

Anchor bolt A steel bolt used to hold down a piece of wood against the foundation. The end that goes into the concrete is usually bent.

Asphalt roll roof A roofing material built up of tarred paper and fiber products. It comes in varying thicknesses and the surface is coated with gravel.

Back fill Dirt used to refill an excavation.

Balloon framing A technique of construction in which the studs extend continuously from the foundation sill to the top plates supporting the roof.

Baseboard A trim board placed against the wall next to the floor to hide a joint.

Base course (sometimes called **first course**): The first or bottom row of masonry block or bricks.

Batten A strip of wood used to cover joints between plywood panels or other sheathing material.

Beading A strip of wooden molding used to cover joints.

Beam A horizontal member of wood or steel used to support a floor or roof.

Bearing wall A wall that supports a roof load.

Bed The horizontal layer of mortar on which the first course of masonry is laid.

Bottom plate The lower horizontal stud of a wood-frame wall nailed to the floor for the framing members.

Bridging cross Wooden members that are inserted in a diagonal between adjacent floor or roof joists.

Butt joint The joint made by fastening two pieces of wood together without overlapping.

Caulking A putty-like compound used to waterproof joints.

Circuit An electrical line with up to 12 receptacles on it. Usually protected by one breaker or fuse.

Cornice The overhang on a pitched roof.

Countersink To sink a nailhead below the surface of the wood with a small metal punch.

Course A continuous layer of bricks of masonry.

Crawl space A narrow space between the floor of the house and the ground beneath.

Curing concrete The covering of concrete with wet rags or sheets to affect the proper chemical reaction of cement and water.

Damp-proofing Coating the outside of the foundation with a special water-resistant material. Usually Hydroseal or similar material.

Dowsing The use of a divining rod to find water.

Drywall Interior paneling of **sheetrock, plywood, fiberboard.**

Eave The lower portion of a roof that projects beyond the face of the walls.

Eave soffit The undersurface of the eave.

End grain The lumber surface exposed when the fibers are cut crosswise.

Face nailing Fastening a piece of wood by nailing it at a right angle to the surface.

Fascia board A board nailed around the edge of the eaves.

Feathering Gradually thinning to a fine edge.

Firebox The interior surface of the fireplace that reflects the heat and smoke of the fire. It is usually a metal unit designed to be covered up with wood or brick.

Fire stop (sometimes called **fire blocking**): A 2×4 placed between the studs to retard the spread of flame or gases.

Flashing Sheet-metal used in roof or wall construction underneath the shingles or other covering to assist water run-off and prevent leakage.

Footing The base section of a concrete wall foundation.

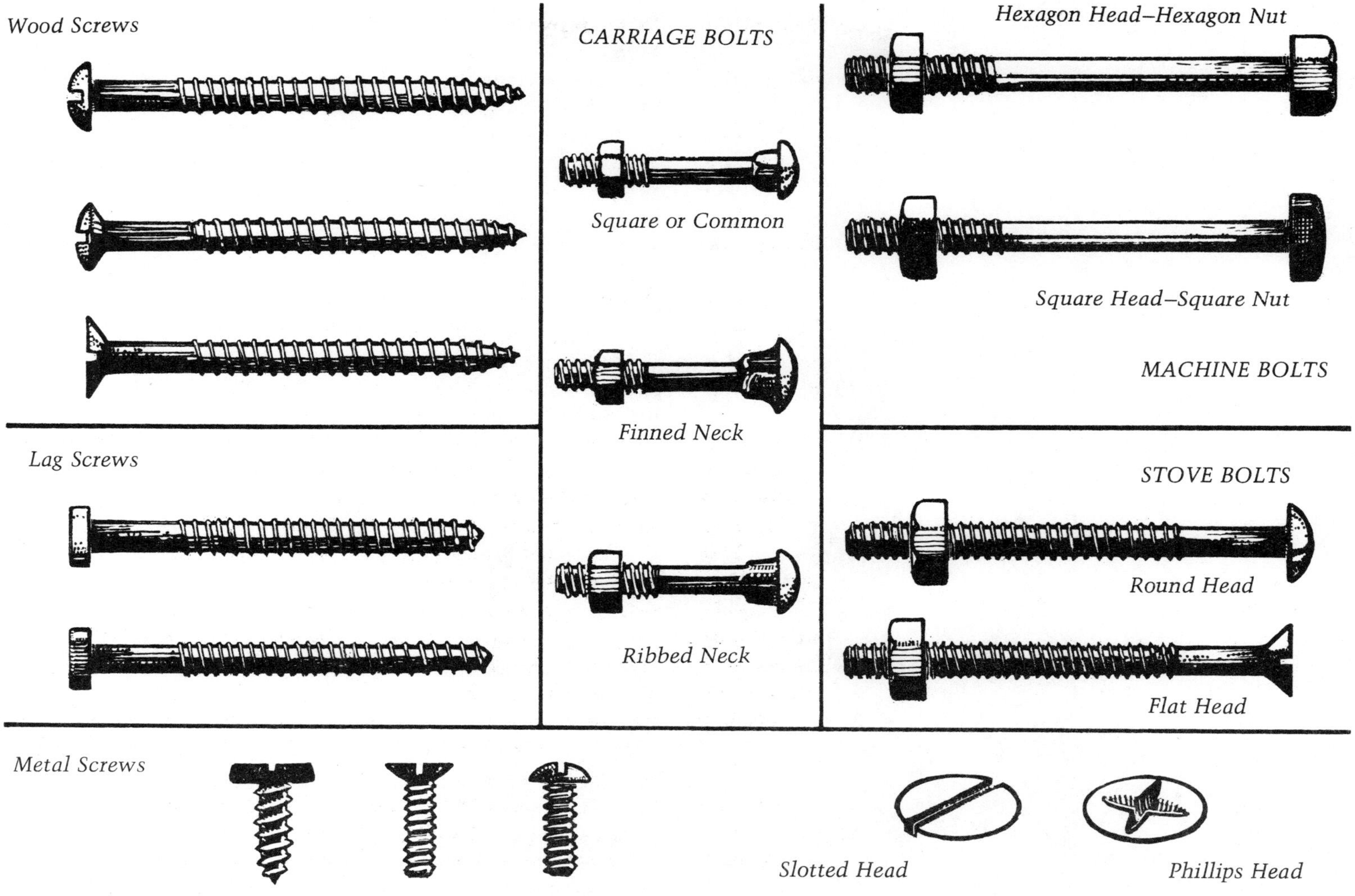

Examples of Screws and Bolts

Foundation The lower portion of masonry that supports the weight of the building.

Gable The upper triangle-shaped section of the wall.

Gable end The entire end wall of a house having a gable roof.

Grades (lumber) Numbers used to separate lumber into different quality classifications, with #1 being the best.

Grade A slope.

Grout A thin gruel of cement and water.

Gusset A plywood or metal piece used to tie-in two or more members of wood into a rigid unit.

Header (framing) A wood timber placed at a right angle to a series of joists or rafters, at which the joists or rafters end.

Hip The sloping portion of a roof formed by two intersecting slopes.

Hot-mop roof Usually consists of several layers of hot tar and tarpaper built up and topped off with asphalt roll roofing. A type of roof that should be applied by professional roofers.

I-Beam A steel beam with a cross-section resembling the letter *I*.

Interior load-bearing wall A wall designed to support roof beams and the weight of a roof.

Jamb The wooden lining of a doorway, window, or passageway.

Joint cement A powder that is mixed with water and applied to the joints of drywall construction.

Joists Usually 2×6 wood members used to support a roof, ceiling, or floor.

Joist hanger A metal stirrup used to fasten a beam to another beam or wall.

King-post truss A rafter system using one vertical supporting member running from the apex to the bottom chord for structural rigidity.

Ledger strip A strip of wood fastened to the bottom side of a beam, on which joists rest.

Lintel A horizontal beam that supports the load over an opening such as a door or window.

Lookout rafters Wooden beams cantilevered over a wall to support an overhanging roof.

Miter box A wooden box slotted for use with a special saw (miter saw) to cut angles.

Miter joint A joint made by cutting two pieces of board on a line bisecting the angle of their junction.

Mortar A cement substance made by mixing cement agents, aggregates, and water.

Mortar bed A layer of mortar on which masonry or tile is bedded or laid.

Mudsill A timber or beam placed on the ground as a foundation for a structure.

Nonbearing partition A wall that divides space into rooms but does not support any vertical load.

O.C. (On center) A term used to signify measurements. Usually from the center of one member to the center of an adjacent member, as in spacing of studs, joists, or nails.

Panel A large sheet of lumber, plywood, or other building material.

Particle board Board made of ground wood and an adhesive. Often found in 4-foot by 8-foot panels.

Pier A masonry structure, usually rectangular, that is used to support beams.

Pipe dope A gray paste used to seal pipes.

Pitch Inclination of a roof.

Plumb To make vertical.

Rafter Usually a 2×6 designed to support roof loads.

Receptacle (electric) An electrical outlet mounted in the wall.

Ridge beam Horizontal structural member, usually 2 inches or more thick, supporting the upper ends of the rafters.

Ridge board Horizontal member at the upper end of the rafters, to which these rafters are nailed.

Road Easement A portion of land allowed for use at a later date, if desired by the county or state. Usually deeded into the records.

Roof pitch The slope of your roof.

Rout To cut out wood. Usually refers to hinges, locks, and fixtures.

Sash board Pieces of wood around the edges of a foundation.

Shake A shingle split from a block of wood. These are often used for roofing and siding.

Sheathing paper Paper treated with tar or asphalt and used under wall paneling to protect against moisture penetration.

Shed roof A simple one-slope roof.

Shim To adjust a door jamb to the proper width and height; or, a small piece of wedge-shaped wood used to do this.

Shingles Roofing materials that can be obtained in various sized rectangles, usually 12 inches by 18 inches. Applied in rows over the roof decking. Can be either wood or compound materials, such as fiberglass and asphalt.

Siding Any material used to cover the exterior walls, except masonry or stucco.

Sill The horizontal member that forms the bottom of an opening such as a door or window.

Snub-out To bring a plumbing pipe out of the wall.

Soffit The underside of things such as roof overhangs, beams, and staircases.

Span The horizontal distance between supports for beams, rafters, and joists.

Stoop A small porchlike platform at the entrance of a house.

Stud One of a series of 2×4's used in supporting walls and partitions.

Subfloor Boards or plywood laid down on joists to make a floor.

Taping Making joints between the sheets of drywall, using paper tape and joint cement.

Threshold A strip of metal designed to be used at the junction of two different floor finishes, under doors, or on the top of the doorsill.

Toe-nailing Driving a nail at a 45-degree angle through the edge of one piece of wood into another piece of wood.

Tongue-and-groove lumber Any lumber machined so that there is a groove on one edge and a corresponding tongue on the other.

Top plate With wood construction, the horizontal 2×4 nailed to the top of the wall studs.

Tread The horizontal part of a stair.

Trimmer A beam or joist running alongside a window or door opening, into which a header is framed.

Valley The angle formed at the junction of two sloping roofs.

Vapor barrier Any material used to arrest the passage of water or moisture.

W-truss A complex rafter system using an internal bracing configuration that looks like the letter *W*, and made of wooden members.

Weather stripping Strips of felt, rubber, or plastic placed along the edges of doors and windows to stop drafts and keep out rain and snow.

Well point A screening device placed over a water-intake pipe to keep out sand and gravel.

Will's Suggested Reading

Low-Cost Wood Homes for Rural America—Construction Manual 1969 Agriculture Handbook No. 364. U.S. Dept. of Agriculture, Washington D.C. 20250

Canadian Wood-Frame House Construction 1969 Canadian Central Mortgage Corp., 650 Lawrence Ave., West Toronto, Ontario, Canada

The Owner-Built Home *Ken Kern* 1975 Charles Scribner's Sons, New York

Build Your Own Low-Cost Home *L. O. Anderson* 1972 Dover Publications, New York

Do-It-Yourself House-Building *Charles Neal* 1973 Stein & Day, New York

Modern Carpentry *William Wagner* 1976 Goodheart-Wilcox Co, Illinois

Illustrated Housebuilding *Graham Blackburn* 1974 Overlook Press, New York

The Practical Handbook of Plumbing and Heating *Richard Day* 1969 Arco Publishing Co, New York

Plumbers & Pipe Fitters Library *Jules Oravetz Sr.* 1976 Audel & Co, Indiana

Wiring Simplified—32nd Ed. 1978 Based on latest 1975 code Park Publishing, Minneapolis, Minnesota

More Unity Press books to further an integration with our earth!